Selected Issues in Logic and Communication

Selected Issues in Logic and Communication

Trudy Govier

University of Calgary

Wadsworth Publishing Company
Belmont, California
A Division of Wadsworth, Inc.

Philosophy Editor: Kenneth King
Production Management: Richard Mason, Bookman Productions
Print Buyer: Ruth Cole
Copy Editor: Celia Teter
Compositor: Omegatype Typography, Inc.
Cover: Stephen Osborn

Printed in the United States of America
  2 3 4 5 6 7 8 9 10——92 91 90 89

ISBN 0-534-08694-2

Library of Congress Cataloging-in-Publication Data

Selected issues in logic and communication.

  Bibliography: p.
  1. Logic. 2. Communication.   I. Govier, Trudy.
BC71.S435   1987   160   87-14792
ISBN 0-534-08694-2

To my children

Contents

Preface

For a number of years, I have sensed that there are fascinating issues at the intersection of two fields: applied logic and modern communications. Such topics as the nature of bias and propaganda, the distinction between fact and opinion, the effects of television and visual presentations on critical thinking, the reliability of experts, and the nature of intellectual "balance" between two sides—these are but a few of many important subjects in this area. There are a number of contexts in which such topics could profitably be studied, including, most obviously, university and college courses in informal logic, critical thinking, communications, and journalism.

In this collection, I have brought together a number of essays bearing on these and related issues. In my opinion all the essays are fascinating, important, relevant, and easy to read. I hope that others will feel the same way, and that this collection will help to draw further attention to the issues described and discussed in this book.

I am grateful to all of the contributors for generously allowing their work to be used. Special thanks are due to Dennis Rohatyn, Ralph Johnson, and Maryann Ayim, who kindly undertook new work for the volume. I benefitted greatly from a careful review by Thomas Moody (California State University, San Bernardino), and from the comments and encouragement of Wadsworth's Philosophy Editor, Kenneth King.

About the Contributors

MARYANN AYIM is a philosopher in the Faculty of Education at the University of Western Ontario, London, Ontario. She has written on the philosophy of C.S. Peirce and on feminism, as well as on logic and the theory of argument.

ANTHONY BLAIR is a philosopher at the University of Windsor in Windsor, Ontario. He is co-editor of *Informal Logic,* co-author of *Logical Self-Defense,* a text on informal fallacies, and a leading figure in the informal logic movement.

JERRY CEDERBLOM is a philosopher at the University of Nebraska and co-author of *Critical Reasoning,* a textbook on argument analysis.

ALEXANDER COCKBURN is a journalist who has written extensively for the *Village Voice, The Nation, Harper's,* the *New York Review,* and other publications. He is Irish by nationality but lives in New York City.

CARL COHEN is a philosopher at the University of Michigan. His interests include DNA research, public affairs, and university adminis- tration. He has published in *Commentary* as well as in philosophical journals.

WILLIAM DORMAN is a professor of journalism at California State University, Sacramento. His special interest is United States press coverage of foreign affairs. He has written extensively on U.S. mass media coverage of the Soviet Union, the Iranian hostage crisis, and the developing world.

MURRAY EDELMAN is a political scientist at the University of Wisconsin in Madison. His special interests are the role of symbols in politics and the nature of and remedies for poverty.

STEPHEN JAY GOULD is professor of paleontology at Harvard University. A frequent contributor to the *New York Review,* he has also written books and essays on a wide variety of topics including recent trends in Darwinism, the evolution-creation controversy, and the mea- surement of human intelligence.

TRUDY GOVIER is a philosopher at the University of Calgary, Alberta. Her interests include moral theory, peace studies, and the theory of argument. She is author of a textbook, *A Practical Study of Argument,* and a number of papers on ethics, applied logic, and nuclear issues.

JOHN HARDWIG is a philosopher at East Tennessee University in Johnson City, Tennessee, and is author of several articles on collective rationality.

GARY JASON is a philosopher at Washburn University in Topeka, Kansas.

RALPH JOHNSON is co-editor of *Informal Logic,* co-author of *Logical Self-Defense,* and a leading figure in the informal logic movement. He currently chairs the Philosophy Department at the University of Windsor in Windsor, Ontario.

JACK MACINTOSH, a philosopher at the University of Calgary, Alberta, is author of many articles on philosophy of mind and early modern philosophy, and a co-editor of the *Canadian Journal of Philosophy.*

DAVID PAULSEN is a philosopher at Evergreen State College in Nebraska and co-author of *Critical Reasoning.*

NEIL POSTMAN is a Professor of Communication at New York University and a widely read critic of American culture and media. His many books include *Teaching as a Subversive Activity, Teaching as a Conserving Activity, The Disappearance of Childhood,* and most recently, *Amusing Ourselves to Death.*

DENNIS ROHATYN is a philosopher at the University of San Diego in Alcala Park, California. He is the author of several books on contemporary culture, teaches courses on communications and applied logic, and hosts a weekly local radio show.

PERRY WEDDLE is a philosopher at California State University, Sacramento. He is author of a text and several articles on informal logic and founding editor of *C.T. News,* a circulating newsletter on the teaching of applied logic and critical thinking.

Trudy Govier
Calgary, Alberta
Canada
April, 1987

Introduction

We are said to live in an Information Society. Yet many distrust the so-called information, and others feel overwhelmed at the sheer quantity of it. Information can give power. So too, alas, can disinformation: the power only shifts its base.

Recently the cultivation of critical thinking has been widely applauded as a key educational goal. Courses, texts, and tests have been developed—at every level from elementary school to college and university. Conferences, workshops, and seminars have been held. Many points of intersection exist between an analysis of modern mass communications and the pursuit of critical thinking as a skill and disposition. In a society of mass communications, the media do much to structure and affect our thoughts about everything from personal health to evolution to nuclear power. We are not independent solitary thinkers collecting evidence autonomously, but members of a vastly complicated society exploding with images, suggestions, innuendo, questions, hypotheses, and arguments. Many of these emerge not from the experience of single individuals but from the decisions, policies, and actions of institutions whose goals are multiple and include profit and persuasion as much as information and argument.

The popular notion of a "free marketplace of ideas" presumes a critical capacity on the part of the consuming public, a capacity to arrive at well-founded beliefs when a variety of beliefs are disseminated and defended. This concept is still used to defend freedom of expression. Yet it now operates in a context quite different from the nineteenth-century world in which it originated. Then even quite small towns had several newspapers representing diverse political views. People got their information from print or from speeches at public meetings. Television, film, and videocassettes, where images predominate and provide little opportunity or incentive for rational thought, did not yet exist. In his classic defense of freedom of speech, "On Liberty," John Stuart Mill wrote of such a world. For better or for worse, that world is not ours. It is a real question how mass media in contemporary times affect understanding and critical thought, and how and whether the free marketplace of ideas is still a viable concept today. The essays collected here are, in various ways, contributions to this general theme.

One pessimistic analysis is that of Neil Postman, who has written often about the media and their influence on modern life. His scathing analysis in *Amusing Ourselves to Death* is a prolonged attack on the idea that television can provide anything like real information. In the essay reprinted here, Postman examines the information content of even the "best" television and comes to essentially pessimistic conclusions. He sees the visual and fast-paced character of television as a disincentive to critical analysis, tending to encourage decision by image. Postman contends that even so-called debates include little serious examination of issues and small opportunity for participants to respond rationally to positions put forward by others.

Fallacious moves can be prominent and powerful in debates of great public significance. Gary Jason, in his essay on two United States presidential debates, quotes extensively from the transcripts of the Nixon-Kennedy debate (1960) and the Reagan-Mondale debate (1984) to show that in each case both participants dodged key issues, resorted to questionable causal reasoning, and committed various other fallacies. This essay raises the issue of the relation between format and content. A televised debate in which people are given a fixed, short time in which to state positions on a vast array of complex and contentious problems is not conducive to accurate and subtle thought, nor to precise reasoning. The poor content and logical quality of the discussions, emphasized by Jason, may be attributable as much to the nature of the medium and competence and expectations of the audience as to any limitations of the participants. Whichever is the cause, watchers receive intellectually shabby material as the result.

A conspicuous aspect of much serious television coverage of public issues is the attempt to achieve balance and objectivity. This is often done by presenting two sides of an issue. Journalist and author Alexander Cockburn offers a witty satire of the "two-sides" format of programs such as the popular McNeil-Lehrer report. The model falsely neutralizes and oversimplifies issues, he claims, making any position look as rationally respectable as any other. According to Cockburn, McNeil and Lehrer could have made the Crucifixion itself look routine and morally respectable. The view that issues typically have two sides, which must be presented for an objective understanding, is also discussed by Govier. A useful label for the view is "binary objectivity." This is the idea that we get objectivity by presenting the two sides of an issue and realizing that the truth is somewhere in between. According to Govier, there are some reasons for seeing this view as plausible, but it has its pitfalls. Errors and distortions by one side are not necessarily highlighted or detected by an advocacy account from another. In addition, the apparent neutrality of a two-sides analysis can be deceptive in its implication that the two sides depicted represent all possible reasonable positions on the matter. Identifying two positions is itself a substantive structuring that may omit significant alternatives. Binary objectivity is neither as simple nor as neutral as it first appears.

In a related discussion, Perry Weddle scrutinizes the two concepts of fact and opinion. We often presume mistakenly that everything humans believe falls either into the category of fact or into the category of opinion. Such a distinction is still taken seriously in many critical thinking programs. As Weddle points out, each year hundreds of thousands of schoolchildren in California are asked to distinguish fact from opinion on standardized tests that are supposed to measure their critical thinking ability. The distinction appears to be a liberating one: People must respect the facts, but they have a right to their own opinions. In fact, this use of the distinction undermines the idea of serious rational discussion and debate. There is no need to construct rational arguments to defend known statements of fact. And if opinions are regarded as pure issues of preference, where people should have complete freedom to believe untrammeled by considerations of logic and evidence, argument will be irrelevant to matters of opinion as well. If everything believed is either fact or opinion, and argument is unnecessary for fact and irrelevant for opinion, then argument must be irrelevant to the establishment of human beliefs. This is surely an unsatisfactory conclusion.

This peculiar dilemma already suggests that there is something wrong with a simple dichotomy of fact and opinion. We do argue about scientific, moral, and policy questions, and we do not regard all that argument as useless. Weddle explores many ways of drawing the distinction between fact and opinion and comes to the conclusion that none will work neatly. He suggests avoiding the problem by attending instead to the quality of evidence available for a claim or hypothesis. This is what really counts—not whether the matter is one of fact or opinion.

Extensive coverage of dramatic events may provide neither reliable evidence nor rational deliberation about what that evidence indicates. William Dorman reflects on the coverage of the Iranian hostage problem. Although millions of television hours and column inches were devoted to this prolonged and painful event, little information was given about the historical background of the problem. Coverage of the Iran hostage crisis did not include reference to the American involvement in dislodging the popular Iranian leader Mossadegh in 1953, nor did it include any serious examination of United States support of repressive aspects of the Shah's regime. That U.S. weaponry was used to buttress the power and prestige of the Shah, for example, was given virtually no attention. Dorman's account suggests that the so-called problem of information overload may be misnamed. There may be image overload, paper overload, and time and inch overload, but insofar as relevant historical and political background is missing, there is no information overload.

Bias and distortion in information need not come from outright falsehood nor from intent to deceive. They can be the result of a selective presentation of evidence, arguments, and hypotheses. This selectivity need not be intentionally self-serving or malicious. It can result—as it may have in this case—simply from the unconscious and uncritical adoption of socially prevalent assumptions and goals.

Bias in the media and elsewhere is often defended on the grounds that it is inevitable. At a recent satellite conference on journalism and coverage of international affairs, Canadian participants in Calgary complained of American bias. The major preoccupation of the prominent speakers featured in the video coverage seemed to be with attitudes and responses of the American public to events deemed important because of their ramifications for American policy. A commentator acknowledged the problem, saying this is why a Canadian communications policy is so necessary for Canada. Then he added that, of course, if Canadians had more of their own international coverage instead of relying on American agencies and reporters, there would inevitably be another bias—a Canadian bias.

Is bias inevitable? What is bias? The notion that every person and group is of necessity biased is both plausible and strange. It may seem plausible on the basis of experience. Yet it is strange because it seems incompatible with our common belief that bias is something negative, which is a fault. In his essay on bias, Anthony Blair seeks to clarify these questions. He explains three common senses in which the word "bias" is used and gives clear examples fitting each sense. One kind of bias is objectionable, another is neutral—because it is inevitable—and a further is actually good. Excusing the "negative" bias of distortion of interpretation and self-serving selectivity of facts and evidence on the grounds that bias in some other sense is inevitable is a mistake. It goes unnoticed, sometimes, because we fail to understand the different senses of bias and fail to see that the argument results on a confusion of two distinct meanings.

If Blair's account is accepted, we could say that Canadian coverage of international affairs would inevitably be biased in the sense that it would be from a distinct point of view—a Canadian point of view. One cannot avoid having some point of view. Whether a Canadian view would be biased in the sense of selecting facts and hypotheses favorable to Canadian government policy and Canadian interests is another question.

Some critics have attacked both Canadian and American coverage of foreign affairs and other controversial matters, alleging that people's opinions are hastily formed on the basis of selective data. Such critiques raise important issues about the nature and powers of institutions related to communication and the compatability of their power with genuine democracy. Noam Chomsky and others have gone so far as to accuse American mass media of disseminating propaganda, a kind of propaganda that is so pervasively accepted that it is seldom recognized as such. Of what moral and political significance is consent of the people if that consent can be molded, even manufactured, by institutions controlled, in the final analysis, by economic elites?

The notion of propaganda is something like the notion of bias: We are inclined both to think of it as a serious fault that sometimes appears and to think (inconsistently) that it is an inevitable feature of all accounts. Propaganda is a negative concept most of the time—even when we believe in a cause we are likely to feel uneasy about defending it by means of propaganda. In 1983, the United States Department of Justice ruled that three films made by Canada's government-funded National Film Board were Canadian government propaganda and had to be labelled as such when shown in the United States. This ruling drew attention to the concept of propaganda—and probably attracted a wide audience to the films! Two were about acid rain; the third was Helen Caldicott's *If You Love This Planet*, an anti-nuclear film contending that there is a serious risk of nuclear war and urging that ordinary citizens act to prevent such a catastrophe. Many observers were outraged at the Justice Department's statement. Eventually the accompanying administrative policy of having groups who had seen the film register with the government was challenged in U.S. courts.

However, several participants on a Canadian Broadcasting Corporation "Ideas" show on the topic of propaganda readily granted the Reagan administration's claim that two of the shows constituted propaganda. They adopted a definition of propaganda as a selective advocacy presentation of facts with a view to persuading the audience to make a commitment to action. By such a definition Caldicott's film would constitute propaganda. (So would most documentary films; the medium is not conducive to a careful analysis of alternative accounts.) Caldicott's film omitted any rational considerations of opposing views and presented facts quite selectively.

Dennis Rohatyn's provocative dialogue on propaganda raises the problem of determining what is and what is not propaganda in a mass culture loaded with slogans, advertisements, images, and innuendo. Rohatyn describes such noteworthy classics of propaganda as Leni Riefenstahl's 1934 "Triumph of the Will" film and Richard Nixon's 1952 "Checkers" speech. The dialogue reveals that propaganda has effects within groups that are not easily detected except from an external standpoint. When we look at propaganda from past decades, it seems so silly that it is hard to believe it was ever effective. Only with difficulty can we gain a comparable perspective on the slogans and images of our own times. Yet the recognition of propaganda as such remains crucially important.

Of necessity, communities share habits of speech and mind. Usually these are not examined reflectively. In the context of discussing and debating public issues, it is far easier and more natural to think in language than to think about it. Nevertheless, sensitivity to the language used in communication is fundamentally important. By adopting a jargon—colloquial or technical—we often move substantially toward a stance or orientation on an issue. Language selects some features of reality for attention and if it selects, it must necessarily omit. Language connotes attitudes, emotions, and traditions, as well as descriptive features of things, people, and events. It presumes assumptions we may never notice. It links things to organizing frameworks, to disciplines, to experts, and to power structures. Image as a substitute for language merely inserts new selection and attitude problems. It does not avoid issues of interpretation and is even more susceptible to propagandistic uses than are words. To the cliche "a picture is worth a thousand words," one observer responded "a word is worth a thousand pictures." Language is potent and indispensable. Yet it can carry us unwittingly to unexpected destinations.

To his anti-Utopian novel *1984*, George Orwell added an appendix describing an imaginary language, Newspeak, which would severely restrict thought in a totalitarian society. A minimum number of words was used in that language and every meaning was to be fixed as rigidly as possible. Words were either very concrete and everyday (such as "bed," "table"), heavy with ideological meaning of a fixed nature ("goodspeak," "Ingsoc"), or technically specific and used by specialists. Orwell commented, "The intent was to make speech, and especially speech on any subject not ideologically neutral, as nearly as possible independent of consciousness . . . a Party member called upon to make a political or ethical judgment should be able to spray forth the correct opinion as automatically as a machine gun spraying forth bullets."

In his famous essay "Politics and the English Language," Orwell argued that even in a nontotalitarian society, language and thought are in a relationship of mutual support. If we think clearly, we will speak and write clearly. Poor thinking will result in sloppy and unclear use of language. But poor language is more than the effect of poor thought. It is, eventually, its cause as well. Repetition of cumbersome, abstract, vague, and virtually meaningless phrases can become a substitute for real thought. Abstractions such as "the rectification of the frontier" can cover up cruel evictions of thousands of suffering peasants from villages. The vague and abstract character of such language disguises ugly realities from our consciousness, leading reasonable people to condone barbarities they would never accept if they faced them for what they really are.

Orwell insisted that real thought is concrete, based on a specific fresh image that precedes words. Good language, preceded by real thought, should be simple and vivid. Language is a potent force in politics. It will not be a force for the good unless we refuse to blanket reality in cliché, euphemism, and abstract jargon.

Jack MacIntosh develops a closely related theme in dealing with the language of nuclear strategy. Unlike Orwell, MacIntosh does not see meaning as a product of prior thought in terms of concrete images. Rather, he relates meaning to standard contexts of use and the mutual expectations of speaker and audience. An audience will assume that words are used as they are in other standard contexts and that the speaker aims to convey maximum information. On this view, intentions and images on the part of the speaker are not enough to ensure meaning. Many of the terms used to describe nuclear weapons and nuclear strategy convey assumptions and expectations that, upon analysis, are easily shown to be incompatible with the realities of the nuclear age. These associations are evoked by the users of language because they normally are associated with terms typically used in less horrifying contexts. Language thus ties thought to the pre-nuclear age and cloaks the risks and realities of a nuclearized present.

Like Orwell, MacIntosh firmly rejects euphemism and abstraction in political discourse. He argues that the language that has been cultivated for nuclear weapons and related policy is far too abstract, bland, and mundane to convey the awesome possibilities. Usually when old language is used for new objects and events, an accompanying shift in meaning occurs. But with nuclear weapons and nuclear war, the possibilities are so threatening that this does not seem to happen. Instead, we have, in effect, used pre-nuclear language to save ourselves from thinking about the hideous possibilities of the nuclear age, with the result that nuclear weapons seem more rational and usable than they would if language more accurately reflected the potential for global damage and unprecedented death that these weapons embody. There is no possibility of a vivid image here that would be anything adequate to the realities. Experienced contexts and expectations may not be adequate until it is too late.

There is little point in criticizing abstraction as such, for with the exception of proper names, all language is necessarily abstract. Harmful abstraction merits criticism, and abstraction becomes harmful when omitted aspects are pertinent to our understanding. Any vocabulary to discuss people, their problems, tools, and politics will necessarily be abstract in that it will gloss over many details of a specific case. Even mundane words like "table," not easily susceptible to rhetorical manipulation, are abstract. Though closer to common perceptual experience than "democracy," "justice," "gender," "race," "nation," and many other politically and ethically sensitive terms, mundane words such as "table" necessarily fail to connote our full range of experiences, attitudes, and evaluations that we may feel with regard to tables. Saying that a cup is on the table, we are not typically moved to reflect on the height or color or type of wood constituting the table, nor on the loves and quarrels we may have experienced while sitting beside it. The word "table" can apply to many objects and does not discriminate between them as to color, style, age, and many other features. The abstraction is there, to be sure, but it is almost always harmless.

Following in the tradition of Orwell, MacIntosh criticizes abstractions that are not harmless. Aspects omitted from consideration are the very ones we need to attend to to have a proper understanding and appreciation of the things we are trying to talk about. Vague, pompous, technical, or jargonistic language spins on while aspects of reality crucial to our appreciation of human well-being and potential are hidden from view. Language helps to ossify thought and perpetuate stereotypes.

Different interests and perspectives stimulate persons and groups to form different conceptual maps of the world. A danger even in pluralistic and open societies is that when deep underlying assumptions and interests are taken for granted by nearly everyone, valuable alternative ways of thinking and acting may escape our attention.

The potency of organizing frameworks of language and thought is nicely illustrated by Murray Edelman, who explores the beliefs, attitudes, and world views implied by language in therapy and social work. Edelman points out how alternative terms can each seem in their way correct and yet have different implications. A high school student might be described as "unorthodox," "disturbed," or "predelinquent." Quite distinct courses of action and pertinent "expert" communities are suggested by such terms. Words from technical language are sometimes taken over by "clients" (victims?) themselves, with resulting changes in self-image and self-understanding.

Categorization is as necessary in politics, ethics, and social science as everywhere. But it is often more than a stage of science: It is a political act, one which begins to establish status and power hierarchies. Edelman quotes a civil rights lawyer who said, "While psychiatrists get angry, patients get aggressive; nurses daydream, but patients withdraw." He repeats Orwell's warning that abstraction can hide abuse. This abstraction, cloaking abuse, can provide a wide range of discretionary power to professionals who may abuse it. Formal technical language can mark disciplinary territory, within which specialists like to claim their own monopoly, seeking power over laypeople and rival specialists.

The role of experts in modern knowledge and belief appears both potent and problematic. Knowledge is said to be exploding—increasing at a rate faster than at any time in past history. Yet we may become puzzled about this claim if we ask just whose knowledge is increasing. Disciplinary explorations are limited in perspective; people are typically trained to be narrow specialists and to be cautious and modest about venturing outside their areas of specialization. Perhaps no one individual, not even the best educated, knows more than well-educated individuals a hundred years ago. To say that knowledge is expanding and assert something correctly, we must mean somehow that the social pool of knowledge is greater. Individuals potentially have access to the accumulation of work by vast numbers of experts.

John Hardwig examines this topic in his essay "Relying on Experts." Hardwig contends that our reliance on experts is so great that the individualist model of thinking for oneself is jeopardized. Intellectual autonomy is just not feasible in our time. Much of our evidence is indirect in the sense that we can only have good reasons to believe things if we adopt beliefs vicariously from experts, assuming that these experts themselves have good direct reasons for their beliefs. For instance, we believe that the Salk vaccine is effective against polio, but few directly understand the evidence for this statement. What we do know is that medical experts believe this. We assume they do so on good evidence, and we take over the belief vicariously. In fact, Hardwig submits, modern knowledge now cumulates in such a complex way that even specialists working in their own areas sometimes cannot understand all aspects of the research problems they study. Vividly illustrating his point by citing a recent physics paper with ninety-nine authors, Hardwig concludes by suggesting that trust is more fundamental in the accumulation of knowledge than has commonly been recognized.

Hardwig was not intending to argue for skepticism, but for many reflective persons, this would seem the natural conclusion to draw from his account. To accept conclusions on the basis of indirect and cooperative evidence, we have to trust other people, as Hardwig points out. If knowledge and rationality depend on trust, and trust is frequently unwarranted, then perhaps knowledge and rationality do not exist. People are notoriously not always reliable sources of information. They may make mistakes, misperceive, reason poorly, or even lie. Even so-called experts have been known to make serious mistakes. They often have vested interests. They may be limited in their understanding by specialization. Though human knowledge, or so-called knowledge, is more and more compartmentalized, reality is not. Yet the autonomous individual who can rationally appraise any and every statement and argument without trusting in experts is a myth in contemporary times. Renaissance men may have existed in the Renaissance, but Renaissance people are extinct in our time.

Philosophers Jerry Cederblom and David Paulsen grapple with this problem in their essay on amateurs in an age of specialization: People can neither think entirely for themselves nor rely confidently on experts. They recommend partial strategies for coping with the dilemma, recognizing the limitation both of would-be autonomous thinkers and of experts. Appeals to experts are a problematic but inevitable feature of the epistemology and rhetoric of our specialized age.

Carl Cohen writes about another powerful rhetorical move that he terms "the heavy question" technique. Following a debate between molecular biologists, environmentalists, and concerned members of the public on DNA and the manipulation of genetic material, Cohen found some twenty instances in which speakers and writers used this ploy to imply without argument that experimentation would bring unwarranted risks. Cohen explains how such questions as "Have we the right to counteract, irreversibly, the evolutionary wisdom of millions of years, in order to satisfy the ambition and the curiosity of a few scientists?" employ questionable assumptions and loaded language and serve to block rational discussion. A rhetorical question is not in itself an argument. Yet it can function as an effective argumentative ploy. Reflecting on the issue of experts versus laypeople, it is worth noting that this technique was used by very well-established scientists. Specialized knowledge does not prevent logical lapses.

There is, of course, wide recognition that many issues call for public input that cannot be achieved by consulting experts. A common technique of getting information on public opinion is the opinion poll. Governments often use polls to guide policy, especially close to the time of elections. Polls on all sorts of issues—from sex to church-going to nuclear armaments—are frequently cited in the press and elsewhere. In fact, so common is polling that many analysts fear it is coming to replace independent policy analysis by those governing and to dominate coverage of election campaigns.

Ralph Johnson offers a clear essay about extracting information from polls. To know what a poll means, we need information about sampling, and we need to understand the question asked in the context of background knowledge of the problem and the immediate circumstances in which the poll was taken. Expressions of opinion are sensitive to the knowledge of persons questioned and also to the precise wording of questions. In fact, variations in wording can elicit varied responses to polls, so that public opinion on a given topic can actually look as though it is inconsistent.

A poll on the issue of a nuclear freeze taken in April 1982, for instance, showed that 83 percent of respondents agreed that "it doesn't matter if the U.S. or the Soviet Union is ahead in nuclear weapons because both sides have more than enough to destroy each other no matter who attacks first." Yet another poll, only one month later, indicated that 43 percent of respondents believed it "very important that the U.S. produce as many nuclear weapons as the Soviet Union."[1] Clearly such results as these need careful interpretation if they are to be of any significance for public policy.

Stephen Jay Gould's essay provides an example of reasoning from a more academic context—that of social scientific research. It is well known that purely correlational data cannot establish a causal conclusion. Yet in some contexts, this knowledge seems easily forgotten. When such topics as sexual urges, seasons, and crime are concerned, human interests and even passion make it easy to forget or misapply such logical standards temporarily. When such errors can slip into scientific research, it is no surprise that they are widely repeated in the media and often go undetected by the ordinary public.

A fascinating aspect of thought and reasoning concerns the relation of metaphor to literal, "direct" thought. Metaphor is more deeply embedded in thought than we typically realize. In fact, argumentation itself is commonly understood in terms of one particularly deep metaphor—that of war. In *Metaphors We Live By,* authors George Lakoff and Mark Johnson mention the "argument is war" metaphor as common and basic in western culture.[2] They point out that people are said to "stake out" and "defend" positions, to "attack" positions of an "opponent," to claim "victory" when they "win" an argument., to "retreat" from a "claim" when they cannot hold up under "attack," and so on. Maryann Ayim places such metaphors in a broader context in her essay on dominance and violence as metaphors in academic discourse. Science is regarded as a way of achieving dominance over nature, which may even be described as something feminine that has to be attacked and penetrated. Philosophical styles are especially combative, and even critical thinking texts seem insensitive to the metaphors of opposition and attack their wordings perpetuate. In recent theories of education as growth, cooperation, and nurturance, Ayim finds some basis for optimism.

This concluding essay raises provocative questions about critical thought itself. How seriously do we take the metaphorical language Ayim documents, and how much does it affect our practice of discussion and debate and our efforts accurately to understand our world? If the ways of speaking she documents encourage aggressive and unconstructive attitudes, should we work toward their elimination? Or should we rather seek to supplement the models they presuppose with others such as nurturance? Ayim's essay reveals that the academic culture that provides the basis for critical analysis of mass media and popular attitudes poses questions and problems in its own right.

Notes

1. Cited in *Living with Nuclear Weapons,* Harvard Nuclear Study Group (New York: Bantam Books, 1983), 8.

2. George Lakoff and Mark Johnson, *Metaphors We Live By* (Chicago: The University of Chicago Press, 1980).

1

Critical Thinking in the Electronic Era*

Neil Postman

In the nineteenth century, most people received information in written form. In the twentieth, they receive it increasingly in the form of visual images. Television often presents misleading information in a visual form, and there is little opportunity or encouragement to evaluate such information critically.

On September 25 in the year 1690, a newspaper called *Publick Occurrences Both Domestick and Foreign* was published in Boston. It is acknowledged to be America's first newspaper; its editor, Benjamin Harris, America's first journalist. In his prospectus for the paper, Harris indicated that such a newspaper was necessary to combat the spirit of lying which then prevailed in Boston and, if I am not mistaken, still does. Harris pledged himself to exposing those who maliciously give false reports. He concluded his prospectus with the following sentence: "It is suppos'd that none will dislike this Proposal but such as intend to be guilty of so villainous a crime."

Harris was right about who would dislike the proposal. The second issue of *Publick Occurrences* never appeared. The Governor and Council suppressed it, complaining that Harris had printed "reflections of a very high nature," by which they meant that they had no intention of admitting any impediments to whatever villainy they wished to pursue. And so, in the New World, began the struggle for freedom of information which, in the Old, had begun a century before. Bacon and Milton had already stated the essential relationship between liberty and information, the case being summed up for the millionth time by Walter Lippmann in 1920. He wrote, "There can be no liberty for a community which lacks the information by which to detect lies."

I want to advance here the cause of a slightly different proposition, namely, that there can be no liberty for a community which lacks the critical skills to tell

---

*"Critical Thinking in the Electronic Age" by Neil Postman first appeared in *National Forum*, vol. LXV, no. 1 (Winter 1985), 4–8. Printed here by permission of the author.

the difference between lies and truth. Lippmann assumed that if citizens merely had information available to them they would have the good sense to sort out the true from the false. Most of us here, I take it, do not make that assumption. We are inclined to believe that even when information is abundantly available people require a serious education in how to think, without which they are as vulnerable to tyrants and knaves as those who are deprived of information. And so, we must reflect on the nature of that education.

But before we proceed too far, I think we would be wise to consider what is the nature of the information we want to be critical about. Information may come in many different forms—through the spoken word, the written word, the printed word, the painted image, or the electronic image, to suggest only a few. What critical equipment we think it essential to have may, therefore, vary, depending on what form of discourse is dominant in one's culture. If, for example, we were living in a culture where all forms of important public discourse were a product of the printing press and an oratory rooted in the printed word, then it would make sense to educate our students in logic, rhetoric, and semantics, and leave it at that. In fact, these subjects worked tolerably well in the eighteenth and nineteenth centuries in America, which is why in one of Henry Steel Commager's many books about that period, he referred to America as The Empire of Reason. Studies in logic, rhetoric, and semantics still have their uses, of course, but it must be obvious to everyone here that the imperial dominance of typography has come to an end in America; that the printed word has moved to the periphery of our culture, and the electronic image has taken its place at the center. If educators have not yet acknowledged this fact, television executives certainly have: for example, Leonard Goldenson, chairman of the Board of the ABC television network. Speaking at the commencement exercises at Emerson College in 1981, Goldenson said,

> [We] can no longer rely on our mastery of traditional skills. As communicators, as performers, as creators—and as citizens—[the electronic revolution] requires a new kind of literacy. It will be a visual literacy, an electronic literacy, and it will be as much of an advance over the literacy of the written word we know today as that was over the purely oral tradition of man's early history.

By looking at the preceding sentences, you will note, I am sure, that Goldenson has already lost some of the mastery of traditional skills to which he refers. But putting that aside, we must admit that his claim is difficult to refute. Goldenson speaks with great assurance because he knows that American children watch, on the average, 5000 hours of TV before they ever show up at school. He knows that they watch about 16,000 hours by high school's end. He knows that in the first twenty years of their lives they will see about 800,000 television commercials, at the rate of 800 to 900 a week. He knows, in short, that television is winning the competition with typography for the time, attention, and cognitive predispositions of our youth, as well as of ourselves.

It seems very clear to me, therefore, that we ought not to proceed in our discussion of critical thinking as if we were living in the nineteenth century: That is, we cannot assume that the *form* of information which now comprises most public discourse is not different from what it was in the nineteenth century. Advertising provides a pathetic illustration of how educators can be led down the path of irrelevance when they do not take into account the nature of the new media.

Many teachers try to teach their students how to distinguish between false or misleading claims and authentic ones. All of us, of course, want our students to know how to protect themselves from phony advertising. But a claim, whether true or false, must be made in language. More precisely, it must take the form of a proposition, for that is the universe of discourse from which such words as true and false come. If that universe of discourse is discarded, an advertisement is immune to the rigors of logical analysis or empirical tests. And indeed, when one looks at modern advertising, one sees at once that propositions are as scarce as unattractive people.

The fact is that advertisers just about stopped using propositions seventy-five years ago. Today, the truth or falsity of their claims is simply not an issue. A McDonald's commercial, for example, is not a series of testable, logically ordered assertions. It is a drama, a mythology, if you will, of handsome people selling, buying, and eating hamburgers, and being driven to near ecstasy by their good fortune. Is this a claim? Is this true or false? I submit that such questions do not apply to the world of visual images. One can like or dislike a television advertisement, but one cannot refute it. And because this is so, not only has the symbolic arena of advertising changed but, more important, so has the symbolic arena of politics and political information.

Surely the most obvious fact about our present situation is that through television the visual image, embedded in a variety of dramatic formats, has now emerged as our basic unit of political conversation. Politics today is not *The Federalist* or the *The Federalist Papers*. It is not the Lincoln-Douglas debates. It is not even Roosevelt's fireside chats. In all of these, language was the central ingredient. In the age of TV, the ideas of political leaders are not, for the most part, expressed in the form of subjects and predicates and therefore are not susceptible either to refutation or logical analysis, any more than are McDonald's commercials.

A particularly sobering illustration of the primacy of the visual image in our age came to me as a result of a personal experience of a few years back, when I played a small role in Ramsey Clark's Senate campaign against Jacob Javits in New York. A great believer in the public's right to know, Clark carefully prepared a small library of brilliantly articulated position papers on a variety of subjects from race relations to nuclear power to the Middle East. He filled each paper with historical background, economic and political facts, and, I thought, an enlightened sociological perspective. He might as well have drawn cartoons. In fact, Jacob Javits did draw cartoons, in a manner of speaking. If Javits had a position on any issue, the fact was unknown to me or the voters. Javits built his campaign on a series of thirty-second TV commercials in which he used visual imagery, in much the same way as McDonald's, to project himself as a man of experience, virtue, and piety. For all I know, Javits believed as strongly in the public's right to know as did Ramsey Clark, but he believed more strongly in retaining his seat in the Senate. And he knew full well in what century we are living. He understood that in a world of TV and other visual media, "knowing" means having pictures in your head more than sentences. I need hardly say that he won the election by the largest plurality in New York state history.

I will not labor the commonplace that any serious candidate for political office in America requires the services of an image manager to design the kinds of pictures that will lodge in the public's collective head. I do, however, wish to remind you of Richard Nixon's reply to a reporter who asked him in 1982 what he thought of Ted Kennedy's chances in the 1984 presidential race. Nixon remarked that Kennedy's first order of business, if he is serious, is to lose forty pounds. In other words, Nixon knows that through television Americans have been transformed into the sort of people who will not elect a fat person to high political office. He knows that on TV the grossness of, let us say, a dual-chinned, 230-pound image would easily overwhelm whatever wisdom that might issue forth from its mouth. I might add that Nixon probably also knows that the dishonor that shrouds him now is a result not of the fact that he lied but that on television he looked like a liar, a fact which ought not to give comfort to anyone, not even veteran Nixon-haters. For among the alternative possibilities are that one may look like a liar but be telling the truth, or even worse, may look like a truth-teller but, in fact, be lying.

What I am saying is that exposition, explanation, and argument—the instruments of rational discourse—are less and less used as a means of expressing political ideas, and therefore the traditional means of educating people in critical thinking are less and less relevant. What is happening is that the use of extended and complex language is being rapidly replaced by the gestures, images, and formats of the arts of show business, toward which most of the new media especially television, are powerfully disposed. The result is that in the political domain, as well as in other arenas of public discourse—religion and commerce, for example—Americans no longer talk to each other; they entertain each other. They do not exchange ideas; they exchange images. They do not argue with propositions; they argue with good looks, celebrities, parables, and public opinion polls. Because of this, it was even possible for a movie actor to become president of the United States.

One of the more revealing acknowledgments of this shift in the form of public information came not long ago—and I dare say inadvertently—from the late Jessica Savitch, the NBC correspondent. "Voters and viewers," she said, "have come of age in the '80s. Viewers have a tremendous amount of visceral smarts." She went on to observe that these visceral smarts allow viewers to know what is real, what has merit, and what is true. Now, the point to be insisted upon here is that the replacement of the brain by the viscera in political judgment was entirely unanticipated by the Founding Fathers. When Madison, Hamilton, and their colleagues wrote the Constitution, they assumed that mature citizenship necessarily implied a fairly high level of literacy and its concomitant analytical skills. For this reason, the young, commonly defined as those under twenty-one, were excluded from the electoral process by most states, because it was further assumed that the achievement of sophisticated literacy required training over a long period of time, as indeed it does. These assumptions were entirely fitting in the eighteenth century in a society organized around the printed word, where political discourse was conducted largely through books, newspapers, pamphlets, and an oratory very much influenced by print. As Alexis de Tocqueville tells us, the politics of America was the politics of the printed page.

Whatever other assumptions guided the development of America's political structure, none was more deeply ingrained than that visceral smarts were the enemy of sound political judgment, which is why Jefferson, for example, saw universal education and the discipline of literacy as the essential ingredients in the great American experiment.

The assumptions of Jefferson and his colleagues were weakened in the nineteenth century with the emergence of what Daniel Boorstin calls The Graphic Revolution—that is, the beginnings of a visual culture, in which discourse about commerce, religion, and politics was conducted in posters, photographs, advertisements, and drawings. In the twentieth century, with the Electronic Revolution, the assumptions of the Founding Fathers have lost most of their coherence. And so there is a sense, in which a remark made by an old professor of mine, George Counts, has to be taken quite seriously. In 1954, Counts astonished our seminar at Columbia University by saying that the media have repealed the Bill of Rights. But the media have not done this in a way for which most civil libertarians and educators are prepared. Like Walter Lippmann, we have been deeply concerned, for example, with assuring people access to information. But TV does not limit anyone's access. In fact, it increases access. But it does so, as I have suggested, by changing the *form* in which information becomes available. We see this not only in commerce and politics but even in religion, which on television is presented to us as a kind of Las Vegas production (see Postman, "The Las Vegasizing of America," *National Forum,* Summer 1982). There are handsome people both in the audience and on stage. There are floral displays and expensive sets. The audience is never troubled by rigorous demands. There is no dogma, no ritual, no tradition, no principles, no theology. We are required to respond only to the charisma of the preacher.

And we find the same thing in TV's presentation of what is called the daily news. A typical TV news show is put together in much the same way as a David Merrick stage show. There is always a musical theme to excite the audience. There are handsome performers, a fast tempo, comic relief provided by the weatherperson, and always interesting although fragmented film footage to insure continuous visual stimulation. There are between ten and fifteen stories, none taking more time than 100 seconds, most fewer than forty-five seconds, and all presented without context, explanation, continuity, or theory—that is, presented as essentially meaningless. For those inclined to think I am exaggerating, consider, for example, the case of Iran during what was called the "Iranian Hostage Crisis." I don't suppose there has been a story in years that received more continuous attention from the media. And now, I put these questions to you: Would it be an exaggeration to say that not one American in a hundred even knows what language the Iranians speak? Or what the word "ayatollah" means or implies? Or knows any details of the tenets of Iranian religious beliefs? Or the main outlines of their political history? Or knows who the Shah was and where he came from? Nonetheless, everyone had an opinion about this event, for in America everyone has a right to an opinion, and it is certainly useful to have a few when a pollster shows up.

But these are opinions of a quite different order from eighteenth- or nineteenth-century opinions. It is probably more accurate to call them emotions rather than opinions, which would account for the fact that they change from week to week, as the pollsters tell us.

I will not comment at length on the intriguing matter of what the phrase "public opinion" might mean today. Most pollsters seem to think it is self-evident. In this, I am sure they are mistaken, especially if they believe that the phrase suggests opinions based on a rational analysis of information. What does, however, seem to me self-evident is that television and other modern media have degraded the meaning of information by creating a species of it that might properly be called *disinformation*. I am using this word almost in the precise sense in which it is used by spies in the CIA or KGB. Disinformation does not mean false information. It means misleading information—misplaced, fragmented, irrelevant, or superficial information—information that creates the illusion of knowing something but which, in fact, leads one away from knowing. In this sense, almost all advertising is disinformation, and so is most everything on television, insofar as it concerns serious social and political discourse.

To illustrate this point, I offer the case of the eighty-minute discussion provided by the ABC network on November 20, 1983, following its controversial movie "The Day After." I choose this case above many other possibilities because, clearly, here was television at its most serious and responsible. Indeed, everything that made up this event recommended it as a critical test of television's capacity to depart from an entertainment mode and rise to the level of public instruction. In the first place, the subject under discussion was the possibility of a nuclear holocaust, not exactly a theme about which anyone would be inclined to flippancy. Second, the film itself had been attacked by several influential bodies politic, including Jerry Falwell's Moral Majority. Thus, it was important that the network display television's value and serious intentions as a medium of information and coherent discourse. Third, on the program itself, no musical theme was used as background. This is not an insignificant point, since almost all television programs, regardless of their content, are embedded in music as a way of announcing to the audience what emotions are to be called forth. This is a standard theatrical device, and its absence on television is always ominous. Fourth, there were no commercials during the discussion, thus elevating the tone of the event to the state of reverence usually reserved for the funerals of assassinated presidents. And finally, the participants included Henry Kissinger, Robert McNamara, and Elie Wiesel, each of whom is a symbol, of sorts, of serious discourse. Although Kissinger has since made an appearance on the hit show "Dynasty," he was then and still is a paradigm of intellectual sobriety; and Wiesel is practically a walking metaphor of social conscience. Indeed, the other members of the cast—Carl Sagan, William Buckley, and General Brent Scowcroft—are, each in his way, men of intellectual bearing who are not expected to participate in trivial public matters.

Now, what I want to demonstrate is that it is in the nature of television that public discourse will almost always be trivialized, that all information will almost always be transformed into disinformation, and that television cannot prevent itself from doing this even when its theme and its people mean it to do otherwise.

The program began with Ted Koppel, the master of ceremonies, so to speak, indicating that what followed was not intended to be a debate but a discussion. And so people like ourselves, who are interested in the philosophy of discourse, had an excellent opportunity to observe what television means by the word "discussion." Here is what it means: Each of six people was given approximately three or four minutes to say something about the subject.

But as the discussion proceeded, we soon discovered there was no agreement on exactly what the subject was, and no one felt obliged to respond to anything anyone else said. In fact, even if one were so inclined, it would have been difficult to do so. The participants were called upon seriatim, as if they were finalists in a beauty contest, each being given his share of minutes in front of the camera. Thus if Wiesel, who was called upon last, had a response to Buckley, who was called upon first, there would have been four commentaries in between, occupying about fifteen minutes, so that the audience (if not Wiesel himself) would have had difficulty remembering the argument which prompted his response. In fact, the participants—most of whom are no strangers to television— largely avoided addressing each other's points. They used their initial minutes and then their subsequent ones to intimate a position or to give an impression. Kissinger, for example, seemed intent on making viewers feel sorry that he was no longer their Secretary of State by reminding everyone of books he had once written, proposals he had once made, and negotiations he had once conducted. McNamara informed the audience that he had eaten lunch in Germany that very afternoon and went on to say that he had at least fifteen proposals to reduce nuclear arms. One would have thought that the discussion would turn on this point, but the others seemed about as interested in it as they were in what he might have had for lunch in Germany. Later, McNamara took the initiative to mention three of his proposals, but they were not discussed. Elie Wiesel, in a series of quasi parables and paradoxes, stressed the tragic nature of the human condition. But because he did not have the time to provide a context for his remarks, he seemed quixotic and confused, conveying an impression of an itinerant rabbi who had wandered into a coven of Gentiles.

In other words, this was no discussion, as we normally use the word. There were no arguments or counterarguments. No scrutiny of assumptions. No explanations, no elaborations. Carl Sagan, in my opinion, made the most coherent statement—a four-minute rationale for a nuclear freeze—but his statement was not carefully examined; apparently, no one wanted to take time from his own few minutes to call attention to another's position. Koppel, for his part, felt obliged to keep the show moving, and though he occasionally pursued what he discerned as a line of thought, he was more concerned to give each man his fair allotment of time.

But it is not time constraints alone that produce such fragmented and discontinuous language. When a television show is in progress, no one is permitted to say, "What do you mean when you say . . . ?" or "Let me think about that," or "I don't know." This form of language not only slows down the tempo of the show but creates the impression of uncertainty or lack of finish, and it tends to reveal people in the *act of thinking*. But thinking does not play well on television. There is not much to *see* in it, which is to say, it is not a performing art. But television demands a performing art and so, no matter how serious the countenances of the performers, what we get is a picture of men not so much thinking as acting the role of concerned intellectuals. One's impulse is to review their performances, not their ideas—mainly because there are no ideas to review.

Television, in other words, does not direct our attention to ideas, which are abstract, sequential, slowmoving, and complex. It directs us to respond to images, which are holistic, concrete, and simplistic. That is why it rarely matters what anyone says on television. Neither does it matter in what context anyone appears. Gerald Ford and Henry Kissinger show up on "Dynasty." Ralph Nader and Edward Koch are hosts on "Saturday Night Live." Tip O'Neill does a guest shot on "Cheers." Billy Graham exchanges one-liners with George Burns on an NBC special.

This being the case, the problem facing educators who are concerned with critical thinking is formidable. We are no longer talking about providing students with technical apparatus with which they can uncover the unwarranted assumption, the carelessly expressed fact, the logical mishap, or even the demagogic generalization. We are talking about how to help students protect themselves and their culture from a new kind of epistemology, a new kind of discourse— indeed, from a culture on the verge of amusing itself to death.

When educators gather to discuss critical thinking, their thoughts inevitably turn to George Orwell and his book *1984*. In this, I believe, they are making a mistake. There was another, somewhat earlier, prophecy that comes much closer to the mark than Orwell's. I refer to Aldous Huxley's *Brave New World*. Its prophecies are quite different from those of *1984*. As Huxley saw it, no Big Brother will be required to deprive people of their freedoms. People, he believed, will come to like their oppression. They will come to love the technologies which deprive them of their capacities to think. Orwell feared we would be oppressed by tyranny. Huxley feared we would be oppressed by triviality. Orwell feared we will be controlled by pain. Huxley feared we will be controlled by pleasure.

May I suggest that you consider the possibility that Huxley, not Orwell, was right?

Questions for Reflection and Discussion

---

1.   How does Postman think most Americans gain their beliefs and attitudes? What is his evidence for this view?

2.   On what grounds does Postman believe that the truth or falsity of statements or claims is no longer a primary issue in advertising?

3.   How does Postman see the comparative significance of image and policy position in contemporary United States political campaigns?

4.   How would you understand the statement by George Counts, that the media have repealed the Bill of Rights? Would you tend to agree or disagree? Why?

5.   What is unsatisfying about televised discussions such as that following "The Day After"? How, if at all, could arrangements for such debates and discussions be changed so as to encourage a more thorough and closely reasoned examination of issues?

6.   If you were to make three proposals to improve prospects for critical analysis of materials presented on television, what would they be?

2

Are Fallacies Common? A Look at Two Debates*

Gary Jason

Two United States presidential debates (Nixon/Kennedy and Reagan/ Mondale) provide a number of examples of logical fallacies, confirming the hypothesis that fallacies of reasoning are fairly frequent. Ignoring issues by evading questions, using humor to divert attentions, and appeals to patriotism are especially common. Inferring that a government is responsible for everything that occurs during its tenure, due to its actions or inactions, amounts to committing the fallacy of "false cause" and is also common.

T he last decade has seen a healthy debate regarding the nature of fallacies. The "standard textbook account" has been criticised extensively, and new theoretical approaches have been tried, centering around the formal theory of dialogue. The debate has taken on added importance since the recent widespread adoption of "critical thinking" requirements at many colleges.

One aspect of the standard textbook account has drawn considerable criticism: the claim that fallacies are "commonly made" errors in reasoning. Such a claim has struck some scholars as an exaggeration, or as perhaps mere motivational remarks to induce the student to study harder. Maurice Finocchiaro has put this criticism with special sharpness:

> What is wrong with such accounts of fallacies? One problem concerns the paucity of actual examples. . . . It is in fact puzzling that logic textbooks shouldn't be able to come up with more examples of fallacies actually committed given that fallacies are supposed to be *common* errors in reasoning. One gets the suspicion that logically incorrect arguments are not that common in practice, that their existence may be largely restricted to logic textbook examples and exercises.[1]

*Are Fallacies Common? A Look at Two Debates" by Gary Jason is due to appear in *Informal Logic*. It appears here with the consent of the author and of the editors of *Informal Logic*.

He concludes:

> The conclusion I wish to draw from such "consultations" is not that errors in reasoning are probably not common in real life, but that there probably are no common errors in reasoning. That is, logically incorrect arguments may be common, but common types of logically incorrect arguments probably are not.[2]

In this article I wish to give empirical evidence that fallacies are indeed common. I will use the term "fallacy" to mean the sort of errors in reasoning labeled in standard logic texts. Whether the standard definitions should be altered or clarified by means of formal dialectic is a question I will not address.

It would be wise to get clear on what the claim "fallacies are common" really involves. Clearly, nobody means to suggest that fallacies occur commonly in all aspects of our daily lives. Most of our waking hours are spent on entertainment, transportation, recreation, and so on. Fallacies are not common in such activities for the trivial reason that no argumentation bad or good takes place in those activities. If we are to test fairly the claim that fallacies are common, we must focus on contexts of argumentative persuasion.

Focusing on these contexts generally rules out not only fiction but a good deal of nonfiction as well. After all, most mainstream newspapers tend simply to describe events, except in the opinion/editorial pages. Quite a bit of nonfiction is devoted to simply explaining current developments in science, say, or computers.

What then are clear contexts of argumentative persuasion? Your list may differ from mine, but I would include: advertisements, editorials, position papers, essays, letters to the editor, debates, and books and articles that advocate some position. It is to these sorts of contexts that the claim that fallacies are common is meant to apply.

It is easy to get the impression that fallacies are uncommon if one reads scientific or philosophical journals or books. Such literature is by its nature closely reasoned. Even if the fallacies are not commonly present in such writings, that does not mean that fallacies are not common; rather, it only shows that careful reasoners can avoid what are otherwise common errors in reasoning. Indeed, those of us who teach the standard material hope that eventually those fallacies will be uncommon precisely because people will become more careful thinkers.

It is equally easy to get the impression that not only are fallacies common but *nonfallacious* reasoning is *uncommon,* if you read the tabloids. *The National Enquirer* is the best-selling newspaper in the country, and its numerous clones also sell well. A typical issue is loaded with fallacies of the traditional sort: ads that appeal to popular sentiment or contain fallacious appeals to authority ("this diet is doctor tested!"); editorials filled with invective, personal attacks, and loaded language; amphibolous headlines intended to make uninteresting stories interesting ("NUN WALKS HUNDREDS OF MILES—TO LOSE WEIGHT!" and the story describes a perfectly banal case of a nun who walks several blocks every evening for exercise, which over the years adds up to hundreds of miles); ads with key clauses put in fine print ("accent"); and so on.

However, if the claim that fallacies are common is to be tested fairly, we should avoid extremes—contexts either especially "clean" or especially "dirty." If the claim that fallacies are common is taken fairly, it clearly is meant to apply to ordinary contexts of argumentative persuasion: opinion/editorial pieces in good-quality newspapers and newsmagazines; letters to the editors of good-quality newspapers, newsmagazines, opinion political journals (such as *National Review, New Republic,* and *Atlantic*), and other nonfiction magazines (such as *Byte,* and *Car and Driver*); political debates; position papers; and so on.

I propose empirically to investigate the claim that fallacies as standardly defined are common by selecting a fair context of argumentative persuasion, one that clearly influences the opinions of millions of Americans: political debates. Political debates are quite common in American political life. You can think immediately of classical debates such as the ones between Lincoln and Douglas; but of course such debates have had even wider impact since their advent of television (starting with the Richard Nixon/John Kennedy debates, then Jimmy Carter/Gerald Ford, Carter/Ronald Reagan, and Reagan/Walter Mondale). To make this investigation more useful, we will look at two debates, separated widely in time but being similar in importance: the third Kennedy/Nixon debate (October 13, 1960) and the second Reagan/Mondale debate (October 21, 1984). Both debates were important in their respective elections; indeed, both resulted in turnarounds in the polls for the candidates who eventually won their respective races. In what follows, I will select fallacies falling in certain recurring categories for commentary, rather than reproducing the whole debates. Although each debate has between forty and fifty readily identifiable standard fallacies, I have tried to select the most instructive for analysis.

Fallacies of Ignoring the Issue

In examining the tests of the two debates, you can be immediately struck by the large number of times in which the candidates ignore the issue. Some examples:

> *Mr. Nixon:* Now, looking to the U-2 flights, I would like to point out that I have been supporting the president's position throughout. I think the president was correct in ordering these flights. I think the president was correct, certainly, in his decision to continue the flights while the conference was going on. I noted, for example, in reading a particular discussion that Senator Kennedy had with Dave Garroway shortly after the uh—his statements about regrets, that uh—he made the statement that he felt that these particular flights were ones that shouldn't have occurred right at that time, and the indication was how would [Premier Nikita] Khrushchev have felt if we had had a flight over the United States while he was visiting here. And the answer, of course, is that Communist espionage goes on all the time. The answer is that the United States can't afford to have an espionage lack—or should I say an intelligence lag—any more than we can afford to have a missile lag.

It is clear from the passage that Kennedy had raised the issue of whether U-2 flights should have been conducted while Khrushchev was visiting here, and Nixon addressed the different issue of whether the United States should engage in espionage. I do not think I am being uncharitable in interpreting Nixon's remarks as having evaded the issue; indeed, Kennedy rebutted him shortly after Nixon made his comment.

> *Mr. Kennedy:* Number two, on the question of the U-2 flights. I thought the U-2 flights in May just before the conference were a mistake in timing because of the hazards involved, if the summit conference had any hope for success. I never criticized the U-2 flights in general, however. I never suggested espionage should stop. It still goes on, I would assume, on both sides.

In the preceding example, the candidate ignored the issue by "setting up a strawman"—that is, distorting his opponent's position. Also common in the debates are cases in which candidates did not answer the questions put to them, but instead raised irrelevant issues or reverted to earlier issues.

> *Mr. McGee:* Mr. Vice-President, some of your early campaign literature said you were making a study to see if new laws were needed to protect the public against excessive use of power by labor unions. Have you decided whether such new laws are needed, and, if so, what would they do?

> *Mr. Nixon:* Mr. McGee, I am planning a speech on that subject next week. Also, so that we can get the opportunity for the questioners to question me, it will before the next television debate. I will say simply, in advance of it, that I believe that in this area, the laws which should be passed, as far as the big national emergency strikes are concerned, are ones that will give the president more weapons with which to deal with those strikes. Now, I have a basic disagreement with Senator Kennedy, though, on this point. He has taken the position, when he first indicated in October of last year, that he would even favor compulsory arbitration as one of the weapons the president might have to stop a national emergency strike. I understand in his last speech before the Steelworkers Union, that he changed that position and indicated that he felt that government seizure might be the best way to stop a strike which could not be settled by collective bargaining. I do not believe we should have either compulsory arbitration or seizure. I think the moment that you give to the union, on the one side, and to management, on the other side, the escape hatch of eventually going to government to get it settled, that most of these great strikes will end up being settled by government, and that will be in the end, in my opinion, wage control; it would mean price control—all the things that we do not want. I do believe, however, that we can give to the president of the United States powers, in addition to what he presently has in the fact-finding area, which would enable him to be more effective than we have been in handling these strikes.

Are Fallacies Common? A Look at Two Debates 23

Nixon did not answer the question whether he would propose new laws restricting the power of unions, and if so, which ones. He said he would give a speech the next week on the subject, he criticized Kennedy's position on compulsory arbitration, but aside from saying that the president needed greater powers to deal with national emergency strikes, he said nothing. Speaking in generalities is one way candidates ignore the specific issue raised by a questioner. Another example:

> *Mr. McGee:* Senator Kennedy, a moment ago you mentioned tax loopholes. Now your running mate, Senator Lyndon Johnson, is from Texas, an oil-producing state and one that many political leaders feel is in doubt in this election year. And reports from there say that oil men in Texas are seeking assurance from Senator Johnson that the oil depletion allowance will not be cut. The Democratic platform pledges to plug loopholes in the tax laws and refers to inequitable depletion allowance as being conspicuous loopholes. My question is, do you consider the 27½ percent depletion allowance inequitable, and would you ask that it be cut?

> *Mr. Kennedy:* Mr. McGee, there are about 104 commodities that have some kind of depletion allowance—different kinds of minerals, including oil. I believe all of those should be gone over in detail to make sure that no one is getting a tax break, to make sure that no one is getting away from paying the taxes he ought to pay. That includes oil; it includes all kinds of minerals; it includes everything within the range of taxation. We want to be sure it's fair and equitable. It includes oil abroad. Perhaps that oil abroad should be treated differently than the oil here at home. Now the oil industry recently has had hard times. Particularly some of the smaller producers. They're moving about eight or nine days in Texas. But I can assure you that if I'm elected president, the whole spectrum of taxes will be gone through carefully, and if there are any inequities in oil or any other commodity, then I would vote to close that loophole. I have voted in the past to reduce the depletion allowance for the largest producers, for those from $5 million down, to maintain it at 27½ percent. I believe we should study this and other allowances, tax expense, dividend expenses, and all the rest, and make a determination of how we can stimulate growth, how we can provide the revenues needed to move our country forward.

Note that Kennedy never specifically answered the questions whether the present 27½ percent depletion allowance was inequitable and whether he would cut it. In many of their other answers, Kennedy and Nixon both spoke in generalities.

Ignoring the issue is a prominent feature of the Reagan/Mondale debate—occurring fifteen times or more. Again, some examples:

> *Questioner:* Mr. Mondale, two related questions on the crucial issue of Central America. You and the Democratic Party have said that the only policy toward the horrendous civil wars in Central America should be on the economic developments and negotiations with, perhaps a quarantine of, Marxist Nicaragua. Do you believe that these answers would in any way solve the bitter conflicts there? Do you really believe

that there is no need to resort to force at all? Are not these solutions to Central America's gnawing problems simply again too weak and too late?

Mr. Mondale: I believe that the question oversimplifies the difficulties of what we must do in Central America. Our objectives ought to be to strengthen the democracy, to stop Communist and other extremist influences, and stabilize the community in that area.

To do that, we need a three-pronged attack. One is military assistance to our friends who are being pressured. Secondly, a strong and sophisticated economic aid program and human rights program that offer a better life and a sharper alternative to the alternative offered by the totalitarians who oppose us. And finally, a strong diplomatic effort that pursues the possibilities of peace in the area.

The crucial question about whether military force was needed was never specifically addressed. Instead, Mondale spoke in generalities.

Questioner: Mr. Mondale, if I could broaden the question just a little bit. Since World War II, every conflict that we as Americans have been involved with has been in nonconventional or irregular terms and yet we keep fighting in conventional or traditional military terms. The Central American wars are very much in the same pattern as China, as Lebanon, as Iran, as Cuba in the early days. Do you see any possibility that we are going to realize the change in warfare in our time or react to it in those terms?

Mr. Mondale: We absolutely must, which is why I responded to your first question the way I did. It's much more complex. You must understand the region, you must understand the politics in the area, you must provide a strong alternative, and you must show strength— and all at the same time. That's why I object to the covert action in Nicaragua. That's a classic example of a strategy that's embarrassed us, strengthened our opposition, and undermined the moral authority of our people and our country in the region.

Again, Mondale ignored the central question (how the United States should handle unconventional wars) by speaking in glittering generalities.

Questioner: Mr. President, I want to ask you about negotiating with friends. You severely criticized President Carter for helping to undermine two friendly dictators who got into trouble with their own people, the Shah of Iran and President [Anastasio] Somoza of Nicaragua. Now there are other such leaders heading for trouble, including President [Augusto] Pinochet of Chile and President [Ferdinand] Marcos of the Philippines. What should you do and what can you do to prevent the Philippines from becoming another Nicaragua?

Mr. Reagan: Morton, I did criticize the president because of our undercutting of what was a stalwart ally, the Shah of Iran. And I am not at all convinced that he was that far out of line with his people or that they wanted that to happen.

Are Fallacies Common? A Look at Two Debates   25

The Shah had done our bidding and carried our load in the Middle East for quite some time, and I did think that it was a blot on our record that we let him down. Had things gotten better, the Shah, whatever he might have done, was building low-cost housing, had taken land away from the mullahs, and was distributing it to the peasants so they could be landowners, things of that kind. But we turned it over to a maniacal fanatic who has slaughtered thousands and thousands of people calling it executions.

The matter of Somoza, no, I never defended Somoza. And as a matter of fact, the previous administration stood by and so did I—not that I could have done anything in my position at that time. But for this revolution to take place and the promise of the revolution was democracy, human rights, free labor unions, free press. And then just as [Fidel] Castro had done in Cuba, the Sandinistas ousted the other parties to the revolution. Many of them are now the Contras. They exiled some, they jailed some, they murdered some. And they installed a Marxist-Leninist totalitarian government.

And what I have to say about this is, many times—and this has to do with the Philippines also—I know there are things there in the Philippines that do not look good to us from the standpoint right now of democratic rights. But what is the alternative? It is a large Communist movement to take over the Philippines.

They have been our friend for—since their inception as a nation. And I think that we've had enough of a record of letting, under the guise of revolution, someone that we thought was a little more right than we would be, letting that person go and then winding up with totalitarianism pure and simple as the alternative, and I think that we're better off, for example, with the Philippines of trying to retain our friendship and help them right the wrongs we see rather than throwing them to the wolves and then facing a Communist power in the Pacific.

Note that Reagan ignored the issue of what he would do to prevent the Philippines from becoming another Nicaragua.

Why do candidates so often ignore the issues raised by the interviewers and the opposing candidates? We must remind ourselves that attributing a fallacy to someone is not necessarily to accuse that person of dishonest argumentation. In a sense, political candidates in a televised debate are prisoners of the format. They cannot say "I don't know, I'll have to think about it" to a new and difficult issue. Nor can they tell an interviewer that the question is hopelessly naive, or impertinent, or asinine, for fear of appearing churlish. The fault for such logical lapses may lie not in our politicians but in ourselves, for making up our minds about for whom to vote on the basis of one or two short debate performances.

False Cause

In reading the transcripts of the debates, you can be struck also by the number of times candidate A will argue that since bad things happened when candidate

B (or his party) was in office, that B was the cause of those bad things, or that since good things happened while A (or his party) was in office, that A was the cause of those good things. Such arguments are fallacies of false cause (specifically *post hoc ergo propter hoc*). Examples:

> *Mr. Nixon:* Yes. As a matter of fact, the statement that Senator Kennedy made was that—to the effect that there were trigger-happy Republicans, that my stand on Quemoy and Matsu was an indication of trigger-happy Republicans. I resent that comment. I resent it because it's an implication that Republicans have been trigger-happy and, therefore, would lead this nation into war. I would remind Senator Kennedy of the past fifty years. I would ask him to name one Republican president who led this nation into war. There were three Democratic presidents who led us into war. I do not mean by that that one party is a war party and the other party is a peace party. But I do say that any statement to the effect that the Republican party is trigger-happy is belied by the record.

We might interpret this passage charitably by taking Nixon's statement, "I do not mean by that that one party is a war party . . . " at face value. However, since Republicans such as Ford, Dole, and Bush have made the same point in later debates, that all wars in this century were started under Democratic presidents, I think we may fairly suspect that Nixon was attempting to paint the Democrats as being responsible for wars.

> *Mr. Nixon:* One last point I should make. The record in handling strikes has been very good during this administration. We have had less man-hours lost by strikes in these last seven years than we had in the previous seven years, by a great deal. And I only want to say that however good the record is, it's got to be better. Because in this critical period of the sixties we've got to move forward, all Americans must move forward together, and we have to get the greatest cooperation possible between labor and management. We cannot afford stoppages of massive effect on the economy when we're in the terrible competition we're in with the Soviets.

A fair construal of Nixon's remarks is that since fewer man-hours were lost by strikes during the Republican administration, it (and by some further inference, *he*) therefore should be given credit. But any number of other factors may be the cause of reduced strike activity.

> *Mr. Kennedy:* On the question of the cost of our budget, I have stated that it's my best judgment that our agricultural program will cost $1½ billion, possibly $2 billion less than the present agricultural program. My judgment is that the program the vice-president put forward, which is an extension of Mr. Benson's program, will cost $1 billion more than the present program, which costs about $6 billion a year, the most expensive in history. We've spent more money on agriculture in the last eight years than the hundred years of the agricultural department before that.

Are Fallacies Common? A Look at Two Debates

A fair construal of Kennedy's remarks is that because more money has been spent on agriculture during the years the Republicans were in the White House, they must be responsible for that increased spending. But again, other factors, such as Congressional actions, may have been the actual cause of the increase.

> *Mr. Nixon:* I am never satisfied with the economic growth of this country. I'm not satisfied with it even if there were no Communism in the world, but particularly when we're in the kind of race we're in, we have got to see that America grows just as fast as we can, provided we grow soundly. Because even though we have maintained, as I pointed out in our first debate, the absolute gap over the Soviet Union; even though the growth in this administration has been twice as much as it was in the Truman administration; that isn't good enough. Because America must be able to grow enough not only to take care of our needs at home for better education and housing and health—all these things we want.

Nixon asserted that he would not be content with the growth rate achieved under the current Republican administration, even though it was double the rate of the previous (Democratic) administration. It is reasonable to view this passage as implying that because under the Republican administration the growth rate was double what it was under the Democratic one, that the Republicans were responsible for the higher rate. Later in the debate, Nixon reiterated the argument:

> *Mr. Nixon:* America has not been standing still. Let's get that straight. Anybody who says America's been standing still for the last seven-and-a-half years hasn't been traveling around America. He's been traveling in some other country. We have been moving. We have been moving much faster than we did in the Truman years. But we can and must move faster, and that's why I stand so strongly for programs that will move America forward in the sixties, move her forward so that we can stay ahead of the Soviet Union and win the battle for freedom and peace.

An example from the Reagan/Mondale debate:

> *Mr. Mondale:* Where I part with the president is that despite all of those differences, we must, as past presidents before this one have done, meet on the common ground of survival.
> And that's where the president has opposed practically every arms control agreement, by every president of both political parties, since the bomb went off.
> And he now completes this term with no progress toward arms control at all, but with a very dangerous arms race underway instead.
> There are now over 2000 more warheads pointed at us today than there were when he was sworn in, and that does not strengthen us.

Mondale seems to be arguing that since there were no arms control agreements under Reagan, Reagan must be the cause. But other causes are possible; for instance, the instability in the Soviet government because several premiers died during Reagan's first term.

In the following exchange, several instances of false cause are committed.

> *Mr. Mondale:* One of the biggest problems today is that the countries to our south are so desperately poor that these people who will almost lose their lives if they don't come north, come north despite all the risks. And if we're going to find a permanent, fundamental answer to this, it goes to American economic and trade policies that permit these nations to have a chance to get on their own two feet and to get prosperity so that they can have jobs for themselves and their people.
>
> And that's why this enormous national debt, engineered by this administration, is harming these countries and fueling this immigration.
>
> These high interest rates, real rates, that have doubled under this administration, have had the same effect on Mexico and so on, and the cost of repaying those debts is so enormous that it results in massive unemployment, hardship, and heartache. And that drives our friends to the north—to the south—up into our region, and the need to end those deficits as well.

> *Moderator:* Mr. President, your rebuttal.

> *Mr. Reagan:* Well, my rebuttal is I've heard the national debt blamed for a lot of things but not for illegal immigration across our border, and it has nothing to do with it.
>
> But with regard to these high interest rates, too, at least give us the recognition of the fact that when you left office, Mr. Mondale, they were twenty-two-and-a-half, the prime rate; it's now twelve-and-one-quarter, and I predict it'll be coming down a little more shortly. So we're trying to undo some of the things that your administration did.

The national debt grew under Reagan, so Reagan caused it (and that, curiously, caused the illegal immigration from Mexico!), to which Reagan responded by saying that the interest rates were high under President Jimmy Carter, so Carter caused that problem (and so, curiously, that Mondale is to blame).

Again, we must be fair and realize that giving a candidate one minute to explain what causes, say, high interest rates is not a way to encourage in-depth causal analysis.

Ad Populum

Quite unsurprising is the large number of appeals to patriotism, "us-versus them" emotions and so on. These sorts of appeals are apparent in many of the sample passages cited earlier, especially in the passages appealing to our collective fear of the Soviets. Some additional examples:

> *Mr. Nixon:* Now what do the Chinese Communists want? They don't want just Quemoy and Matsu; they don't want just Formosa; they want

the world. And the question is if you surrender or indicate in advance that you're not going to defend any part of the free world, and you figure that's going to satisfy them, it doesn't satisfy them. It only whets their appetite; and then the question comes, when do you stop them? I've often heard President [Dwight] Eisenhower in discussing this question, make the statement that if we once start the process of indicating that this point or that point is not the place to stop those who threaten the peace and freedom of the world, where do we stop them? And I say that those of us who stand against surrender of territory—this or any others—in the face of blackmail, in the face of force by the Communists are standing for the course that will lead to peace.

In this passage, Nixon associated himself with the popular President Eisenhower and places himself in the class of those who oppose Communistic blackmail, who favor peace.

> *Mr. Nixon:* Beyond that, as far as the gold supply is concerned and as far as the movement of gold is concerned, we have to bear in mind that we must get more help from our allies abroad in this great venture in which all free men are involved in winning the battle for freedom.

Again, grandiose appeals to freedom are used to, somehow, buttress a position.

> *Mr. Nixon:* Of course, both Senator Kennedy and I have felt Mr. [Harry] Truman's ire; and consequently, I think he can speak with some feeling on this subject. I just do want to say one thing, however. We all have tempers; I have one; I'm sure Senator Kennedy has one. But when a man's president of the United States, or a former president, he has an obligation not to lose his temper in public. One thing I've noted as I've traveled around the country are the tremendous number of children who come out to see the presidential candidates. I see mothers holding their babies up, so that they can see a man who might be president of the United States. I know Senator Kennedy sees them, too. It makes you realize that whoever is president is going to be a man that all the children of America will either look up to, or will look down to. And I can only say that I'm very proud that President Eisenhower restored dignity and decency and, frankly, good language to the conduct of the presidency of the United States. And I only hope that, should I win this election, that I could approach President Eisenhower in maintaining the dignity of the office; in seeing to it that whenever any mother or father talks to his child, he can look at the man in the White House and, whatever he may think of his policies, he will say, "Well, there is a man who maintains the kind of standards personally that I would want my child to follow."

Ah, the mothers and their babies!

The closing statements in the Reagan/Mondale debate also brought out some appeal to the crowd. Two short examples:

Mr. Mondale: I want this nation to protect its air, its water, its land, and its public health. America is not temporary. We're forever. And as Americans, our generation should protect this wonderful land for our children.

I want a nation of fairness, where no one is denied the fullness of life or discriminated against, and we deal compassionately with those in our midst who are in trouble.

And above all, I want a nation that's strong. Since we debated two weeks ago, the United States and the Soviet Union have built 100 more warheads, enough to kill millions of Americans and millions of Soviet citizens.

Mr. Reagan: We shouldn't be dwelling on the past or even the present. The meaning of this election is the future, and whether we're going to grow and provide the jobs and the opportunities for all Americans that they need. Several years ago I was given an assignment to write a letter. It was to go into a time capsule and would be read in 100 years when that time capsule was opened. I remember driving down the California coast one day. My mind was full of what I was going to put in that letter about the problems and the issues that confront us in our time and what we did about them, but I couldn't completely neglect the beauty around me—the Pacific out there on one side of the highway shining in the sunlight, the mountains of the coast range rising on the other side, and I found myself wondering what it would be like for someone, wondering if someone 100 years from now would be driving down that highway and if they would see the same thing.

Not only do deceitful politicans stoop to *ad populum* appeals, even decent politicans engage in such rhetoric. But *ad populum* appeals should be recognized as such, even if we condone their usage in contexts such as the one under consideration.

Ad Hominem Attacks

Less frequent in the two debates are *ad hominem* attacks. I find this surprising, given how frequently personal attacks occur in ordinary arguments and letters to the editor of magazines and newspapers. Perhaps candidates in a nationally televised debate are reluctant to attack the other too blatantly, lest the debate turn into a mud-slinging contest. But sly digs are managed.

Mr. Kennedy: Mr. Griffin, I believe, who is the head of the [Ku Klux] Klan, who lives in Tampa, Florida, indicated in a statement, I think, two or three weeks ago that he was not going to vote for me and that he was going to vote for Mr. Nixon. I do not suggest in any way, nor have I ever, that that indicates that Mr. Nixon has the slightest sympathy, involvement, or in any way imply any inference in regard to the Ku Klux Klan. That's absurd. I don't suggest that. I don't support it. I would disagree with it.

Kennedy protested too much—he himself brought up that the head of the Ku Klux Klan came out in support of Nixon, and it is not uncharitable, I think, to believe that Kennedy was arguing that since the Klan supported Nixon, Nixon was suspect (guilt by association).

> *Mr. Nixon* [responding to Kennedy's point that the United States had slipped in prestige, as evidenced by Gallup polls taken in other countries and U.N. votes] : Well, I would say first of all that Senator Kennedy's statement that he's just made is not going to help our Gallup polls abroad, and it isn't going to help our prestige either. Let's look at the other side of the coin. Let's look at the vote on the Congo, the vote was seventy to nothing against the Soviet Union. Let's look at the situation with regard to economic growth as it really is. We find that the Soviet Union is a very primitive economy. Its growth rate is not what counts; it's whether it is catching up with us, and it is catching up with us. We're well ahead and we can stay ahead, provided we have confidence in America and don't run her down in order to build her up. We could look also at other items which Senator Kennedy has named, but I will only conclude by saying this: In this whole matter of prestige, in the final analysis, it's whether you stand for what's right. And getting back to this matter that we discussed at the outset, the matter of Quemoy and Matsu. I can think of nothing that will be a greater blow to the prestige of the United States among the free nations in Asia than for us to take Senator Kennedy's advice to go against what a majority of the members of the Senate, both Democrat and Republican, did—said in 1955, and to say in advance we will surrender an area to the Communists.

Nixon insinuated that Kennedy's point is suspect because it hurt our reputation, and that those who want America held in high regard should avoid such comments.

Other standard fallacies are discernible in the two debates, including loaded questions by the questioners, appeals to authority, false analogies, "slippery slope" arguments, and hedging.

Some of the candidates—Kennedy and Reagan, in particular, deflected questions by humorous diversion. It is plausible to suggest that those candidates who are by nature witty will use their wit to get out of answering questions they do not wish to answer. Examples:

> *Mr. Von Fremd:* Senator Kennedy, I'd like to shift the conversation, if I may, to a domestic political argument. The chairman of the Republican National Committee, Senator Thurston Morton, declared earlier this week that you owed Vice-President Nixon and the Republican party a public apology for some strong charges made by former President Harry Truman, who bluntly suggested where the vice-President and the Republican party could go. Do you feel that you owe the vice-President any apology?
>
> *Mr. Kennedy:* Well, I must say that Mr. Truman has his methods of expressing things; he's been in politics for fifty years; he's been president

of the United States. They are not my style. But I really don't think there's anything that I could say to President Truman that's going to cause him, at the age of seventy-six, to change his particular speaking manner. Perhaps Mrs. Truman can, but I don't think I can. I'll just have to tell Mr. Morton that. If you'd pass that message on to him.

Questioner: Mr. President, I want to raise an issue that I think has been lurking out there for two or three weeks and cast it specifically in national security terms. You already are the oldest president in history, and some of your staff say you were tired after your most recent encounter with Mr. Mondale. I recall, yes, that President Kennedy, had to go for days on end with very little sleep during the Cuba missile crisis. Is there any doubt in your mind that you would be able to function in such circumstances?

Mr. Reagan: Not at all, Mr. Trewhitt, and I want you to know that also I will not make age an issue of this campaign. I am not going to exploit for political purposes my opponent's youth and inexperience.
   If I still have time, I might add, Mr. Trewhitt, I might add that it was Seneca, or it was Cicero, I don't know which, that said if it was not for the elders correcting the mistakes of the young, there would be no state.

This was perhaps the most famous moment in the Reagan/Mondale debate. The President turned aside the question with a quip that made everyone including Mondale laugh, and it did much to defuse the "age issue."
   In both the debates examined, roughly forty to fifty standard fallacies are discernible, without, it must be admitted, being overly charitable. The numbers are reduced if we bend over backwards to be charitable, but the clear fallacies are still sufficiently numerous to justify the claim that the standard fallacies are common.
   Traditional categories of logical error, seemingly discerned by scholars of many different cultures over millenia, are no illusion.

Questions for Reflection and Discussion

   1. Do Jason's examples suggest that the intellectual content of United States presidential debates is rather poor? Why or why not?

   2. Could you spot the sorts of fallacies Jason finds in these debates if you were just watching the debates on television and did not have access to the written transcript?

   3. To what extent do you think the format (time limitations, television lights, camera, make-up, importance of visual imagery, need to keep material simple) might be responsible for the poor intellectual quality of these debates? What would Postman (in the previous article) say about this question?

4. Several times Jason refers to the possibility of being more charitable in his analysis. ("Charitable" in this context means giving the speaker more benefit of doubt when the meaning might be taken several ways, so that remarks are interpreted as coming out as sensible as possible.) Do you think Jason is not charitable enough? Why or why not?

Notes

1. Maurice Finocchiaro "Fallacies and the Evaluation of Reasoning," *American Philosophical Quarterly* vol. 18, no. 1 (January 1981): 14.

2. Ibid., 15.

3

The Tedium Twins*

by Alexander Cockburn

The view that there are two sides to every question can be satirized by imagining politely-conducted television interviews on such topics as the Crucifixion, slavery, and cannibalism. This view discourages serious analysis and intense response and encourages complacency. Always avoiding "extreme" positions will not lead to a correct understanding.

T onight: Are there two sides to every question? Back to you, Robin.

(Tease)

ROBERT MACNEIL (voice over): *A Galilean preacher claims he is the Redeemer and says the poor are blessed. Should he be crucified?*

(Titles)

MACNEIL: *Good evening. The Roman procurator in Jerusalem is trying to decide whether a man regarded by many as a saint should be put to death. Pontius Pilate is being urged by civil libertarians to intervene in what is seen here in Rome as being basically a local dispute. Tonight, the crucifixion debate. Jim?*

JIM LEHRER: *Robin, the provinces of Judaea and Galilee have always been trouble spots, and this year is no exception. The problem is part religious, part political, and in many ways a mixture of both. The Jews believe in one god. Discontent in the province has been growing, with many local businessmen complaining about the tax burden. Terrorism, particularly in Galilee, has been on the increase. In recent months, a carpenter's son from the town of Nazareth has been attracting a large following with novel doctrines and faith healing. He recently entered Jerusalem amid popular acclaim, but influential Jewish leaders fear his power. Here in Alexandria the situation is seen as dangerous. Robin?*

MACNEIL: *Recently in Jerusalem on a fact-finding mission for the*

---

*"The Tedium Twins" by Alexander Cockburn originally appeared in *Harper's Magazine* in August, 1982. Copyright 1982 © by *Harper's Magazine*. All rights reserved. Reprinted from the August issue by special permission.

Emperor's Emergency Task Force on Provincial Disorders was Quintilius Maximus. Mr. Maximus, how do you see the situation?

MAXIMUS: *Robin, I had occasion to hear one of this preacher's sermons a few months ago and talk with his aides. There is no doubt in my mind that he is a threat to peace and should be crucified.*

MACNEIL: *Pontius Pilate should wash his hands of the problem?*

MAXIMUS: *Absolutely.*

MACNEIL: *I see. Thank you. Jim?*

LEHRER: *Now for a view from Mr. Simon, otherwise known as Peter. He is a supporter of Christ and has been standing by in a Jerusalem studio. Robin?*

MACNEIL: *Mr. Simon Peter, why do you support Christ?*

SIMON PETER: *He is the Son of God and presages the Second Coming. If I may, I would like to read some relevant passages from the prophet Isaiah.*

MACNEIL: *Thank you, but I'm afraid we'll have to break in there. We've run out of time. Good night, Jim.*

LEHRER: *Good night, Robin.*

MACNEIL: *Sleep well, Jim.*

LEHRER: *I hope you sleep well, too, Robin.*

MACNEIL: *I think I will. Well, good night again, Jim.*

LEHRER: *Good night, Robin.*

MACNEIL: *We'll be back again tomorrow night. I'm Robert MacNeil. Good night.*

Admirers of the "MacNeil/Lehrer Report"—and there are many of them—often talk about it in terms normally reserved for unpalatable but nutritious breakfast foods: unalluring, perhaps, to the frivolous news consumer, but packed full of fiber. It is commended as the sort of news analysis a serious citizen, duly weighing the pros and cons of world history, would wish to masticate before a thoughtful browse through the *Federalist Papers,* a chat with spouse about civic duties incumbent on them on the morrow, and final blameless repose.

The promotional material for the "Report" has a tone of reverence of the sort usually employed by people reading guidebooks to each other in a French cathedral: "The weeknightly newscast's unique mix of information, expert opinion, and debate has foreshadowed an industry trend toward longer and more detailed coverage, while at the same time helping to reveal a growing public appetite for informational television. Nearly 4.5 million viewers watch the 'MacNeil/Lehrer Report' each night during the prime viewing season . . . "

"A program with meat on its bones," said the Association for Continuing Higher Education, in presenting its 1981 Leadership Award. "The 'MacNeil/ Lehrer Report' goes beyond the commercial networks' rushed recital of news to bring us in-depth coverage of single issues . . . There is a concern for ideas rather than video images . . . and they accord us the unusual media compliment of not telling us what to think, but allowing us to draw our own conclusions after we weigh conflicting views."

And the handout concludes in triumph with some findings from a 1980 Roper poll: "Three quarters of those polled said they had discovered pros and cons on issues on which they had not had opinions beforehand."

ROBERT MACNEIL (voice over): *Should one man own another?*

(Titles)

MACNEIL: *Good evening. The problem is as old as man himself. Do property rights extend to the absolute ownership of one man by another? Tonight, the slavery problem. Jim?*

LEHRER: *Robin, advocates of the continuing system of slavery argue that the practice has brought unparalleled benefits to the economy. They fear that new regulations being urged by reformers would undercut America's economic effectiveness abroad. Reformers, on the other hand, call for legally binding standards and even for a phased reduction in the slave force to something like 75 percent of its present size. Charlayne Hunter-Gault is in Charleston. Charlayne?*

HUNTER-GAULT: *Robin and Jim, I have here in Charleston Mr. Ginn, head of the Cottongrowers Association. Robin?*

MACNEIL: *Mr. Ginn, what are the arguments for unregulated slavery?*

GINN: *Robin, our economic data show that attempts at regulation of working hours, slave quarters, and so forth would reduce productivity and indeed would be widely resented by the slaves themselves.*

MACNEIL: *You mean, the slaves would not like new regulations? They would resent them?*

GINN: *Exactly. Any curbing of the slave trade would offer the Tsar dangerous political opportunities in western Africa and menace the strategic slave-ship routes.*

LEHRER: *Thank you, Mr. Ginn. Robin?*

MACNEIL: *Thank you, Mr. Ginn and Jim. The secretary of the Committee for Regulatory Reform in Slavery is Eric Halfmeasure. Mr. Halfmeasure, give us the other side of the story.*

HALFMEASURE: *Robin, I would like to make one thing perfectly clear. We are wholeheartedly in favor of slavery. We just see abuses that diminish productivity and reduce incentives for free men and women to compete in the marketplace. Lynching, tarring and feathering, rape, lack of holidays, and that sort of thing. One recent study suggests that regulation could raise productivity by 15 percent.*

MACNEIL: *I see. Thank you, Mr. Halfmeasure. Mr. Ginn?*

GINN: *Our studies show the opposite.*

MACNEIL: *Jim?*

LEHRER: *Charlayne?*

HUNTER-GAULT: *A few critics of slavery argue that it should be abolished outright. One of them is Mr. Wilberforce. Mr. Wilberforce, why abolish slavery?*

WILBERFORCE: *It is immoral for one man . . .*

MACNEIL: *Mr. Wilberforce, we're running out of time, I'm afraid. Let me very quickly get some other points of view. Mr. Ginn, you think slavery is good?*

GINN: *Yes.*

MACNEIL: *And you, Mr. Halfmeasure, think it should be regulated.*

HALFMEASURE: *Yes.*

MACNEIL: *Well, I've got you to disagree, haven't I?* (Laughter) *That's all we've got time for tonight. Good night, Jim.*

LEHRER: *Good night, Robin.*

MACNEIL: *Did you sleep well last night?*

LEHRER: *I did, thank you.*

The Tedium Twins 37

MACNEIL: *That's good. So did I. We'll be back again tomorrow night. I'm Robert MacNeil. Good night.*

The "MacNeil/Lehrer Report" started in October 1975, in the aftermath of Watergate. It was a show dedicated to the proposition that there are two sides to every question, a valuable corrective in a period when the American people had finally decided that there were absolutely and definitely *not* two sides to every question. Nixon was a crook who had rightly been driven from office; corporations were often headed by crooks who carried hot money around in suitcases; federal officials were crooks who broke the law on the say-so of the president.

It was a dangerous moment, for a citizenry suddenly imbued with the notion that there is not only a thesis and antithesis but also a synthesis, is a citizenry capable of all manner of harm to the harmonious motions of the status quo.

Thus came the "MacNeil/Lehrer Report," sponsored by public-television funds and by the most powerful corporate forces in America, in the form of Exxon, "AT & T and the Bell System," and other upstanding bodies. Back to Sunday school went the excited viewers to be instructed that reality, as conveyed to them by television, is not an exciting affair of crooked businessmen and lying politicians but a serious continuum in which parties may disagree but in which all involved are struggling manfully and disinterestedly for the public weal.

The narcotizing, humorless properties of the "MacNeil/Lehrer Report," familiar to all who have felt fatigue creep over them at 7:40 Eastern time, are crucial to the show. Tedium is of the essence, since the all-but-conscious design of the program is to project vacuous dithering ("And now, for another view of Hitler . . . ") into the minds of viewers until they are properly convinced that there is no one answer to "the problem" but two or even three, and that since two answers are no better than none, they might as well not bother with the problem at all.

The techniques employed by the show enhance this distancing and anesthetizing. The recipe is unvarying. MacNeil and Lehrer exchange modest gobbets of information with each other about the topic under discussion. Then, with MacNeil crouching—rather like Kermit the Frog in old age—down to the left and peering up, a huge face appears on the screen and discussion is under way. The slightest discommoding exchange, some intemperate observation on the part of the interviewee, causes MacNeil to bat the ball hastily down to Washington, where Lehrer sedately sits with his interviewee. By fits and starts, with Jim batting back to Robin and Robin batting across to Charlayne, the program lurches along. The antagonists are rarely permitted to joust with one another and ideally are sequestered on their large screens. Sometimes, near the end of the show, the camera will reveal that these supposed antagonists are in fact sitting chummily, shoulder to shoulder, around the same table as Lehrer— thus indicating to the viewer that, while opinions may differ, all are united in general decency of purpose. Toward the very end, MacNeil's true role becomes increasingly exposed as he desperately tries to suppress debate and substantive argument with volley after volley of "We're nearly out of time," "Congressman, in ten seconds could you . . . ," and the final, relieved "That's all for tonight."

It's even important that MacNeil and Lehrer say good night to each other so politely every evening. In that final, sedate nocturnal exchange everything is finally resolved, even though nothing has been resolved. We can all go to bed now.

And so to bed we go. The pretense is that viewers, duly presented with both sides of the case, will spend the next segment of the evening weighing the pro against the con and coming up with the answer. It is, in fact, enormously difficult to recall anything that anyone has ever said on a "MacNeil/Lehrer Report," because the point has been to demonstrate that since everything can be contradicted, nothing may be worth remembering. The show praised above all others for content derives its attraction entirely from form: the unvarying illustration that if one man can be found to argue that cannibalism is bad another can be found to argue that it is not.

Actually, this is an overstatement. "MacNeil/Lehrer" hates such violent extremes, and, by careful selection of the show's participants, the show tries to make sure that the viewer will not be perturbed by any views overly critical of the political and business establishment.

> ROBERT MACNEIL (voice over): *Should one man eat another?*
> (Titles)
> MACNEIL: *Good evening. Reports from the Donner Pass indicate that survivors fed upon their companions. Tonight, should cannibalism be regulated? Jim?*
> LEHRER: *Robin, the debate pits two diametrically opposed sides against each other: the Human Meat-Eaters Association, who favor a free market in human flesh, and their regulatory opponents in Congress and the consumer movement. Robin?*
> MACNEIL: *Mr. Tooth, why eat human flesh?*
> TOOTH: *Robin, it if full of protein and delicious too. Without human meat, our pioneers would be unable to explore the West properly. This would present an inviting opportunity to the French, who menace our pioneer routes from the north.*
> MACNEIL: *Thank you. Jim?*
> LEHRER: *Now for another view of cannibalism. Bertram Brussell Sprout is leading the fight to control the eating of animal fats and meats. Mr. Sprout, would you include human flesh in this proposed regulation?*
> SPROUT: *Most certainly, Jim. Our studies show that some human flesh available for sale to the public is maggot-ridden, improperly cut, and often incorrectly graded. We think the public should be protected from such abuses.*
> MACNEIL: *Some say it is wrong to eat human flesh at all. Mr. Prodnose, give us this point of view.*
> PRODNOSE: *Robin, eating people is wrong. We say . . .*
> MACNEIL: *I'm afraid we're out of time. Good night, Jim, etc., etc.*

Trudging back through the "MacNeil/Lehrer" scripts, the hardy reader will soon observe how extraordinarily narrow is the range of opinion canvassed by a show dedicated to dispassionate examination of the issues of the day. The favored blend is usually a couple of congressmen or senators, barking at each other from either side of the fence, corporate chieftains, government executives, ranking lobbyists, and the odd foreign statesman. The mix is ludicrously respectable, almost always heavily "establishment" in tone. Official spokesmen of trade and interest groups are preferred over people who only have something interesting to say.

This constriction of viewpoint is particularly conspicuous in the case of energy, an issue dear to the "MacNeil/Lehrer Report." "Economics of Nuclear Power," for example, was screened on November 25, 1980, and purported to examine why a large number of nuclear utilities was teetering on the edge of bankruptcy. Mustered to ponder the issue we had the following rich and varied banquet: the president of the Virginia Electric and Power Company; the vice-president (for nuclear operations) of Commonwealth Edison of Chicago; a vice-president (responsible for scrutinizing utility investments) at Paine Webber; and the president of the Atomic Industrial Forum. The viewers of "MacNeil/Lehrer" did not, you may correctly surmise, hear much critical opinion about nuclear power on that particular evening.

On May 1, 1981, the "Report" examined "the problems and prospects of getting even more oil out of our ground." Participants in the discussion about oil glut included some independent oil drillers and "experts" from Merrill Lynch, Phillips Petroleum Company, and the Rand Corporation.

At least on May 1 the viewers had more than one person saying the same thing ("regulation is bad"). On March 27 they were invited to consider the plans of the Reagan administration for a rebuilt navy. The inquiring citizen was offered a trip around the battleship *Iowa* in the company of MacNeil and an extremely meek interview, conducted by both MacNeil and Lehrer, of Secretary of the Navy John Lehman. No dissenting views were allowed to intrude, beyond the deferential inquiries of MacNeil and Lehrer, both of whom, it should be said, are very bad interviewers, usually ignorant and always timid. By contrast, Ted Koppel of ABC's "Nightline"—a far better show covering the same sort of turf—is a veritable tiger in interrogatory technique.

The spectrum of opinion thus offered is one that ranges from the corporate right to cautious centerliberal. One should not be misled, by the theatrical diversity of views deployed on the program, into thinking that a genuinely wide spectrum of opinion is permitted. Moldering piles of "MacNeil/Lehrer" transcripts before me on my desk attest to the fact.

The show would be nothing without Robert ("Robin") MacNeil. Canadian, of course, with a layer of high seriousness so thick it sticks to the screen, MacNeil anchors the show to tedium and yanks at the hawser every time the craft shows any sign of floating off into uncharted waters. He seems to have learned—on the evidence of his recent memoir, *The Right Place at the Right Time*—the elements of his deadly craft in London, watching the BBC and writing for Reuters.

MacNeil is a man so self-righteously boring that he apparently had no qualms in setting down the truth about his disgraceful conduct in Dallas on November 22, 1963. MacNeil was there covering Kennedy's visit for NBC. The shots rang out and he sprinted to the nearest telephone he could find. It so happens that he dashed, without knowing its significance, into the Texas Book Depository.

"As I ran up the steps and through the door, a young man in shirt sleeves was coming out. In great agitation I asked him where there was a phone. He pointed inside to an open space where another man was talking on a phone situated next to a pillar and said, 'Better ask him.' I ran inside . . . "

Later, MacNeil writes, "I heard on television that a young man called Oswald, arrested for the shooting, worked at the Texas Book Depository and had left by the front door immediately afterward. Isn't that strange, I told myself. He must have been leaving just about the time I was running in . . . "

Later still, William Manchester demonstrated that there was a 95 percent certainly that MacNeil had met Oswald. Any reporter, any human with anything other than treacle in the veins, would naturally make much of the coincidence and divert children, acquaintances, and indeed a wider public with interesting accounts of Oswald's demeanor at this significant moment. Not MacNeil. With Pecksniffian virtuousness, he insists that the encounter was merely "possible" and that "it is titillating, but it doesn't matter very much."

Such is the aversion to storytelling, the sodden addiction to the mundane, that produced "MacNeil/Lehrer." Like an Exocet missile, MacNeil can spot a cliché, a patch of ennui, and home in on it with dreadful speed. Witness his proclamation of political belief:

> Instinctively, I find it more satisfying to belong with those people in all countries who put their trust in Man's best quality, his rational intellect and its ability to recognize and solve problems. It is distressing that the recent course of American politics has caused that trust to be ridiculed or dismissed as some sort of soft-headedness, inappropriate to a virile nation confronting the dangerous world. It will be unfortunate if being a "liberal" remains an embarrassment, if young Americans should begin to believe that conservatives are the only realists.
>
> Each has its absurd extreme: liberalism tending to inspire foolish altruism and unwarranted optimism; conservatism leading to unbridled selfishness and paranoia. Taken in moderation, I prefer the liberal impulse: It is the impulse behind the great forces that have advanced mankind, like Christianity. I find it hard to believe that Jesus Christ was a political conservative, whatever views are espoused in his name today.
>
> For all my instinctive liberalism, my experience of politics in many countries has not left me wedded to any particular political parties. Rather, I have found myself politically dining à la carte, on particular issues.

This is the mind-set behind "MacNeil/Lehrer." "I have my own instinctive aversion to being snowed," he writes at another point. "The more I hear everyone telling me that some public person is wonderful, the more I ask myself, Can he really be all that wonderful? Conversely [for MacNeil there is always a "conversely" poking its head around the door], I never believe anyone can be quite as consistently terrible as his reputation."

Hitler? Attila the Hun? Pol Pot? Nixon? John D. Rockefeller? I'm afraid that's all we have time for tonight. We've run out of time. Good night.

Questions for Reflection and Discussion

1. In the imaginary interview on the Crucifixion, Cockburn has MacNeil break off when Simon Peter says, "He is the Son of God and presages the Second Coming." What general problem is Cockburn trying to bring out when he structures his imaginary interview this way?

2. What is wrong with the two positions on slavery, around which most of the second imaginary discussion is centered?

3. Cockburn thinks that a danger of such supposedly neutral shows as the MacNeil/Lehrer report is that a people will conclude that the suggested two answers are equally valid and that they might as well not bother to think further about the problem at all. Do you think this is a real danger? Why or why not?

4. If we received a categorically-stated and extreme-sounding judgment on the morality of Hitler or Pol Pot (responsible for between one and two million deaths in Cambodia, 1975–79, in pursuit of a pure form of Communism), would we be right or wrong if we suspected that it was incorrect because it was so extreme, according to Cockburn? Do you agree? Why or why not?

4

Are There Two Sides to Every Question?

Trudy Govier

Presenting two views does not always provide objectivity or intellectual balance, because each view can contain serious errors that may not be corrected in the presentation of the other view. A well-worded, well-reasoned, and careful statement of one view often can provide more solid understanding of an issue than opposed presentations of two different views, even when an issue is quite controversial. In addition, for many issues there may be more than two important positions. When we select two views and claim to give "both sides," we imply that every important position is represented, which is not so.

I n January 1984, an Alberta social studies teacher, James Keegstra, was charged under Section 281.2 of Canada's Criminal Code with willfully promoting hatred against an identifiable group. Eventually Keegstra was found guilty and fined $5000. Many fascinating themes surfaced at his trial, which was surely one of the most bizarre spectacles in Alberta's legal history. Keegstra had lost his position as a teacher due to the strange anti-Semitic views he had been promulgating in his social studies classes. The trial provided a platform for him to continue his exposition of an account of modern history according to which a conspiracy of communists, Jews, Zionists, and bankers has worked since 1776 to promote violence and revolution, with the ultimate goal of Jewish domination of the earth. The Holocaust never happened, on this analysis. Adolf Hitler was a hero who perceived real dangers others did not see.

In the face of Keegstra's testimony, sensible commentary was hard to come by. A division director in the Alberta educational system said that his concern was with the one-sidedness of Keegstra's teachings. He reported having written to Keegstra to warn him not to teach one interpretation of modern history as though it were fact. This strangely understated view presumes a model of objectivity as a balance between two opposed sides. The director suggested that the problem was not with the content of Keegstra's position—according to which Franklin D. Roosevelt was a lackey of Communists and Zionists, bankers collude with Communists, Jews persecuted in the Soviet Union are in league with their persecutors, and the testimony of hundreds of thousands of people about World War II experiences is an orchestrated plot to deceive the world about Hitler. Rather, the problem arose because Keegstra taught only this view. He was one-sided and ignored other interpretations. Taking the director's comment literally, we could conclude that if Keegstra had offered an alternative to his highly idiosyncratic view of the world, there would have been no problem. Thus, a rival analysis attributing all the same world events to the efforts of a secret conspiracy of Japanese thugs and African tribesmen would have given proper balance to the teaching.

There must be more to balance and objectivity. But our liberal institutions and ideas often seem to presume such a model, according to which fairness and lack of bias will result when both sides of an issue are presented by advocates. In the fall of 1985, Bill Cosby nearly walked off the set of his television series "The Cosby Show" because NBC was nervous about the appearance of an "Abolish Apartheid" sign he had placed in the household of his television family. The network did not wish to be seen to advocate a controversial position about apartheid in South Africa. Cosby insisted that for American black families such as the Huxtables depicted in the show, there are no two sides to South African apartheid. The network apparently worried that it would be accused of bias if something else did not appear on the show, advocating apartheid! Objectivity would have meant equal play for both sides.

An official in the Canadian Department of External Affairs revealed a similar commitment to the "two sides for balance" model when he articulated a requirement that groups and activities funded under a special disarmament fund administered by his department be "balanced." If sponsored groups have someone speak out against Star Wars, he said, they must have someone else speak out in favor of it. That is what balance means: Both sides must be presented. The analysis seems to work towards self-annihilation for sponsored groups. If one person argues for X and is followed by another who argues for not-X, what has been presented is, in effect, X and not-X. This is everything or nothing—depending on how we look at it.

Something is seriously wrong with the idea that a balanced objective account is one in which two sides of an issue are represented. It does not force us to look at the quality of hypothesis, evidence, and interpretation within an account (Keegstra); it suggests misleadingly that for any issue one side is as credible and worthy of attention as another (Cosby); and it can function to disempower institutions and groups (the disarmament fund). This model is seriously flawed. We need to understand objectivity in another way. However, let us consider briefly some of the factors that may have functioned to make this model seem plausible.

Factors Supporting the Two-Sides Model

The idea of balance is, at root, metaphorical. The image suggests that of an old-fashioned scale, where items are placed on each side. If the items are of equal weight, the scale is balanced. A state of equilibrium has been reached. Similarly, we might think we can reach intellectual equilibrium by balancing opposed accounts. When one advocate presents a number of considerations indicating one thing, and another presents an equal number of considerations indicating the opposite, we can weigh these and reach equilibrium. The popular idea that the truth is usually some kind of compromise between two extremes may well be related to this underlying metaphor.

Much political life, especially in North America and Britain, has been organized primarily around two opposed parties. Given this framework, fairness in political contexts means giving equal time to each. When there are two parties that take opposing positions, this strengthens the idea that issues have two sides, each of which must be heard in approximately equal measure. We can easily confuse fairness in politics with objectivity in intellectual matters.

The advocacy system in law courts may have a similar impact. Each of two sides is represented and argues as strongly as possible for its own case. The idea is that this procedure will best enable judges and juries to find out the facts of the matter, ascertain what are relevant laws and precedents, and resolve the issue. The system is based on the belief that such advocacy will ultimately result in a fair trial with an optimal chance of arriving at a legally correct decision.

Logic itself is founded on the basic duality between truth and falsehood. Each well-formulated statement must be either true or false. This format suggests two sides for every issue: either a statement S is true, or its denial, not-S, is true. If the statement really is well-formulated, it looks as though this is all there is to say.

Such background phenomena no doubt affect our thinking and our social institutions so as to reinforce the two-sides model. However, if we think about it, it is clear that this support is less than compelling. Debate and discussion are not similar to a weigh scale. Many countries have more than two political parties, and existing parties often fail to represent all reasonable opinions and beliefs on issues of social importance. The courts are a special case because the question they address has been restricted very specifically (Is the accused guilty or innocent, according to the law?) and their procedures also are carefully specified.

Logical dualities exist, of course—but only provided that the statement in question is accurately formulated. For many real issues, the precise formulation of a problem, with proper qualifications respecting context, predicted ramifications, and degrees of knowledge is a major part of the difficulty.

There is a more plausible defense of the idea of a two-sides balance. Often a strongly committed advocate is biased in favor of a single position. Learning this from experience, many of us become suspicious of strongly committed people. Hearing them, we think "There must be another side to the issue," and we react skeptically. On any topic, a vast number of facts can be brought forward and can be described in numerous ways. Different facts, and different descriptions of facts, will suggest different approaches and resolutions to problems. Alternate explanatory hypotheses can be proposed. The significance of objections can be weighed differently. Counterarguments known to an advocate can be omitted. The possibilities at so many points are endless. Knowing this, we may suspect the strongly committed advocate of having selected just those interpretations, explanations, and premises that will support the case being advocated. The presentation of an opposed view can provide an opportunity to see how some of these choices might have been made. If facts are prejudicially selected in one case, and then again in another but with a different prejudice, we may be able to correct each account in terms of the other. Surely, we might think, there is a greater likelihood of detecting bias, selectivity, special pleading, and error in an account if we have a competing account available. (More on this later.)

There are many problems with the two-sides model. It remains to be seen whether the idea that one prejudiced account can serve as the basis for correcting another retains sufficient plausibility to serve as a good reason for adopting this model. The incidents described make it clear that something must be wrong with the idea that presenting two sides makes for objectivity. What has gone wrong?

There Are Often More Than Two Sides to an Issue

On many issues—scientific, political, ethical, interpretive—there are more than two reasonable positions. This fact becomes obvious when we consider an example. Consider the issue of the role of religion in public education. Informed and conscientious people hold a number of distinct positions on this question, all of which can and have been defended by arguments, and all of which, if understood, can contribute something to our understanding of the issue as a whole. Here are just some of the possibilities:

1.　　Religion has no place in public schools.

2.　　Religion has no place in public schools except in programs about world religions (descriptive comparative religion) or about the history of some major religions.

3.　　Religion may occupy a minor place in education in public schools, but parents should be able to remove children from any classes on religion in a way that will not embarrass them.

4.　　Religion has a large role in education. In a pluralistic society, public monies should be given to a variety of religious groups so that each can sponsor its own educational system within which religion will have what that group sees as its proper educational role.

5.　　Religion has a large role to play in education. Only the religion of the majority can and should be taught in public schools. Minority religions can opt for private systems to teach their own religion in schools.

6.　　Religion has a large role to play in education. There is only one true religion, and it is that religion that should be taught in public schools.

(Our example is moral and political, but its point holds true for more purely intellectual issues as well.)

Obviously these positions do not exhaust the possibilities. Cramming the question of what is the proper role for religion in a pluralistic society with public education into just two opposed positions would omit a great many possibilities. In fact, such a move would severely restrict and prejudice the nature of inquiry and debate into the problem. The many possibilities here could not all be explored with equal seriousness, perhaps, for practical reasons. Yet when a selection is made, there is no magic about the number two. The great variety of possible and actual positions reveals how important is the agenda of inquiry and debate.

Identifying a position as a possible one that is held by someone does not automatically give it equal credibility and intellectual respectability with other positions that are held. A major concern about such trials as that of James Keegstra is the apparent respectability conferred on the theory that the Holocaust did not occur. That theory had to be discussed at length in court and, apparently, taken seriously by serious-minded and well-educated people. The legal necessity to discuss the view seriously in court might suggest that it was a reasonable position as a matter of history. But such status in a legal forum should not be confused with logical or historical integrity. The fact that a position is held by a significant individual or group may be sufficient reason to discuss and examine it seriously. It is not in itself a reason to think it has logical or intellectual integrity equal to that of other positions.

Many liberal-thinking people take pride in understanding and communicating the two sides of an issue because they see this as an advance on the dogmatism of others who can see only one side. Often it is an advance; but it is only a partial advance. Selecting two sides can oversimplify and falsely polarize debate. Sometimes it gives pseudocredibility to outrageously implausible positions. Usually, understanding two sides is better than dogmatically sticking to one— but it is not enough in itself.

The Two-Sides Model Includes No Restrictions on What Is Presented by Either Side

Two advocates of opposed positions may both speak or write very prejudicially— using distorted facts, loaded language, false statements, questionable hypotheses, inappropriate authorities, fallacious arguments, tendentious rhetorical questions, and much else. If so, neither can offer a correct account of a problem. Many people think that two incorrect accounts will somehow balance and cancel each other out, leading to a roughly correct compromise. However, there is no guarantee that this will be the case. Juxtaposing two opposed but biased accounts often leads to confusion, skepticism, a perpetuation of previous ignorance, or even persistence of dogmatically-held convictions. Those antecedently convinced of one of the positions may sense only the inadequacies of the opposed one and rest even more secure in their dogmatic beliefs.

The naiveté of thinking that one prejudicial account can serve to highlight the errors of another can be illustrated by examining imaginary speeches by an atheist and a fundamentalist on the issue of religion in education.

> *Atheist:* Religion is all superstition, and superstition has absolutely no place in modern life. Religion has caused the suffering and death of millions of people in gruesome wars. Religious people are bigots who think that others who do not share the one true faith will suffer eternally in hell for a matter of belief. The sooner religion disappears from the world, the better. There is no need or place for it in the modern scientific age. Keep it out of the schools. No modern citizen should have to support bigotry and superstition with tax dollars.

> *Fundamentalist:* The humanists are trying to play God by preempting God's knowledge and claiming it for themselves. They condone pornography, child abuse, and abortion. They are evil incarnate as they do not recognize the need of mankind to be saved from sin. Education based on secular humanism is no education at all. Teaching is meaningless unless we save our children from the fires of hell. There is only one true religion, and it is the primary function of the schools and the rest of society to teach it to our children. No aspect of life is intelligible unless it is understood in the aspects of God's creation and God's rules for man.

Imagine the Atheist and the Fundamentalist on a panel. Superficially, the panel is balanced; two sides of an issue are represented. But not only do such spokespersons fail to represent a broad range of opinion, both their accounts are extremely inadequate judged from an internal point of view. Both use loaded language. The Atheist uses such terms as "superstition" (for religious belief), "bigots" (for religious believers), and "modern" and "scientific" as emotionally positive words to label his own secular position. The Fundamentalist uses "evil" and "playing God" to brand his opponents and "true religion" as a tendentious phrase to select his own religion as the single correct one. Both the Atheist and the Fundamentalist make very questionable, even false claims, unsupported by any argument. The Atheist links all religion with superstition, though some theological systems are carefully reasoned and articulated and disassociated from magic and even from miracle. The Fundamentalist says that humanists seek to play God, ignoring the fact that those humanists who do not believe in God cannot possibly be trying to fill a role they do not think exists at all. Both use facts in a misleading way. The Atheist says that religion has caused wars without acknowledging that many religious people have worked for peace and that there have been many nonreligious causes for wars—economic and nationalist causes, for instance. The Atheist ignores the fact that some religious believers see heaven as an open possibility for nonbelievers and others do not believe in heaven and hell at all. The Fundamentalist ignores the fact that many humanists oppose pornography, child abuse, and abortion. The Fundamentalist fails even to consider ways of understanding human life that would find meaning and intelligence in nondivine aspects.

Given such gross internal flaws, we cannot advance our understanding of the role of religion in education by listening to the Atheist or to the Fundamentalist. Nor can we advance our knowledge by listening to the Atheist followed by the Fundamentalist—not even if both look and sound important and appear on television! The rhetorical tricks and cognitive failings of these accounts are seen by looking at them with a critical eye, scrutinizing the language and use of facts, looking for the presence and quality of argument, and bringing our own background knowledge to bear on the account. In this case, though, nothing in either account can serve to correct the other. The correction comes from a critical hearing or reading of the account by an alert audience—not from the opposed account. Hearing an atheist suggest that religion has caused all war does not correct, or even help to correct, the misleading suggestion by a fundamentalist that all humanists condone child abuse!

This is an extreme case, of course. But the imaginary statements are not entirely unrealistic. In two real cases, the content is much better, but there is little contact of opposed views, and confusion and skepticism are the net result.

On May 15, 1986, at about 8:30 AM, the CBC (Canadian Broadcasting Corporation) FM network in Calgary broadcast a discussion of the safety of North American nuclear reactors in Hanford, Washington. This discussion took place in an atmosphere of public concern about the safety of reactors in the aftermath of the Soviet disaster in Chernobyl, April 1986. Patrick Moore, chairman of Greenpeace in Vancouver, was interviewed. Representing "the other side" was Steve Irish, a spokesperson for UNC—nuclear industries in Hanford, Washington, where there are a number of nuclear reactors, some dating back to the Manhattan Project in the forties. Moore said that there was corrosion in these reactors, that there could be and have been fuel leaks, that $81 million has been requested to fix these leaks, and that a disaster comparable to that at Chernobyl could happen in Hanford. (Calgary is about as far from Hanford as Warsaw is from Chernobyl; citizens in Warsaw were throwing away fresh fruits, vegetables, and milk in the wake of the Chernobyl disaster.) Irish said there are some problems with fuel lines at Hanford, but these are quite routine. He said that as many as ten leaks at a time can be easily repaired, and that the reactors have been checked by inspectors from the United States Department of Energy and found to be all right. He also said the reactors will be checked by an independent (sic) committee of scientists and engineers again in four months. The reactors have been working safely for twenty-five years and are differently designed from the Chernobyl reactors, Irish said. A disaster like that in Chernobyl could not occur in Hanford, according to him.

Despite the fact that I listened carefully to the discussion and—having by coincidence read several books about nuclear developments in Hanford—was almost certainly better equipped to absorb details than the average listener, I gained little information. An interviewer questioned both people; they did not debate directly with each other. Moore was not asked to defend his analogy between Hanford and Chernobyl. He was not asked to explain how the fuel leaks could lead to a disaster as serious as that in Chernobyl. Irish was not asked about the $81 million, what makes leaks "routine," or about the matter of natural aging of reactors. The audience is left with one party saying "it could happen here" and another saying "it could not."

Radio, television, and film are typically heard or seen only once. (Taping is changing this, to some degree.) The product is gone when we come to reflect and analyze it. With print media, we have an opportunity to look back, to see exact statements made, to find arguments, and to compare evidence. Even so, the combination of two opposed accounts often produces little real contact between them, and the net effect on our understanding may be as trivial as with more ephemeral media.

An example appeared in the *Herald Tribune,* June 7–8, 1986, concerning Kurt Waldheim's candidacy for the presidency of Austria. An essay "Why the Critics are Unfair," by Gerhard Waldheim, son of the candidate and active in his presidential campaign, was printed beside another, "He Shares in the Collective Guilt" by Menachem Rozensaft, founding chairman of the International Network of Children of Jewish Holocaust Survivors. Both concerned the issue of whether Kurt Waldheim, then a candidate for president of Austria (elected the next day), was guilty of involvement in war crimes because of his connections with the German army during the World War II. Gerhard Waldheim urged that his father had not deceived the public about his military service, though he naturally did not like to discuss this aspect of his past. He claimed that Waldheim and his family had, prior to 1939, been against the Nazis and had been penalized for their protests. Kurt Waldheim was an interpreter and liaison officer to the Italian army. He had no combat role, according to Gerhard Waldheim, and no involvement in atrocities. Furthermore, he said his father consistently showed sympathy for Jews after the war. He was not a Nazi and was not guilty of war crimes. In contrast, Rosensaft stated that Kurt Waldheim was a willing and apparently enthusiastic servant of Hitler between 1939 and 1945. He closed his eyes to deportations and atrocities he must have known about. He was accused by the United Nations War Crimes Commission of having participated in atrocities. Rosensaft argued that all who supported Hitler by allowing his government to function share guilt for the annihilation of European Jews. Rosensaft said Waldheim was involved and bears responsibility for a regime that was one of "absolute evil."

The accounts were both well written and contained plausible arguments. They did not really contradict each other as to facts, in the strict logical sense. They were based on different interpretations and selections of facts and differed in their concepts of citizen responsibility for government atrocities. Both authors could be said to have interests prejudicing their credibility. More information about what Waldheim knew and did and more reflection on the options citizens had and the responsibility they bear for involvement in the Nazi regime would help to resolve the issue. As presented, the two accounts were interesting and articulated key historical and moral issues. But as stated, they offered the reader no resolution and no indication as to how to go about finding one.

These examples indicate that diametrically opposed accounts will not always serve to correct each other. In general, there is no good reason to believe that the truth or anything close to it will emerge from a consideration of two such accounts.

Institutions Seeking Balance May Restrict Their Roles as Conveyors of Information and as Political Agents by Communicating Nothing

A familiar kind of anthology can soothe the hearts and minds of anxious educators: pro and con. One author argues that genes cause criminal behavior, followed by another who argues that the cause is environmental. A third author argues that genes cause behavior differences between the sexes; followed by a fourth who argues that they emerge due to environmental factors. And so it goes on. In the hands of students and instructors willing to sift through the arguments and reach an independent stance, such anthologies can serve a purpose. But much analysis is necessary to avoid pure confusion and ignorance as the result of such a treatment. "There is no real answer. These people are experts, and obviously, they disagree," readers will say. The two-sides treatment can lead to unreasoning agnosticism, to a nihilistic kind of effect intellectually.

Unconsciously, such endeavors are often conservative in their impact. No stance is demonstrated; no one has a basis for disagreeing with what is actually being done; hence things may as well be left as they are. When ostensibly critical and independent institutions and individuals are compelled to present both sides of an issue, to achieve balance and objectivity, skeptics may well suspect that such a requirement severely will limit the political and educational impact of the endeavors these agents undertake. When established policy is X, and would-be critics have to balance their materials and presentations by arguing in effect for X as well as for not-X, the eventual effect is likely to be no effect.

This is not to say that media presentations and educational materials should never present several sides. They should frequently present several sides—often, more than just two. However, this will not be sufficient for objectivity and will not necessarily lead to a careful rethinking of issues. Whenever possible, steps should be taken to provide for critical analysis of each case and efforts made for genuine cross-dialogue. In addition, we should be sensitive to the implicitly conservative effect such approaches may have in some contexts.

Two Views May Both Be Founded on a Mistaken Assumption and Thus May Both Be Mistaken

People sometimes argue as to whether the United States should exercise world leadership by military might or by political and economic influence. What is ignored here is the assumption that the United States should exercise world leadership at all. This assumption, which may be difficult for many Americans to question, needs to be critically examined. Perhaps the world does not need leadership from any one country. It is possible that aspirations to leadership role by various countries (for example, Britain in the nineteenth century and the United States and the Soviet Union presently) only serve to make global problems worse. Or perhaps, leadership is necessary, and some country other than the United States is best fit to exercise it. Scrutinizing the background assumption is useful. Even if eventually we wish to endorse it, we are forced to see other alternatives and to understand that reasons are needed to back up a previously unexamined idea.

This kind of example reveals again the crucial role of the setting of agenda, both in inquiry and in public debate. If two sides are identified and share a common assumption that is either controversial or just plain wrong, then following a debate or inquiry based on that idea is unlikely to serve us well.

Examples seem obvious if we look at another time or place. In nineteenth-century Europe and America, considerable debate raged as to how masters should treat their slaves. Some said they should treat them kindly and educate them well; thus the slaves would be healthy, competent, and loyal. Others said slaves should be treated brutally to exploit their labor for maximizing profit and that they would only take advantage of kind, indulgent masters. Nearly any modern citizen looking at this debate would regard it as crazy: We deny the assumption that masters and slaves should exist at all. Perhaps in another century the current debate as to whether nuclear weapons should be targetted against military installations or against cities will appear similarly bizarre.

Presenting two sides of an issue is clearly not sufficient to provide an accurate, objective understanding, free from bias, prejudice, propaganda, and distortion. It may in some contexts be better to do this than to present only one side, but we should not deceive ourselves into thinking that we have corrected for selectivity and represented a full range of positions. Important positions may be omitted; bias and distortion internal to accounts may go uncorrected; confusion, ignorance, or dogmatism can naturally result; and key underlying assumptions may go unscrutinized.

What Factors Make an Account Fair and Balanced?

In fact, a single account, even an advocacy account from someone with a committed stance, can often better serve the ends of objectivity provided it meets certain conditions. We gain a better, more just understanding from a fairly-worded analysis that allows for and reasonably handles alternative interpretations and counterarguments than we do from two or more propagandistic accounts. "Balance" can be achieved within a single discourse that expresses fair and careful thinking.

Can an advocate think fairly? I submit that this is possible. To think it is not is to presume that judicious, fair, and rational analysis will always lead one to a skeptical or neutral position. There is no reason to think that this true. In fact, in practical life, we all presume the opposite.

I suggest that an account is fair and balanced when it satisfies all or most of the following conditions:

1. The language used is relatively neutral. (Example: a speaker opposing religion in public schools refers to religious people as believers or adherents, not as bigots or fanatics.)

2. Facts that would tend to support an interpretation or evaluation different from that of the speaker or writer are acknowledged. Their apparent impact is either recognized or argued against and accounted for. (Example: A speaker defending religion as making a contribution to human progress acknowledges wars in Ireland and Lebanon as an apparent counterexample to his thesis. But the speaker contends that broader economic and political issues exist behind these conflicts so that, appearances notwithstanding, they are not fundamentally religious conflicts.)

3. The point is acknowledged where expert opinion is cited and the relevant experts differ from each other. Either the case developed does not depend entirely on citing expert opinion or good reasons for selecting particular experts are given. Those experts whose views are not accepted are not attacked on irrelevant personal grounds.

4. Controversial interpretations of events or texts, explanations for which there are plausible alternatives, disputable predictions, estimations, or value judgments are acknowledged as such. Reasons for them are given and, where appropriate, the impact on the analysis of making another such judgment is recognized.

5. The speakers or writers do not insidiously introduce their own special point of view as being the one the audience would naturally adopt. (Example: If a feminist is speaking in favor of equal pay for work of equal value, the speaker does not refer to the audience as "we in the feminist movement.")

6. Sources are indicated and, where practically feasible, quoted so that they may be checked in contexts where this is sufficiently important.

7. Arguments are careful and well reasoned, not fallacious.

8. Where time and space permit, alternative positions are stated, explained, and considered. Reasons are given as to why these positions are seen to be less satisfactory than the one advocated. Alternative positions are fairly and accurately represented and described in nonprejudicial language. People holding them are described accurately, politely, and respectfully.

9. The point is acknowledged where evidence and reasons offered are less than rationally compelling. An explanation is given as to why the position taken nevertheless seems the most nearly correct or appropriate in the context.

Advocacy accounts can be biased and misleading. They can also be objective and fair. Presentations of two sides can be biased and misleading. They can also be objective and fair.

No, there are not two sides to every question. In some ultimate sense, there are far more than two—an indefinitely large number when all the different alternative descriptions, explanations, predictions, hypotheses, and recommendations are taken into account. Considering two sides does not guarantee fairness, genuine understanding, lack of bias, tolerance, or accuracy in conclusions. It sometimes facilitates these, but not if opposed accounts are propagandistic or when little scope for cross-dialogue and genuine critical analysis is allowed. We must remember that there is nothing necessarily objective either about our own favorite account or about the two sides of an issue that may constitute society's agenda in a particular immediate situation. We must think carefully and flexibly when working out and expressing our own beliefs. Showing these capacities and eliciting them in others is more important, I submit, than seeking balance as a virtually automatic by-product of the presentation of the two sides of an issue.

Questions for Reflection and Discussion

---

1. Why does Govier think that endorsement of a two-sides model by television networks and other social institutions will tend to perpetuate status quo thinking? In what sorts of circumstances might her claim about this be wrong?

2. Are there more than two sides for issues such as capital punishment, the draft, prayer in public schools, and bilingualism? Pick any one of these, or another public issue of your own choice, and see how many reasonable positions you can identify and distinguish.

3. How could a press discussion of a controversial subject such as Kurt Waldheim's Nazi connections be made more intellectually significant to readers, according to Govier? Do you tend to agree? Why or why not?

4. What do you think Govier means by the "setting of agenda" in public debate? Does this agenda setting just happen, or do people or institutions consciously plan it?

5

Distinguishing Fact from Opinion*

Perry Weddle

The distinction between fact and opinion is not simple. Opinion, as contrasted with fact, is not always false nor is it always controversial. Nor is it what is believed, what is inferred, what is advocated, or what is judged. That there is no general way of distinguishing fact from opinion does not really matter, though. What does matter is the quality of the evidence or reasons for our beliefs.

For years a well-known publication billed itself as "the newsmagazine that separates fact from opinion." The phrase "fact from opinion" is a staple of education speech and educated speech generally. In this essay, I try to isolate strands of meaning masked by that phrase and its first cousins. Frequently I find ill-braided or discontinuous bits masquerading as sound cordage. My findings are not like a fisherman's backlash snarl, the kind that with patience may be unsnarled into usable line. I also try to provide alternative expression for the "fact from opinion" phrase.

What does it mean to "distinguish fact from opinion"? Let me count the ways.

1. The Distinction as Semantic

Actually, fact and opinion could be separated easily. Whereas facts are states of affairs, opinions are human claims about states of affairs. It may be fact that fewer than five people in the room were born in Bulgaria, but it would not be

---

*"Distinguishing Fact from Opinion" by Perry Weddle is an adaptation of "Fact from Opinion", which first appeared in *Informal Logic* Vol. VII, no 1 (Winter, 1985). It is printed here with permission of the author and the editors of *Informal Logic*.

opinion until someone at least ventured it. Another example: If x is opinion, then x is somebody's opinion, that of a person or body of persons, where if x is fact, then x is not somebody's fact. This would be a mathematician-like way of noting that for opinions the question, "Whose opinion is it?" is germane and that the question, "Whose fact is it?", except as joking, makes no sense. I call this the "Whose?" test. That the "Whose?" test works, yet trivializes the distinction, ought to alert us. There is something suspicious about trying to counterbalance the one category against the other. That there might be a problem, however, seems to have been widely missed. Equally importantly, people are looking for a difference that is more than merely one of semantics.

The "Whose?" test can be short-circuited easily. By replacing "fact" in the distinction with something already somebody's opinion, something such as "statements of fact," we can eliminate the grammatical cue. Indeed, several of the numbered distinctions discussed in this essay almost do this. The substitution, moreover, may move us closer to what we had in mind.

Don't we want to be able to spot slanted journalism, inadequate support, and the differences between description and prescription? Such matters are verbal and very human. But if substituting the likes of "statements of fact" would constitute an advance, it would have corresponding drawbacks. We would no longer have a distinction between fact and opinion. We would have something considerably more modest. There are more facts than are contained in human statements. Untold facts await discovery. There are facts completely forgotten by humanity. There are unknown facts created along with the evolution or invention of conventions and systems. We do not want to confine ourselves to the already stated but also want to make sense of the idea that there are facts waiting to be discovered.

The separation of fact from opinion is not the same as the separation of statements of fact from statements of opinion.

2. The Distinction as Fact Versus Falsehood

From the Greenhaven Press test, *Basic Skills for Critical Thinking,* by Gary McCuen, consider this question:[1]

> Which of the following sentences is a statement of fact rather than of opinion?
>
> **A.** There are no differences between the Democratic and the Republican parties.
> **B.** Democrats and Republicans often disagree over the issue of welfare.
> **C.** Republicans always vote for big business.
> **D.** Democrats always vote for the common man.

The keyed answer is B. Apparently the author felt that because distractors A, C, and D were false, they were relegated to the realm of opinion, whereas that answer B was true, it was relegated to the realm of fact. This would be a misunderstanding, for opinion can be—indeed frequently is—correct. Just possibly the question's author felt that the answer was qualified, and the distractors being the opposite, were relegated to their respective realms. But many statements of fact are unqualified—"Oboes are musical instruments," for example—whereas qualified statements are frequently opinion, or false—for example, "In a right triangle the square of the hypotenuse may perhaps, at least sometimes, equal the sum of the squares of the adjacent sides." It is important to see when we should be qualifying our claims and when the claims of others need qualification. But this has little to do with the relationship between fact and opinion.

With a fact-falsehood interpretation of our subject, further questions would be raised about the educational value of the distinction between fact and opinion. Emphasis would be in the wrong place—as may be brought out by the following. Envision a dispute wherein either side has good but not complete evidence, and one side or the other must be right (say it is a round of dice, both cups having been overturned but with their contents yet to be revealed). Would the outcome make the contentions of the one side fact and those of the other side opinion? To affirm so would be extreme, for the dispute's about exactly the same thing, exactly the same matter of fact, and each side's got about as good a case. The difference would not be educationally important. The difference would be pure luck.

3. The Distinction as Fact Versus Reasoned Judgment

Perhaps the question "Is that a fact or is that his opinion?," where "opinion" would be somebody's careful interpretation, conveys the difference we want. Something may be open to several interpretations, but that same something could not be said to be open to several facts. And interpretations may be closer to or further from fact, but the same would not be true for fact itself. Opinions differ, one might say, facts don't.

Possibly the California State University Chancellor's Office intended something like this version of the distinction in the critical thinking paragraph of Executive Order 338—which mandates that undergraduates in the 300,000-student system be taught to distinguish "between fact and judgment." The 338 language does reflect usage, as in the testimony (reported in the *Sacramento* [California] *Bee*) of Gordon Wade, formerly in the management of Proctor and Gamble:

> When I first arrived there, fresh from Harvard, I kept wanting to say, "In my judgment." I can still hear the response. "Your judgment's no better than the drunk in Lytle park." At Proctor, they pay you for removing judgment.

But there's a problem. A distinction should distinguish, at least in the bulk of the cases it covers, and a fact/reasoned judgment version would not distinguish. Consider the record of my local weatherperson, Stormin' Norman. It is (1) Stormin' Norman's *opinion* that it'll be fair today and (2) a *fact* that it's fair today—Stormin' Norman knows his stuff. But to a great extent don't we all? This would mean that countless opinions would be facts and that countless facts would be opinions. The imagined slash between fact and opinion would become an indefinite, leagues-broad swath.

4. The Distinction as Fact Versus Mere Conjecture

Like Stormin' Norman, most of us when plying our trades, or when cautious, are pretty good at making reasoned judgments. But what of our unguarded moments? What of unfamiliar terrain? What of the fools among us and the fool in each of us? If reasoned judgment turns out frequently to be fact, this scarcely means that mere conjecture does. Accordingly, to appreciate the difference between fact and mere conjecture may seem to be our goal, a goal moreover, well enshrined in usage—as in, "That's just your opinion" and in "One opinion is as good as another." If opinion were mere conjecture, then such dismissals would not infrequently be well taken. And for sure we want to be able to see when somebody states fact and when somebody merely runs off at the mouth.

But that a fact—mere opinion contrast—is the expression we want to give to these desirable abilities, I doubt. Implicit in the fact-conjecture version of the contrast, as in others, is the assumption that fact is superior, that the better half of the distinction lies on the left. But does it? I once overheard a dispute over whether Ireland is west of Scotland. In the course of the discussion it became clear that neither party had the foggiest notion of a true map. Both parties were shooting off their mouths. One party just happened to have stated fact. It was fool's luck. Educationally speaking, that party's no more admirable than the other.

Furthermore, if one ought not automatically to laud statements of fact, neither ought one automatically to downplay conjecture. In its place conjecture, even wild conjecture, can be admirable. We want to be good at imagining, good at free-association, good at creating fusillades of hypotheses. Wild conjecture, one might even say, is the soul of scientific advance, or indeed of any advance. (Along with the creativity, of course, we seek to explore, to conjecture, and to evaluate conjecture.) But whatever ultimately counts does so in direct proportion to the firmness of the grounding—the kind of evidence supporting it.

5. The Distinction as Observation Versus Inference

The California Department of Education is now preparing to administer a multiple-choice social studies test to the state's quarter-million-plus eighth graders. Eventually there will be analogous tests at the sixth, tenth, twelfth and third grades. That's well over a million kids. The commission which mandated the test expressed the desire that 40 percent of the items involve something called critical thinking. The rainbow committee of educators formed to construct the instrument decided, among many things, to test the ability to distinguish fact from opinion, which the committee defined as the difference "between observation and inference."

Although this committee's construal may constitute an advance, I do wonder. Again the version fails to distinguish. Countless facts and opinions are best seen neither as simply observation *nor* inference. Last night on PBS (Public Broadcasting System) Bill Moyers served up the standard explanation of the Depression-era migration to California from the South and Midwest. What Moyers said is fact, at least as far as I know, yet how rich a mixture its backing is. There are sixty-year-olds recalling the motives they had fifty years back. There are diaries, bank records, textbook accounts of farming practices, tree-ring and census data, and the vivifications of Steinbecks and Dorothea Langes. There are professors renowned for their "sense of history." Whatever category one were to try helpfully cramming all such information into would be complex indeed, much more complex than either observation, inference, or both.

There is, furthermore, the implication that observation (fact?) is the privileged category. Frequently it's the other way around. An acquaintance of mine on a backpack trip said, "Saw a twelve-foot pterodactyl swooping down from Rodrigues Ridge." Having just ingested hallucinogenic mushrooms, this person quite properly *inferred* that her observation was less than veridical. Compared to her observation, her inference is in much the firmer epistemic position. Some inferences, moreover, are simply impeccable, such as a valid syllogism, or the correct solution to an algebraic equation.

There are further difficulties. Countless facts are not observations. Consider two examples. *Fact One:* Two plus two equals four. You couldn't observe that two plus two equals four. The equation is general, covering any case, including calculations done tomorrow. Furthermore, what you can observe—for example, a carefully-measured two ounces of bourbon plus a carefully-measured two ounces of water—very often does not equal four. (Alcohol is somewhat soluble in water.) *Fact Two:* "Washington is in the northwest part of the country." This "fact" answer was submitted for the State of California test. The sentence would indeed state a paradigm fact. Yet only an astronaut could *observe* that Washington is in the northwest part of the country.

Of course, one can observe indirectly. This is what Lewis and Clark must have done—using the magnetic compass, the sun, the length of a day's march, and so on to reckon, to deduce, that the wild land they were in lay northwest from where they had commenced. Fact and observation, yes, but inference equally, the pair are intertwined inextricably. And let's ask, I mean really, how do *we* know that Washington is in the northwest part of the country? Didn't we take somebody's word for it? That's how we know most of what we know, by appeal to authority. That's an honorable method—but observation it is not.

6. The Distinction as the Verifiable Versus the Not Verifiable

Recently I saw a draft of a paper being prepared for teachers whose pupils will be taking that Department of Education social studies test, the one which by attempting to measure the ability to distinguish observation from inference attempts to measure the ability to distinguish fact from opinion. In the draft, by Dr. Peter Kneedler, consultant at the department, "fact from opinion" and "observation from inference" are explained as follows. Facts are "statements of observations which can be proved true or verified." Opinions are "expressions of approval or disapproval." I'll call it the "draft," to remember that this is only a draft, and discuss it because it represents a respected view. It's close to the version in the Greenhaven Press test teacher manual, which defines statements of fact as "those which can be demonstrated empirically," and statements of opinion as "beliefs or attitudes which cannot be proved." Let's look at the "fact" halves of these definitions first; and because comments about statements and about observation have already been made, here I'll consider only the fact halves' "verifiability" parts. Afterwards I'll look at the "opinion" halves.

Are statements of fact verifiable? One might say so, but this would not separate them from opinions. Opinions are verifiable, too. For instance, in my *opinion* this paper can be delivered orally in fewer than forty-five minutes, a *fact*, which supposing I were right, would be easy to verify. And herein lies another problem: Suppose that I were wrong. Neither distinction seems to have left room for falsehood. Obviously falsehoods can't go on the "fact" side, but there seems to be no room for them on the "opinion" side either.

Since an important part of critical appraising is detecting falsehood, the fact-opinion dichotomy can be useful in critical analysis only if it allows for the possibility of falsehood.

One more point about the "verifiability" versions' "statements of fact" category: Why should it be confined to the empirical? Many a fact is based not on observations, not on the empirical, but on, for example, adding a column of numbers, or interpreting a passage, or tracing out the implications of a set of assumptions. These aspects of thinking have to be allowed for in a sound version of the fact-opinion distinction.

Now for the "opinion" halves of the two versions. Are opinions statements of either "beliefs or attitudes which cannot be proved" (that's Greenhaven) or "expressions of approval or disapproval" (that's the draft). And does defining them as such separate them in an educationally useful way from fact? Well, clearly some opinions are either, or both. Last month I was told, "The world would be a better place if you were to burn that necktie." Not only can the claim not be proved, since for one thing I refuse to burn the tie, the claim is clearly an expression of disapproval. But there are problems. Countless opinions not only can be proved but do get proved. Countless opinions, moreover, express neither approval nor disapproval. Recall Stormin' Norman's opinion about today's weather. Have we any idea how Stormin' Norman *feels* about today's weather? Nor would it matter how Stormin' Norman felt. Indeed in giving professional opinions, reliable people usually want precisely to avoid expressing approval or disapproval. They are there to give objective interpretations, to state the *facts* as best they can, not to color matters one way or another. Even when we give plain opinions, not professional opinions, we may not approve or disapprove. Whether this paper would run under or over forty-five minutes may or may not be of concern to me, but in any case you knew my opinion before you knew whether I approve, don't, or don't care.

A word had better be said about "expression of emotion," something into which the likes of "beliefs or attitudes" and "expressions of approval or disapproval" sometimes get unfolded. That understanding of "opinion" would not work either, for reasons just considered. Moreover, countless statements of fact also happen to be expressions of emotion. In only unusual circumstances could true accusations like "You molested my child!" be uttered without expressing emotion. The utterers, however, whatever the emotional accompaniments, would of course have been stating fact. Furthermore, countless opinions are delivered unemotionally. This goes no distance toward making them fact. They are or are not fact not because of emotional accompaniments but because of something else.

7. The Distinction as Settled Matters Versus Controversial

The multiple-choice question which pegged the state-of-Washington sentence as fact pegged as opinion the sentence, "Oregon is the most beautiful state in the union." Now there would be no controversy over the Washington claim but plenty over the Oregon claim. Is that the distinction then, settled versus controversial? The suggestion has merit in its connection with another issue—when we need to supply argument for a point, namely when it's controversial or likely to be, and when we need not supply argument for a point—when there's general agreement. We don't want to beg questions or plump at length for the obvious. The suggestion, furthermore, reminds us that controversy or its likelihood is in many circumstances precisely what makes something a matter of opinion. And where there be unanimity this is an indicator that the matter has been settled and relegated, accordingly, to the realm of fact.

But educational considerations and others cloud even this horizon. The suggested version would not well distinguish. Many a controversy is caused by fools, or stirred up by journalists. Furthermore, many an "established fact" has turned out to have been no more than complacency in the community of experts or copycatting among journalists. A settled-versus-controversial version of the fact-opinion distinction would place emphasis in the wrong place, place it, again, on an accompaniment of what counts, and not what really counts. This is partly due, no doubt, to "opinion" having semantic connection with controversy. But for students it won't do. If it were to do, then we should have to say that a dose of adrenaline or of Valium administered to one side or another over an issue would change fact to opinion, or vice versa. That would not be education but chemistry. We don't want to just count heads to make policy. Instead, we want to ask "Regardless of what proportion support this proposition, what are their reasons; what are the facts?"

8. The Distinction as Reporting Versus Advocating

Although I failed to find this version in any obvious source, surely it is quite unoriginal. It's what is assumed to distinguish the main news pages of a newspaper from the editorial pages. In other words, the newsmagazine with the slogan would have been far from original either.. But again I wonder.

Consider the lead story in the June 18, 1984, *Sacramento Bee* under the headline, "Foreign Trade Deficit Record $19.4 billion." Assuming the headline and story accurate, would that make it fact? I would say yes. It taps no questionable sources, succumbs to no obvious sophistry. The statistic could appear in next year's edition of *Facts on File*. But would any such considerations mean that opinion is not also heavily admixed? Wherever the story were rationally placed in the newspaper, somebody would have had to decide that the story, with that size headline, ought to go there, that in that person's opinion that news is prime. The placement expresses a viewpoint. Another viewpoint would have emphasized the story less, big trade deficits being a quite foreseen, and therefore unsurprising, and therefore less newsworthy, simply a negative consequence of the overall Reagan administration policy: The *Bee* story is that of a Democrat paper reporting to its chiefly Democrat readers. Fact, yes, but opinion too. As in many contexts the pair intertwines. And as educators, we would like our clients to understand *all* sorts of such intertwining, as in the present case, not merely to separate the pure one (supposing that it could be done) from the pure other.

And what about the "advocacy," the "opinion" side of this version? Along toward November the big trade deficit became an editorial salvo hurled against the administration. Did that make it opinion or close to opinion? Why say so; it's the same fact?

Now perhaps everyone knows that opinions worth considering are backed by facts. What, however, of editorial bottom lines, the "ought" conclusions borne of facts? Are they then opinion? That will depend. They may be opinion, but not simply because they're advocacy, not simply because they are "oughts." After the first day of starting to build a board fence around my lot, I heeded my neighbor's advice. "You know," he said, "if you want to knock that thing together efficiently you really ought to get yourself a heavier, professional-quality waffle-faced hammer." I did. I proceeded in accordance with my neighbor's opinion. The guy was dead right, and that's a fact.

Now my neighbor's "ought' differs only in degree, and in some cases not even in that, from "oughts" in good newspaper editorials and similar persuadings. The differences in degree are because the cases are worth arguing, because there are alternative opinions; and this makes the journalistic "oughts" opinion. But they may be fact, too. Is a light-rail public transport system for Greater Sacramento financially wise? The *Bee* editorializes so. Looking back from 1994 to 1984, we will be able to see—just as I was able to see about that waffle-faced hammer. The *Bee,* or its opponents, will have stated fact.

Undoubtedly there exist further ways plausibly to construe a contrast between fact and opinion. And although one which does the job perfectly may surface at any time, for two reasons I doubt that one will. First, "fact" and "opinion" each have multiple shades of meaning. This makes essence-hunting difficult if not impossible and exception-finding easy and rich. Think of the differences just between "mere opinion," "professional opinion," "received opinion," "dissenting opinion,' "second opinion," and "difference of opinion." It would take a John Austin to sort them out, and such a list would be but a beginning. The same would hold for "fact," a miasma which only an epistemologist could love. Second, unlike genuine opposites—such as on-off, hot-cold, male-female—this one draws its constituents from mutually compatible but different types, of category. (It could be called a "category mistake.") Claiming to be able in general to ask, "Is that fact or is it opinion?" is like claiming to be able in general to ask of a politician, "Is she a Republican or is she a . . . conservative?" Where we would have expected "Democrat" or something of the same order, we get something of a different order. And so we shouldn't be surprised if the answer turns out to be "Both." Or "Neither." Or "Whaddya mean?"

In our urge to separate fact from opinion, something was undeniably right. We see people adopting or rejecting teachers, diets, student-body presidential candidates, music, or career choices—all on flimsy ground or what masquerades as grounds. We see them swayed by question-begging slogans like "Abortion is baby-killing" and "Abortion is free choice"—as if either stated uncontroversial, established facts. "If only they could see the facts," we think "and ignore the cacophonous gaggle of opinion." Here the contrast makes itself felt. But if my ruminations are close to the mark, the pull is folklore, and if so we suffer from what I once heard described as "hardening of the categories."

We need something better, but what? I fancy the answer is not all that tough. At bottom it is a matter of evidence quality: The existence of complete evidence renders a contention fact or false, though it may also be opinion; the existence of partial or no evidence renders a contention opinion, though it may also be fact. For this reason, the distinction does not matter, although evidence quality matters greatly.

And isn't this what we wanted all along? We wanted to be good at demanding and assessing support for others' claims and mustering strong support for our own assertions. We wanted to ask, "How is that known?" and to be able and disposed to employ all sorts of devices with which to calibrate the likelihood that the contention at issue is correct or false. I am pleased to see many such devices in the several documents cited—guidelines for gauging reliability of sources, for example, for generalizing responsibly, for measuring relevance, and for recognizing common foibles. So if I have been polemical here, it is against neither whole nor parts but only against one part that, in my opinion, deserves tougher-minded scrutiny than it has been receiving. Literally millions are being spent on it, and that is a fact.[2]

Questions for Reflection and Discussion

1. On what grounds does Weddle claim that there are more facts than there are human statements?

2. Give an example of something that is both an opinion and is correct.

3. Why is it more than a matter of observation that people migrated to California from the Midwest during the Depression years?

4. Could something both be a fact and be a matter of conjecture, according to Weddle? Give your own example.

5. Do you agree with Weddle's conclusion that having a tight, neat distinction between fact and opinion does not really matter, provided we pay attention to the quality of evidence and reasons for our beliefs? Why or why not?

Notes

1. Gary McCuen, *Basic Skills for Critical Thinking* (with *Teacher's Manual*) (St. Paul, Minn.: Greenhaven Press, 1979). The question is from Test Form 1.

2. This is a revised version of a paper delivered to a group of educators at the Second International Conference on Critical Thinking and Educational Reform at Sonoma State University, Rohnert Park, California, July 9–13, 1985.

6

Mass Media and International Conflict*

William A. Dorman

Press coverage of Iran and the Soviet Union has not provided American citizens with a good understanding of those countries. It has ignored relevant background information and tends to use loaded language and present data in a selective manner. This is worrisome, because for most people, the media are their primary textbook in foreign affairs.

S ince Vietnam, a sizeable element in the United States appears to be nominally concerned about foreign policy and defense issues in general and the possibility of nuclear war in particular. Although they may not be knowledgeable about the details of foreign affairs, this group of citizens is very much affected by a general mood, a mood that can set the boundaries of policy by producing passivity and acquiescence on the one hand or alarm and active dissent on the other. This mood consists of a generalized sense of whether foreign policy actions taken are in the country's best interests.

The news media have everything to do with shaping this general mood, for it is the press and broadcast journalism that on a day-to-day basis give most Americans a vital sense of what is in the nation's interests and what is not. The media with their labels and frames provide the public with a sense of who is enemy and who is friend, of who are freedom fighters and who are terrorists, and of which countries are allies and deserving of support and which are enemies and deserving of hatred, fear, and contempt. In short, the media are the primary textbook on foreign affairs. It matters greatly, therefore, if the textbook has serious flaws.

*Used with permission of William A. Dorman.

Iran: an Example

Yet the results of an extensive study of how the American press covered Iran from 1951 to 1978, the year of its revolution, are not reassuring for those who have come to depend on the press for a reliable picture of the world. The hostage crisis, of course, was a traumatic affair of unprecedented proportions. But for a moment, try and go back in time to before 1979 and the seizure of the embassy in Teheran, back to a time when most Americans thought an Ayatollah was a small foreign compact that got 35 MPG on the highway. In short, try and go back to a time when the average U.S. citizen did not have particularly strong feelings about Iran.

Iran by 1978 and the coming of the revolution had become the most important client state in United States history. More arms had been delivered by the United States to Iran than had ever been sold by any country in history. The United States had entered into a bilateral trade agreement with Iran that was larger in dollar amount than the total amount of money it took to reconstruct Europe under the Marshall Plan following World War II. Iranians comprised the largest group of foreign students in the United States. The United States had trained Iran's secret police and Army. American advisors and technocrats comprised one of the largest national minorities in Iran by 1978. In many ways, in brief, Iran was America's India. We had our own Raj. Yet Americans knew little if anything about Iran under the Shah Reza Pahlavi, and the revolution of 1978 came as a complete surprise to policymakers as well as the general public.

How did journalism contribute to this failure to understand what is probably the most strategically important country in the gulf region? Although a fully satisfactory answer requires more than a brief essay, some broad generalizations are possible.

From the beginning of direct United States involvement in Iran's affairs in 1953, the American mainstream press did little to give the American public an understanding of this increasingly vital country. For example, in its coverage of Iran's first democratically selected and enormously popular premier, Mohammad Mosaddeq, the press portrayed him as a communist dupe, eccentric madman, and enemy of democracy. He was none of these things, as even no less a luminary than Supreme Court Justice William O. Douglas was often moved to proclaim. Rather he was a staunch nationalist who was attempting to wrest control from foreign hands of the country's only significant natural resource—oil. Such coverage paved the way for the American public's acceptance of the coup, engineered by the Central Intelligence Agency, that overthrew Mosaddeq in 1953, returned the shah to power and made possible a twenty-five-year dictatorship that culminated in today's estrangement between the United States and Iran, a country that remains the most strategically important in the Persian Gulf no matter who rules it.

There is even evidence that the *New York Times,* widely recognized as the newspaper of record in the United States, had knowledge of the fact the United States had mounted the coup, and yet failed to report on it until years later. Moreover, evidence also shows that the *Times* reporter in Teheran in 1954 privately warned his New York editors that the newly returned shah had surrounded himself with what he called bargain-basement fascists—yet there was nothing to this effect in the *Times*.

From 1954 to 1963 when the shah was building a police state, there was only approving discussion in the press of how he was moving to suppress communism—when what he was actually suppressing were any and all political opponents.

From 1963 to 1973, the press was content to publish admiring accounts of how the shah had embarked on a modernization program, the keystone of which was land reform. Yet there was no meaningful land reform: The shah redistributed land his father had stolen to more potentially useful political allies. By the end of his supposed modernization program, he had destroyed the agricultural sector to the extent that the country was importing 80 percent of its foodstuffs, whereas before the country had been largely self sufficient.

Instead of portraying the shah as a despot, which Amnesty International, the International Commission of Jurists, and the International Red Cross had documented that he was, the press persisted in respectfully referring to him only in terms usually reserved for a hereditary monarch. Yet the Pahlavi Dynasty was exactly two generations old. Indeed, an extensive survey turned up only four uses of the term "dictator" used to describe him in the American mainstream press over a period of twenty-five years.

At a time when the shah was being accused in the international court of opinion as having the worst human rights record in the world, the liberal Aspen Institute for Humanistic Studies conferred a Special Award for Humanism on his wife, and a *New York Times* reporter sitting in the audience at the ceremony thought nothing unusual about such a presentation. Indeed, in 1975 at the height of Iran's abuses, the *New York Times* ran exactly three stories on human rights abuses in that country, although there were more than 150 stories in the same year on dissidents in the Soviet Union.

As a result of how the press portrayed Iran before and during the revolution, Americans of all backgrounds had little sympathy for those in revolt in 1978. President Jimmy Carter therefore had a free hand to pursue a disastrous policy that culminated in his allowing the shah into the United States, which precipitated the hostage crisis.

This journalistic failure was enormous. But consider its implications for budding hot spots such as Pakistan, Lebanon, Honduras, and so on where the American people are likely going to be asked to understand equally complex matters. What help can we count on from the press?

The interesting thing is that the media portray similar rebellions so differently. For example, Moslems on the Iran side of the border resisting the shah, a major client of the United States, were "religious fanatics" or "Moslem extremists," while Moslems on the Afghanistan side of the border resisting a Russian-sponsored government are "freedom fighters" or "Moslem militiamen." Journalists, in short, throughout the Cold War all too frequently have allowed "official" Washington to define the terms used to describe peoples in revolt abroad, rather than exercising their own independent judgments.

The result of the different journalistic treatments of these two countries in revolt was predictable: There was no support, only contempt for Iranians, or, as some persisted in calling them during the revolution, the "Ragheads."

Meanwhile, according to an item in the *Oregonian,* the people of Portland were holding car washes to benefit the freedom fighters in Afghanistan. The point, of course, is that by any reasonable standards both peoples were deserving of sympathy.

U.S. Media Portrayal of the Soviet Union

How conflict in the Middle East is portrayed has everything to do with the Cold War standoff between the two so-called Superpowers. And, if anything, the willingness of the press to accept Washington's definitions and interpretations of Middle Eastern politics is exceeded only by its willingness to serve the foreign policy establishment in the portrayal of the Soviet Union.

There can be little doubt that forty years of Cold War rhetoric and sixty-five years of accumulated fear of communism in general and the Soviets in particular have had their effects. In this respect, most people would laugh if someone compared America to revolutionary Iran in its fanaticism, but Americans in many ways have their own Great Satan to hate, to borrow a phrase from Kohmeini's Iran. Their great Satan, of course, is the Soviet Union.

The unprecedented situation in which the United States now finds itself with the Soviet Union significantly differs from past wars in that Americans have been mobilized to support the confrontation without the two adversaries actually having engaged in battle themselves. The Cold War in some fundamental ways, then, has been fought in the trenches of the mind.

Undergirding a sense of never-ending crisis is the threat of nuclear arms. In this respect, it may be well to remember that nuclearism and anti-Sovietism are one and the same thing. When Americans think about nuclear weapons, they have only one adversary in mind, not some vague indeterminate enemy. It matters greatly, therefore, how the media answer the question: What about the Russians?

Under the circumstances posed by the Cold War, the dimensions of press performance that seem most important are these: Does the press use loaded frames and labels to characterize Soviet life, intentions and behavior; do journalists present a range of plausible alternative explanations for the course of international events; do the news media report all that is reasonably knowable at the time of an international confrontation with the Soviets; and perhaps most importantly, do journalists remain independent of the foreign policy establishment in their judgments. Ample evidence indicates that the media have failed all of these tests to one degree or another.

How has the press contributed to a view of the Soviet Union as the Evil Empire? Again, there is not space to document press performance in exhaustive detail, but several examples are representative. These examples are drawn from a study I was commissioned to do at the time of Premier Leonid Brezhnev's death in late 1982. The results were presented at the National Conference on War, Peace, and the News Media at New York University.

First, I found that the press persists in using value-laden language. Stephen F. Cohen of Princeton University has described this tendency: We have a government, a security organization, and allies, the Soviet Union has a regime, secret police, and satellites. Our leaders are consummate politicians; theirs are wily, cunning, or worse. We give the world information and seek influence; they disseminate propaganda and disinformation while seeking expansion and domination. It seems reasonable that such prejudicial language is incompatible with fair-minded analysis.

Such highly charged and prejudicial language is used routinely to portray the Russian leadership in terms suggestive of a deep current of darkness. At the time of Brezhnev's death, for instance, the kindest words *Time* magazine could find for the man were "Hard driving, hard drinking, and exuberant until slowed by illness, Brezhnev was the quintessential Russian, a mix of caution and opportunism, a genial knee-slapper who did not hesitate to crush opponents . . . He was not a cold-blooded fanatic like Lenin. He was not a bloodthirsty tyrant like Stalin. He was not a capricious, mercurial improviser like Krushchev."

Figuring prominently and predictably in media accounts of the specific aspects of Brezhnev's life was the darker side of his eighteen-year rule. A *Washington Post* editorial stated, "The one doctrine to which he lent his name rationalized aggression." A *New York Times* editorialist summed up the consensus view in "The Brezhnev era was repressive at best and brutal at its worst."

Newsweek's twenty-page treatment, insofar as Brezhnev-the-man is concerned, can be summed up by the headline: The Cautious Bully. American media were kindest, if that is the proper term, in describing the late Russian leader's personal qualities. United Press International found the Soviet leader to be "canny," "burly," and "beetle-browed," a favored description in much of the media. The *New York Times* also described Brezhnev as "canny," "burly," "gregarious and talkative," with a "reputation as a lover of good food and drink, fast cars—which he collected—and hunting." The *Times* found Brezhnev to have been "a man of "little humor" and someone who found the "circus more entertaining than the ballet or an opera." (Incidentally, Americans may have their own window of vulnerability on the ballet and culture issues, given the fact President Ronald Reagan did not see his own son perform in ballet until Ron Junior's career was nearly at an end, and given that Reagan once told *TV Guide* that his favorite show was "Charlie's Angels," a show he preferred because the good guys always seemed to win.)

Echoing the *New York Times,* and *Washington Post's* assessment was that the Soviet president was a "burly, beetle-browed hard-liner" with a "fascination with fancy cars." Indeed, the *Post* noted in an editorial farewell to the man, apparently without intended irony, "his most widely reported human quality was a taste for expensive Western cars."

The point to be made here is not that Brezhnev was none of these things; many of the descriptions used apparently were quite accurate. But imagine what a relentlessly anti-American journalist might say in a obituary of Richard Nixon:

> Richard Nixon died today in a country that has known slavery, a massive civil war, the forced collectivization of the American Indian, a brutal

industrial revolution, several devastating depressions and many lesser recessions, and the seemingly routine assassination of presidents, political figures, and labor leaders. He was the perfect leader for a country that has used force abroad as an instrument of foreign policy more than 300 times since its inception as a republic. He ordered the secret bombings of Laos and Cambodia, and compelling evidence exists that indicates Nixon overthrew the democratically-elected Salvador Allende in Chile. Known in domestic politics as "Tricky Dick" for his underhanded campaign tactics, Nixon's administration was scandal-ridden, with some eighteen members serving time in prison. He was known to keep an "enemies" list and was not hesitant to use the Internal Revenue Service or other federal agencies to harass and intimidate his political foes. His vice-president, Spiro Agnew, was the first vice-president in United States history to be forced to resign after having been indicted for income tax invasion stemming from illegal kickbacks. The heavily bearded Nixon, who was almost pathologically paranoid and who drank to excess, by far preferred football to a night at the symphony.

The point of course is that Nixon is more than that. And certainly, the nature, genius, and promise of the United States is far more than the darker pages of our past would suggest. Yet here is how *Time* magazine summed up Russian history since the Bolshevik Revolution:

Tsarist autocracy quickly gave way to the "dictatorship of the proletariat," and the United States began sixty-five years of trying, with a great variety of tactics and theories but with a notable lack of success, to find some way of ameliorating the more maddening, sometimes murderous aspects of Soviet tyranny.

The second area in which the media contribute significantly to suspicion of the Soviet Union deals with Soviet behavior. Again, the argument is not that the news media lie or make things up. What is of far greater concern than the question of journalistic truth or untruths is the interpretation that demonstrable truths receive. Under the American system of law, for instance, determination of the legal truth or totality is not wholly based on an act itself. Such a determination only follows substantive consideration of the context in which the act took place. The motives and behavior of nations are probably best considered and evaluated in a similar way, particularly if an appropriate and measured response to another country's actions is sought. As someone once remarked, the literal truth in politics—as in art—is the most doubtful truth of all. Yet the media persist in treating the Soviet Union as if this were not so, and they choose to interpret Russia's behavior as if its acts can be understood only at the literal level.

In this regard, successful propaganda is not based on lies but rather on truth interpreted in a certain way. For instance, it is no figment of the imagination that the Soviets brutally invaded Afghanistan. But how did the media interpret that truth? From the *New York Times* to the *San Francisco Chronicle*, the consensus was that the Soviets had very likely begun their march through the

Persian Gulf, bent on capturing Arab oil, taking Iran, and threatening Pakistan. In short, the invasion was portrayed as obvious evidence of the Soviet's desire for world domination. It is as if the Soviet media had interpreted America's invasion of Grenada as the first step in the military conquest of the Caribbean.

A final example of how truths, however terrible, can be subject to varying media interpretations involves two instances ten years apart—the downings of civilian airliners. In the first, an Israeli jet fighter in 1973 shot down a Lybian 727, killing 106 innocent men, women, and children. To be sure, the American media in general viewed the tragedy with dismay and to varying degrees condemnation. At the same time, however, the media were careful to put the action into the historical context of the Arab-Israeli conflict and did not suggest that it might have been a deliberate act. *Newsweek,* for instance, headlined its account: "A Deadly Blunder Over Sinai." There was no hysteria, no effort to portray the killing of innocent civilians as evidence of barbarity, no move to drum Israel out of the league of decent nations. Yet here is how *Newsweek* dealt with the Soviet downing of Korean Airlines Flight 007. The cover headline read: Murder in the Air; and the inside subhead was: A Ruthless Ambush in the Sky.

Why the Media Act as They Do

I should be very clear at this point about why I think the press behaves as it does. Nothing that I say here is meant to imply that correspondents are part of a planned conspiracy or that their editors act on instructions directly received from the state department. Rather, the process by which the press over time tends to reflect official foreign policy positions is a function of both the media system's ideological orientation and Cold War conditioning. The behavior is spontaneous and usually unconscious. It is reflexive rather than deliberate.

In short, the Cold War has resulted in the same kind of willingness on the part of the media to suspend the critical function that hot wars have always elicited. The roots of the phenomenon can be found in the establishment of a permanent garrison state of the mind for Americans. This permanent state of psychological siege results from the nuclear crisis with the Soviet Union. This has led to what I call a "journalism of deference" to the National Security State. Whatever its sources, such deference has put the journalistic watchdog, much celebrated in democratic theory, on a rather short tether with consequences that ought to be of serious concern.

The foreign policy bureaucracy, as it is now constituted, seems incapable of the type of understanding demanded by changing conditions in foreign affairs generally and the Third World in particular. Under such conditions, the press, if it maintains an autonomous perspective, can act as a reality check on policymakers by providing a means of gauging whether policy is based on evidence and concrete facts or self-delusions and misperceptions—as so often has been the case since World War II. Moreover, the Reagan White House has gone even farther than usual to politicize the state's formal information gathering apparatus, pressuring intelligence agencies and the foreign service to provide only "facts" that reinforce official assumptions. Under such circumstances, policymakers tend to operate within a closed information loop: The information they receive confirms the policy choices they already have made.

It is precisely when a liberal democracy's state information-gathering apparatus is so highly politicized that the press can make its most important contribution, by providing the public and especially Congress with a candid and independent picture of developments abroad. Yet there is scant evidence that the news media are yet willing to exercise the necessary independence. Theoretically, the press has the material and intellectual resources to comprehend political conflict abroad and transform raw information into knowledge. But before the press can become a corrective force in the foreign policy arena, the journalistic system must come to grips with the effects of world view on its perspective. As well, there must be a determined commitment to rethinking the assumptions and practices of contemporary foreign affairs reporting. Until these goals are achieved, public debate on foreign policy issues is likely to remain dangerously stunted.

Questions for Reflection and Discussion

1. Does Dorman convince you that United States media coverage of the shah's government in Iran between 1953 and 1975 was inadequate? What does Dorman see as the cause of the very selective coverage?

2. How would you distinguish between a religious fanatic and a freedom fighter? Is there any plausible justification for regarding 1978 opponents of the shah as religious fanatics and 1979–80 opponents of the Soviet-backed government of Afghanistan as freedom fighters? What difference do these labels make?

3. Compare Dorman's imaginary obituary notice of Richard Nixon to the real piece he cites from *Time* magazine about Leonid Brezhnev. Are both biased, as Dorman implies? In what specific ways are these pieces similar? How are they different?

4. What do you think Dorman means when he says that "successful propaganda is not based on lies but rather on truth interpreted in a certain way"? Do you tend to agree or disagree, and why?

5. There is an old Yiddish saying that "half a truth is a whole lie." In what ways would Dorman's account of press coverage of Iran and the Soviet Union tend to confirm this saying?

7

Propaganda Talk*

Dennis Rohatyn

Propaganda is hard to define. You cannot even define it in terms of the manipulation of symbols for political purposes. Some propaganda uses images, not symbols. And some propaganda is for commercial purposes, not political ones. We are so surrounded by propaganda that we hardly detect it, even though classic propaganda from other times and places seems blatant. Every instance of propaganda seems to inspire another instance of counterpropaganda, so that it is difficult to avoid propaganda entirely. Even the most skilled propagandists might end up deceived by their own products.

On a recent pilgrimmage to a forbidden place this reporter was privileged to visit the underground offices of Dr. Uve Binad, the world's foremost authority on propaganda and director of the Ministry of Truth. Dr. Binad took time from a busy schedule to grant me an exclusive interview, a concealed tape recording of which I sneaked through customs and stealthily smuggled past the X-ray machine. The transcript is unaltered, except for adding whatever references were needed to clarify Binad's allusions.[1]

Q: *Dr., what is propaganda?*
Social scientists working in tandem with philosophers have long since defined it as " . . . political symbols manipulated for the control of public opinion."[2] But that doesn't begin to tell the full story.

Q: *Why not?*
For one thing, many of the symbols are commercial, not political. A woman seated in a bathtub cooing "Caress . . . when I undress" during a TV commercial is selling soap, not ideology. Of course, she's also selling you a bill of consumer goods, but that's another story.

Q: *You mean, the soap won't get you clean?*
No, I mean that it won't change or improve your sex life, make you alluring or irresistible, or do anything but get you clean.

Q: *But does the ad promise any of those things?*
No, but it suggests them. Advertisers are far too smart to make false promises; they're not about to risk a law suit. So they rely on innuendo.

Q: *Doesn't political propaganda do those things?*
Sure. But political propaganda seeks to convince you, to make you buy its line, whereas commercial propaganda seeks profit, to get you to buy the product. The effects are not the same in each case, though the means of persuasion may resemble each other.

Q: *So there are different kinds of propaganda?*
Yes, depending on the objective. But that's not all that's wrong with the definition I just cited.

Q: *What else?*
The word "symbol" is ambiguous. Narrowly construed, it means words, utterances, in short, language. But most propaganda uses images to make its point: the woman seated in the tub, happy, smiling people drinking Coke or Pepsi, rugged macho men jumping up and down alongside pickup trucks, or gruesome images like starving children, clubbed baby seals, unborn fetuses. Now, an icon or image is a symbol, too, but it's not a verbal symbol. So we have to be careful, especially when it comes to images that lend themselves to diverse interpretations. And that spells trouble, especially between different cultures. Even in the same culture, a given symbol often has different functions.

Q: *For instance?*
A plus sign looks like a Cross. A sheriff's badge resembles a Star of David. A crescent may be the moon, a banana, or an alchemist's hat. Mind you, this is just the physical shape or the syntax. When we get into semantics, things get really complicated. We nod for yes and shake our heads to mean no. Some tribes do just the reverse. A propagandist must be aware of what the audience already believes and try to reinforce it. If you violate people's expectations, you'll just confuse them. That's the point to remember here.

Q: *Don't propagandists use both verbal and visual symbols?*
Yes, and music, too. Every sense organ is involved, and so is every type of symbol. A really skillful propagandist can blend all of these together into a single overpowering experience, like immersing yourself in Wagnerian opera or attending a huge outdoor rally. Propaganda isn't an isolated component or a discrete proposition; it's more like a configuration or Gestalt.

Q: *Why is this so important?*
Because scholars who analyze propaganda tend to overconcentrate on just one

aspect of it. As a consequence they miss the wood for the trees. Even when their analysis is correct, they're still missing something.

Q: *Give me an example.*
Let's start with something manageable. Take the ad that runs "Volvos last an average of eleven years in Sweden." Now, what's the objective? To get you to buy a Volvo. How do they persuade or massage you into it? By giving you a truncated argument, which logicians call an enthymeme.

Q: *What's the argument?*
Probably something like this:

> Volvos last an average of eleven years in Sweden. Sweden is near the North Pole. It has a rugged climate and lots of bad roads. If a Volvo lasts eleven years in Sweden, it should last at least as long where I live. The more reliable and long-lasting a car is, the better buy it is. Therefore, my next car should be a Volvo.

Q: *What's wrong with this argument?*
Maybe nothing. Then again, maybe a lot. If you live in Southern California you don't have to worry about climate or roads. So it doesn't matter whether your car is hardy in winter or not. But the salt air from the Pacific Ocean might bother it. Are Volvos equipped to handle that? Also, how much does a Volvo cost? Is it three times as expensive as some comparable make I can afford? But the ad doesn't discuss the merits or demerits of buying a Volvo. Nor does it draw any conclusions or make its premises explicit. So you've got to fill in all of the relevant details.

Q: *What you're saying is that the Volvo ad hides something from us.*
Yes, and that's what logicians call suppressed evidence. If I knew all the facts, maybe buying a Volvo wouldn't seem like such a terrific idea. This isn't to say anything against the car, just the ad. Of course I'm presuming that Volvos do last an average of eleven years in Sweden. The one you buy may last half as long or twice as long. Suppressed evidence isn't the same as lying. It's more like cheating.

Q: *That suggests something. Why can't we define propaganda as "selective evidence favoring a point of view," be it commercial or political? Wouldn't that suffice?*
No, because for every Volvo ad there's three that are more like the Caress ad. See, the Volvo ad is nice because it gives you something to latch on to, something to critique. Whereas Caress is as slippery as the soap it sells. It doesn't *say* anything, it makes no overt claims, nothing you can point to and say "that's a fallacy" or "that's fraud, misrepresentation, falsehood." Volvo leaves out a lot, but at least there's some evidence there. Hence ads like that attract logicians, because it gives them something to do.

Q: *That's why you maintain that analysis of "symbols" can be misleading or incomplete.*
Exactly. Propaganda is elusive. It isn't something you can pin down. It's like wall-to-wall carpeting or smog in Los Angeles: It's everywhere. So you can't detect it using the usual rational methods. With Volvo you can stand back and say "that's a weakly supported inductive inference" and then solemnly warn your audience against being duped or tricked. But Volvo ads are a fast-disappearing breed. Nowadays, propaganda can't succeed unless it's covert.

Q: *Covert?*
So well disguised that no one notices it. Let me illustrate. If you come out and say "Adolf Hitler was a great man, he didn't have anything against the Jews, he just wanted a better life for his people and to maintain racial purity," no one who isn't already wedded to that way of thinking is going to believe you. I've watched cable television programs hosted by Tom Metzger [the founder of the National Association for the Advancement of White People and former official in the Ku Klux Klan] and believe me, they're duds. They won't convert the unconverted, because their lies are too blatant and their tactics too gross and unsophisticated to fool anyone over seventeen or with a corresponding IQ. That might have been "good" (effective, subtle) propaganda in Hitler's time, but today it's passé. Whether your pitch is popcorn, population control, or Pershing missiles, you've got to be slick.

Q: *So propaganda, like history, marches on?*
Absolutely. It evolves and adapts. Propaganda is dynamic, not static. Only the fittest varieties survive. Take [Richard] Nixon's "Checkers" speech [in 1952]. Now that was a classic; but try it on an audience today, no matter what their age or political affiliation, people will burst into hysterics.

Q: *Isn't that because he disgraced himself as president twenty years later?*
No. Even if Watergate had never happened, Nixon's whole manner would still provoke guffaws. He sits motionless in front of the cameras recalling his poor Quaker upbringing in California, his struggles to get through college, his service in the Navy, his marriage and move to Washington, all this after nearly fifteen minutes during which he does nothing but itemize his monthly income and expenses. That's a quarter hour of laundry bills, mortgage payments, installments on his Oldsmobile, and other boring details. Of course, he had to do that to clear his name [Nixon was accused of accepting illegal campaign contributions]. And in those days prime time [on national television] wasn't as expensive as it is now. Still, if I were his advisor there's no way I'd have let him put on such a monotonous show, so devoid of style and interest. Not to mention the way he's dressed or his overly stiff posture. He's wearing a rumpled suit, and he looks haggard. Strike one. Then he introduces his wife, who's as frigid as he is rigid. Her smile is plastered on, she doesn't say a word or move a facial muscle. Together they look like a retouched version of *American Gothic*. Strike two. The only time Nixon shows any emotion is when he gets up (near the end) and tells the audience that [General, later President] Eisenhower is "a great and good man" who will "fight communism" both in Korea and in the United States

Senate. He gets a mad glint in his eye, clenches his jaw, the whole paranoid bit. He did it spontaneously, because the tape ran out and the network had to cut him off in mid-sentence. That's the only thing he said that he didn't rehearse. Strike three.

Q: *What about the dog after whom the speech is named?*
Actually, that's a minor episode. Somebody gave Julie [Nixon's daughter, at that time a small child] a pet dog, and Nixon tried to milk some sympathy by saying "we're going to keep it." He was also trying to demonstrate how scrupulously honest he was in keeping track of gifts, even a puppy delivered to the train station in Chicago. It was a clever touch, but Nixon already sounds beleaguered, as though the world is against him and his family.

Q: *Isn't that due to hindsight?*
You have to wonder why more people didn't notice it at the time, because it's embarrassingly obvious now. The whole half hour is like that: They're out to get me, and I've got to protect myself before it's too late. It's all there on tape, with no deletions. What we're seeing when we watch "Checkers" isn't the '50s, it's an '80s retrospective on the '50s. That's why it's easy to jeer at Patricia Nixon. Since the late '60s, feminism and the women's movement have made subservience and docility unacceptable. Mrs. Nixon was just trying to help her mate. If she had made "liberated" noises or quoted Simone de Beauvoir, she wouldn't have been on the show. Today she'd be just right for a Virginia Slims poster.

Q: *Did Nixon succeed despite or because of his flaws?*
A little of both. Sometimes propaganda just wears you down. Nixon's appeals to pity are always transparent, yet after a while you do feel sorry for him just because he's so mediocre, a perfect *schlemihl* [born loser] who's also a *shmuck* [detestable].[3] Have you ever given a beggar money just to get rid of them? That's roughly what Americans did with Nixon, only they gave him power. Even that didn't cure him. "Trusting nothing, he could not even trust good fortune. Even at this late date [1972], he was not convinced that the heart of his emptiness would not be penetrated by the press."[4] And so Watergate happened. But Nixon revealed himself as early as '52 when he went on the electronic stump to save himself. He oscillates between "poor me" and belligerence, just as he did throughout his career. The strategy was terrible, yet it worked. The mail ran at least 18–1 in favor, suddenly he was back on the [presidential] ticket and [in November, 1952] the Republicans swept into office. Propaganda like that is obsolete, but it was a success in its day. You have to respect it even though no one would dare to repeat it, least of all someone trying to keep the truth about Nixon hidden from the public.

Q: *So even propagandists learn from their mistakes?*
You bet. Propaganda is just like any other craft, be it shipbuilding, clock manufacture, weaving, or pottery. Propaganda technique is handed down from one generation to the next. But it has to grow, or it can't survive in a competitive world. You can't bake pies like grandma did, because grandma used a stone hearth oven and you've got a microwave. But you can learn from her recipe and

Propaganda Talk

refine her cuisine. The same is true of propaganda. It's a cumulative tradition. It builds on what predecessors have accomplished and tries hard not to repeat old blunders. A propagandist must stay up to date or else be left behind. The self-deprecating commercials Volkswagen did in the 1960s were a breakthrough, because nobody had ever dared to ridicule themselves before.[5] Now that's become commonplace, an overused gambit. So you can't do it, though you can still learn from it.

Q: *Lincoln said, "You can't fool all of the people all of the time." Was he right?*
Absolutely, although he tried to fool all of the people by flattering their intelligence. Audiences are getting smarter all the time, and they have propaganda to thank for their new-found sophistication. Constant exposure to advertising since the advent of radio in the 1920s has made us experts at spotting clumsy, inept propaganda. Just as Eskimos have dozens of words for snow, so the average North American can finely discriminate between sales angles, even if we end up falling for them. Moreover, every day we routinely "tune out" thousands of mass communications, that is, printed and electronic signals, messages between senders and receivers that reach millions of people more or less at once. I don't mean that we turn off the TV or the radio or that we stop reading the magazine or newspaper. We watch, hear, and read all of those things without paying attention—by flatly ignoring most of what's there. If we didn't we couldn't cope with the technological hum, the background noise of our existence.

Q: *So although propagandists select their evidence, we only pay selective attention. Is that it?*
Yes. For propagandists this is a blessing in disguise, because even the best (most cunning) propaganda imaginable betrays itself at crucial moments. When you watch a pro-Nazi epic like *Triumph of the Will* [1934], you wonder why it's classic. Don't those people realize that they're not individuals but ciphers? Can't they see that Hitler is leading them to their doom? Aren't the sheer enormity of the swastikas, the endless columns of soldiers standing at attention saluting the Fuehrer, and the aerial shots of row upon row of human toothpicks lined up single file a graphic clue to Germany's fate? From overhead the throngs assembled in the Nuremberg square and amphitheater look like headstones in a military cemetery. That's both somber and prophetic, but not what [Leni] Riefenstahl intended. Yet the movie, like the real (not staged) events it depicted, was fatally attractive to millions of adherents. Like watching Nixon, today we view it through a prism. It's no longer what it was. To get some idea of what it stirred we have to subtract fifty intervening years from each of our lives and imagine ourselves mentally more blind than we in fact are.

Q: *So both Nixon and Riefenstahl exploit our inability to see things as they are?*
You've got it backwards. If the invention of photography has taught us anything, it's that things are as we see them. Isn't that what [Bishop] Berkeley's [1685–1753] slogan "to be is to be perceived" means? We never see things as they are, only as we want or imagine them to be. That's what propaganda exploits. What propaganda does is to capitalize on our reluctance to change from one mode of

perception to another. Conceptually, we prefer to stay in one frame, rather than to rearrange, experiment, or break out of it.[6] This is because we're creatures of habit, afraid of the unknown and the unconventional. Consequently, anyone who asks us to change frames is destined for trouble.

On the whole, it's far easier to tap some visceral impulse or deep-seated desire than to inculcate a belief system or a set of abstractions. You can get people to parrot an "ism," but inside they remain unchanged.

That's why Riefenstahl edited the Party speeches down to a minimum of footage. Even those sound like machine-gun fire; the words don't matter, but you can't miss the message even if you don't understand a word they're saying at the Party Congress. Primarily she relies on gigantism to convey power, to get across the idea that Germany will no longer be divided or humiliated. So she "documented" what her domestic audience, starved by runaway inflation and still licking its wounds from the first World War, wanted to see and hear. She catered to their desires and aroused their ardor for revenge by feeding them a mental laxative in bulk quantities. Yet if they stared at their plate again or glanced at their meal under a different light, it might suddenly appear inedible, just as McCarthyism eventually did to many Americans after 1954. It's tough to induce radical belief-change, but a 180-degree reversal of beliefs is possible. That's a Gestalt switch.[7] It's rare, but it does happen. Otherwise we'd still believe that the earth was flat.

Q: *Are you implying that Riefenstahl wasn't responsible for her deeds? That she just "gave the public what it wanted," the same excuse network executives give for programming prime-time tripe?*
I'm saying the blame must be distributed equitably between the propagander and (millions of) propagandees. For every propagandist, there's thousands begging to be propagandized. Actually, they've already propagandized themselves. They just don't realize it yet.

Q: *That's awfully cynical.*
Yes, and self-serving, too. I can see your whole litany of objections coming at me, so don't waste your breath. Just ponder the following tidbit. When foreign audiences viewed *Triumph* in the '30s, you know what their reaction was? "This is just Nazi propaganda. The Fuehrer couldn't have that much military strength at his disposal. He's just a pipsqueak." Besides, Hitler had sent Riefenstahl to Hollywood in 1933 to master film technique. That was when they were making Busby Berkeley musicals. She learned how to shoot big, splashy scenes with thousands of extras and state-of-the-art special effects. So when the film appeared, everyone who wasn't loyal to Hitler treated it as art, forgetting that art is truth. They dismissed her undisguised message that Germany was a force to be reckoned with, until it was almost too late! The truth lay before them: Soldiers, weapons, fanatical resolve—yet they collectively ignored it. So much for perceiving things as they are.

Q: *But that could only happen because propaganda made it impossible (or difficult) to distinguish lies from facts.*
Precisely. And facts are much better than lies, not because they're facts but

because they lend themselves to propaganda. Everything Riefenstahl portrays in her film is true, just as everything Nixon tells you about his finances is true. It's only when everything is true that the lies can begin. Then watch out!

Q: *But can't that occur innocently, without deceptive intent?*
Sure. That's just what happened when Orson Welles broadcast "War of the Worlds" [October 30, 1938] and "described" a phony Martian invasion! Several hundred thousand people fled New York and New Jersey, and others went out armed with guns looking for the spaceship that had crashed near Trenton [in the story]. Too bad Welles never became a propagandist. He was a natural.

Q: *And you see nothing wrong with that?*
Welles told the audience four times that it was a joke, a Halloween night prank. The newspapers listed the radio show and summarized the plot that same day. Besides, he adapted the whole thing from H.G. Wells (1866–1946, who wrote *War of the Worlds* in 1898).

Q: *You're saying it was the public's fault?*
Yes, though Welles helped them along by interspersing dance music with [false] news reports and an "interview" with a nonexistent astronomer. But it was all a gag. People who tuned in late after listening to Edgar Bergen and Charlie McCarthy, on another channel didn't pick up the context and reacted as though it were a news report. Besides, Americans were jumpy following [live coverage of] the Spanish Civil War and then Chamberlain's capitulation to Hitler's demands at Munich. And Martians are the same as Reds [Communists]. People were ready to believe anything, without being told, or despite being told just the opposite. Now whose fault is that? Besides, only 10 percent of the audience panicked. The rest stayed home, called the station, or wrote letters to CBS.[8]

Q: *So Welles wasn't guilty.*
The point is, he wasn't trying. Just think what he might have achieved if he had been! The man was a genius. If he had stayed with it, eventually he'd have set or broken every world record for bamboozlement. What a waste of talent!

Q: *I suppose you admire Riefenstahl, too.*
No, I don't, although many respected critics and film historians do. Frankly, I find her dull. Her camera angles are imaginative, but her subjects are not. Colossal size doesn't impress me, and in her case it obeys a law of diminishing returns. Too much of the same thing turns me off, whether it's planes, parades, or goose-steps. Not to mention Heil Hitler salutes or the Fuehrer hugging newborn babies, later to be sacrificed to the Third Reich. And in *Triumph* there's a surfeit of all these things, which gives me indigestion.

Q: *Riefenstahl enjoyed a monopoly on public attention, at least in Nazi Germany. But even Nixon always had to contend with diametrically opposed points of view. Doesn't the checks and balances system of government guard against propaganda's most damaging effects?*

If you mean, does it prevent tyranny, as James Madison hoped it would, the answer is probably yes, so long as you enforce the system and don't mistake pious lip service or on-paper declarations for actual political practices. But when there's too many voices clamoring for attention, the results are as dismaying as when there's too few.

I'm not talking about the two-party system so much as the media blitz that we are compelled to endure. During an average day we may hear or read half a dozen editorials and again as many "op-ed" columns on everything from sewage to immigration to terrorism to AIDS to military appropriations to demonstrations in China to smoking in public places to who's going to pay for the new domed stadium to pre-trial publicity to sex education to . . . It's too much to assimilate, yet it constantly assaults us. So we end up staggering around like punch-drunk boxers who can't find their opponent or their respective corners.[9] No one knows what to believe, except "opinion managers" who are paid to bombard us with more advice on every conceivable subject.[10] So we read or tune in Dr. Ruth, George Will, Ann Landers, Dr. Joyce Brothers, Paul Harvey, and Chef Tel, and by then it's time to go to sleep. The only think we've learned from this surfeit of expertise is that we don't know anything, that we can't trust common sense or our instincts, and that we must leave big decisions to the professionals. And that's what propaganda is and does in a "free" society: it convinces us that we have no right to an opinion, because we aren't smart or informed enough to have one. It negates Emerson's vision of "self-reliance" [1838], which was dying out even as he exhorted Americans to it.

Q: *But people like Dr. Ruth and Dr. Joyce Brothers always are trying to raise people's self-esteem.*
Yes, but their method is self-defeating. Apart from having money, the only way to have self-esteem in our society is to transmit messages rather than receive them. And how do you do that? By having your own TV or radio show or a regular column in the newspapers. Hence the only way that media therapists could improve the self-image of their faceless clientele is if they brought them all into the studio and put them on the tube. This is why call-in shows are so popular. They're the modern equivalent of touching the hem of royalty. Talking to the host temporarily lifts you out of the stream of anonymity and makes you a lord or a lady for a few precious seconds. But the glow wears off fast; as soon as the call is over you plunge back into obscurity. Media fame is like taking cocaine: Either you're constantly high or you're dead. Either way is hopeless. Besides, even the nobility have to share their fame, to move over and make room for each other.

Q: *And that means less of the limelight for each one?*
When they're not arguing with each other, they're bowing to each other. So what do you get? Mostly it's a succession of monologues. The expert guest sits on the couch being interviewed by a talk-show host who knows nothing about the subject and is under pressure to keep the subject light. The alternative is weekly blasts of hot air, either self-caricaturing exchanges like those between Shana Alexander and James Kilpatrick on "60 Minutes" or obnoxious, simulated third-degree torture like "Point/Counterpoint," where the guest never gets a

word in edgewise because the hostile hosts are too busy cutting each other down.

Q: *You make it sound like roller derby or professional wrestling.*
Those sports have more class.

Q: *When there's a cacophony of voices they all tend to disappear, to drown and cancel each other out. So how do we make ourselves heard? How do we get on the tube, not to promote ourselves or relieve our anxiety but to raise the level of public discourse?*
We have to begin, not by shouting but by listening. It's amazing what we don't notice because we're too busy talking. That's why Riefenstahl was able to con Germans into embracing Hitler and nonGermans into disregarding him. That's why Nixon's tics and phobias don't become apparent until three decades later. We're not ready to speak yet. Maybe never.

Q: *But so long as we don't speak, we're letting others represent us: all those Ph.D.s and celebrities you mentioned, the "priestly caste" whose influence dictates trends and persuades us that we are worthless.*
Yes, that is a vicious circle. But I'm a member of that caste, so anything I say is bound to make matters worse! We may need Zen exercises to jolt our awareness and reorient our perception. That's one reason why John Cage composed "4'33"" [4 minutes and 33 seconds of silence]. He wanted people to attend to noise so they'd realize what was floating all around them, from Muzak to occult metaphysics, from jackhammers to jokers like me. And that was back in 1951, when TV was in its infancy and you could count the number of atomic warheads on the fingers of both hands. Once people hear and see what's directly in front of them, they'll be less susceptible to propaganda and able to control their own destiny. But that's a long way off.

Q: *What about ways in which propaganda takes advantage of human physiology, as in subliminal advertising? Isn't that both covert and downright sinister?*
Sinister, yes, though there's not that much of it around." Covert, no. To be covert, propaganda must play a game with your intellect, even challenge you in some way. Whereas, subliminal ads directly "inject" a message below the threshhold of consciousness. They're artless and crude. They operate against your will but without your awareness or complicity. Although propaganda seduces you, subliminals are mental rape. That's why they're no fun. And they're no fun for the propagandist, either. There's nothing more exciting than a prolonged chase, an uncertain conquest, an obstacle to be overcome. It's the prospect of failure that eggs a propagandist on. Subliminals are foolproof, they're not art but perverted science. The only way you could get propagandists to use them is if you injected them first. Then you might as well use force.

Q: *OK, then how does covert propaganda work?*
Look at the back of the Ruffles potato chips bag (distributed by the millions in stores and convenience marts). It's divided into two halves. On the right side it provides nutrition information. On the left it says things like "when you and

your family enjoy RUFFLES brand Potato Chips, you're getting more than great taste. You're getting beneficial nutrients in every ounce. We're not going to tell you that our chips are a primary source of nutrition, because they're not. But they have more to offer than many people think." The ad then goes on to state that Ruffles chips are a good source of Vitamin C, contain "surprisingly" few calories, and contain less salt than either tomatoes or cottage cheese. And they have no cholesterol or preservatives.

Q: *I assume these statements are all accurate, or else the FDA [Food and Drug Administration] would crack down on the manufacturer, in this case Frito-Lay.*
That's just it. Frito-Lay isn't telling obvious lies (like Neo-Nazis), nor do they withhold vital product information. On the contrary, they insist on being honest: "No one said we had to have nutrition labeling. But we thought you'd like to know." So you can't accuse them of suppressing evidence or fudging data. They're not doing a Volvo number on you. Every single thing they say is true, they leave nothing out (except their own motives), yet the whole ad is a model of covert propaganda, designed to trap the unwary. That's way it's wrong to define or identify propaganda strictly in terms of what it omits. It's just not that simple.

Q: *Then why not choose another criterion, like distortion?*
That might work, except that even a Nazi epic like *Triumph* can claim to be "a purely historical film" devoid of "tendentious commentary" or lies of any sort.[12]

Q: *But her self-vindications are worthless, just more propaganda!*
Granted, but she can say them with a straight face. After all, the Nazis did believe they were the master race; that's no lie. Is she to blame for conveying their lie, both to impress and frighten the world? In this respect, nothing has changed since the '30s and '50s except what's being sold. Like the greatest athletes, the finest propagandists of one era could play, compete, and win in another.

Q: *Too bad there's no Hall of Shame. But how can potato chip packages be an unworthy success to* Triumph *and "Checkers"? Isn't that stretching it a bit?*
To the '80s, Coke *versus* Pepsi is what "the battle for men's minds" was in the '50s. The war has changed, but the strategy is similar. Besides, don't ever underestimate multinational corporations. Their propaganda may not be as comical or as devastating as Nixon and the Nazis were; but by making everyone into a conspicuous consumer, they're doing as much psychic damage. It isn't as direct, but that's the beauty of it. Potato chip ads may look undignified, but they're in the best tradition—part of an unbroken line, a continuous flow of mind-molding muck.

Q: *What is their motive? Why are they doing it?*
Because Frito-Lay wants you to believe that their potato chips aren't junk food but part of a normal, healthy diet. Because it wants you to stop feeling guilty about your poor eating habits and buy its brand instead. And because it wants you to regard Frito-Lay as a responsible corporate citizen, one that doesn't have

to be coerced into telling you ingredients or forced to comply with government regulations. Thus Frito-Lay creates a favorable aura surrounding the product, boosting the reputation of the company. (Frito-Lay publishes a similar spiel on packages of their tortilla chips.) None of this is subliminal; it's all out in the open. Frito-Lay even takes you into its confidence, warning you against jumping to false conclusions ("We're not going to tell you that our chips are a primary source of nutrition"). Now that's sinister!

Q: *What if it's all true? What if it's OK to eat potato chips in moderation? What if that brand is superior to the competition?*
You want to buy a bridge? Today only, I'm selling the Golden Gate and the Brooklyn, a two for one special.

Q: *Be serious. Can't propaganda be true?*
It has to be true, or else it can't deceive anybody. That's why advanced propaganda defies rational criticism. You can't reduce propaganda to a set of utterances (p, q, r, s . . .) and then interrogate each one. The whole set is propaganda, not just its members. Yet the whole set is not graspable in the way that mathematics can prove theorems about sets.

Q: *Propaganda as Gestalt or [Rohrschach] ink blots, again?*
Correct. So when you ask, "Does it follow that Ruffles chips are wholesome just because they contain 'only 150 calories in a one-ounce serving'?" don't assume either that the answer is no or that if the answer is yes that puts Ruffles in the clear. Covert propaganda succeeds not by denying the truth or by propounding unsound arguments; it can fulfill every requirement science imposes yet still be vacuous. Unfortunately, both logic and law have fallen far behind the myth makers. You can bet that Frito-Lay will never end up in court so long as the ad agency that handles the account knows and acts on this principle. Propaganda is a cat-and-mouse game, a jousting tournament played both with the audience it preys on and against the rules devised to protect us from it.

Q: *Who would play such a game?*
Well, we all do. Some of us make propaganda for a living, others are willing victims or at least tolerate its presence. Propaganda is both active and passive. It's active to the extent that we manipulate others; it's passive to the extent that we wink an eye or allow others to manipulate us. Most of the time, we acquiesce or let it go; we reserve our outrage for special occasions, when we confront invidious or cruel forms of symbolic behavior (racism, for example) that are not apparent to everyone. To live today you must endure a lot of propaganda without complaining, because there's too much to keep track of. Besides, it isn't something you can measure with a Geiger counter. It's everywhere, and therefore it's nowhere in particular—like God in some theologies.

Q: *That reminds me. You haven't said a word about religious propaganda, yet the Counter-Reformation (in 1622) is where the word propaganda got its start.*
People never tire of bringing that up, as though propaganda can't transcend its origins or adjust to new surroundings. Propagandists don't care whether they

serve God or Mammon, Communism or Catholicism, an ideal or an idol, something they believe in or advocate on behalf of a client. Of course, different objectives demand different techniques, but a professional propagandist has a limitless repertoire of persuasive ploys and will oblige any paying customer. After all, it is a business. Although sincerity and enthusiasm sometimes help, they can also interfere with expert judgment. If I'm what Eric Hoffer called a "true believer," I may not understand why others aren't dying to jump on my ideological bandwagon. If there's one thing a propagandist must avoid, it's propagandizing themselves! There's nothing more pathetic than propagandists who can't be objective about their own work.

Q: *But if propaganda is everywhere, aren't propagandists bound to victimize themselves, sooner or later?*
Yes, but not in the same ways as they victimize their targets. Propagandists must believe that, in general and in principle, propaganda works, or else they couldn't continue plying the trade. This might be the biggest delusion of all, trapping propagandists and their (government, corporate, and individual) clientele in an endless circle. But that's a special kind of propaganda that mesmerizes elites. Call it metapropaganda. That's quite different from master-minding an agency or directing a 30-second spot, where your job is to sell soap by insinuating that it's sexy.[13] *You* might buy soap on those grounds, but *I* wouldn't, because I know too much.

Q: *Familiarity breeds contempt.*
Uh-huh. I'm not saying you can't massage me, just that you can't do it in the same way as I massage others. I might be religious, too, but if I'm hired to compose a sermon for Jerry Falwell or Jimmy Swaggart to deliver on nationwide TV, that doesn't make me an evangelist or one of the faithful: just a hack [speechwriter].

Q: *Yet isn't propaganda a systematic attempt to convert skeptics, to foster faith, and (even) to induce worship? Isn't that what ads for toilet bowl cleanser, election campaign promises, and fundamentalist preachers all have in common?*
I suppose. But then you'll have to say the same thing about Darwin's *Origin of Species* and Newton's *Principia,* which "converted" scientists to believe in what Thomas Kuhn calls paradigms, ways of investigating nature.[14]

Q: *But science gives us testable, verifiable results. It works.*
So does toilet bowl cleaner. So do potato chips, though they taste better.

Q: *Science is more than just devil's advocacy or partisanship.*
I didn't say it wasn't. You're assuming that propaganda necessarily spoils things, that it's an unqualified evil. If it were, either everyone would see through it or no one would put up with it.

Q: *Does that mean that propaganda can be for a good cause?*
Sure. Commercials urging teen-agers not to abuse drugs or alcohol are a case in point. So are skits warning children not to let strangers offer them rides or

give them candy. What you must decide is whether the end (preventing suffering) justifies the means.

Q: *Please explain.*
To fight propaganda, you may have to resort to propaganda as a counter-offensive. This is the lesson the Jesuits taught the world in the seventeenth century. Since then, everyone else has copied their invention, which they couldn't patent. It's as though society were determined to parody Newton's third law: Every act of propaganda creates an opposite (if not equal) propaganda reaction. That's why the air is saturated with verbal, visual, and aural pollution. Now, suppose you're genuinely concerned about teen-agers on dope or little kids being abducted. How will you reach them? The most effective method is to show them that smoking is "uncool" or that getting in a car with someone you don't know (or even an adult who's merely an acquaintance) is not in their best interests. You must do this quickly (on one page or in sixty seconds), without moralizing, lecturing, exceeding their vocabulary, or bypassing their range of experience. And you must repeat the message often and disseminate it as widely and rapidly as possible to prevent further harm from being done. You can see what that adds up to.

Q: *Yes I do.*
So now you approach me, your friendly neighborhood propagandist, who might already be employed to glamorize smoking and drinking saying "Please make me a nice commercial or advertising layout. Here's $1 million dollars. Will that be enough to get on the Super Bowl twice at halftime?" Sure, glad to help. Let me show the kind of quality work we do. Last year we represented Frito-Lay, toilet bowl cleanser and three twenty-four-hour fundamentalist telethons, and this year our special project is polishing up the neo-Nazi image, to make it more upscale and marketable. Care to see our facilities or to sit in on a shooting session?

Q: *Your're exaggerating.*
Just slightly. There are limits to what propagandists will do, because like the rest of us they have a capacity for outrage and a sense of injustice, no matter how dormant. But that's beside the point. My tolerance is virtually infinite. I'll take your money and put on a great show, even though it contradicts my commitments to other sponsors and undermines my private life. I can see you're getting squeamish, too, because you don't like the idea of make a slime like me rich. So there you are with your money and your proposal. Are you going to do business with me, or are you going to go somewhere else and hope the same hypothetical scenario doesn't repeat itself? Whatever you do, you must recognize that by fighting propaganda with propaganda you are administering an eye for an eye, instead of turning the other cheek. If propaganda is morally questionable or wrong to begin with, then two wrongs don't make a right.

Two characters in a 1943 radio play by Ignazio Silone express this dilemma perfectly. One says to the other, "Don't you under*stand* that we can't afford these scruples when we're fighting against Fascists? *They* don't have scruples." The other replies, "I know. That's why I'm not a Fascist." ["The Fox," adapted for the BBC by George Orwell, original in Italian].[15] Whenever you stoop to the level of the enemy you become the enemy, whether your adversary is Mussolini or mouthwash. Yet sometimes this is necessary. And that's the tragedy both of propaganda and of modern life.

Q: *That's a tired cliché. That's like saying, "You cannot make an omelet without breaking eggs" or "You can't go through life without getting your hands dirty." You're up to your neck in corruption, so naturally you think everyone else is, too. But there are still good human beings out there, fighting the good fight, struggling quietly or loudly to make the world a better place. You* can *be a moral man or woman, even in an immoral society. It may be difficult but nobody ever said it was easy.*

Ever think of joining the business? With lines like those you'd have a bright future. Look, if by "moral" you mean being " . . . a warm-hearted and loving human being,"[16] then I agree it's possible. If it weren't, I wouldn't bother with someone like you. But I can't afford to be nice all the time. I have to eat, too. I might be a sweetheart in private, but in public I've got to be tough, mean, and unsentimental. Business is business. And propaganda is very big business. You can't divorce the process from the product.

Q: *Are you a Fascist, or do you have scruples?*
It depends on how much money you're offering. If my belly is full I can be very moral; if it's empty I'll do anything for a fee, and so will you. If you're expecting perfection, forget it. There are no heroes and no role models, just fallible men and women.

Q: *What about saints and martyrs?*
They're the best friends the New Testament public relations guys ever had. They started a propaganda bonanza that has lasted 2000 years. For some reason, even in a secular age people still insist on putting their peers on a pedestal and creating idols to venerate, no matter what logic or evidence discloses to the contrary. Even a media scholar, who should know better, savagely will denigrate every American politician from Eisenhower to Reagan, yet maintain that alone among twentieth-century public figures Dr. Martin Luther King, Jr. (1929–1968), pacifist, civil rights leader, and author of *Letter from the Birmingham Jail* was wholly pure: "We do not know what he liked for lunch, what his office routines were, whether or not he slept in the nude. We cannot imagine a *People* photo of him and Coretta sharing a bubble bath."[17] The more sordid are the facts, the more we need to deny them. So the same writer will say that King's purity made a difference, that when he "used the media to amplify his voice" it was OK, while admitting that when his colleagues and associates did it it was never to advance a Gandhian cause but for "personal aggrandizement."[18]

Q: *Are you criticizing King's philosophy of nonviolence? Are you saying he was a hypocrite?*
No, no, you don't understand. Whether Dr. King was pure is irrelevant. I don't know what the word means. But some people desperately want him to be pure, they insist that he was pure, and they'll deify him against his own wishes, just

as Buddha's [563–483 B.C.] followers did as soon as he was dead. That's how legends grow. By the time they're through with King, they'll negate everything he did and stood for, but there'll be monuments, shrines, and planets named after him. That's just human perversity.

Q: *So everyone is a rat, is that it?*
No. But everyone must make compromises to avoid becoming a rat, especially when you're locked in a cell with rats all around you. Even more important is to acknowledge them for what they are, not pretend that we can evade or justify them. King managed this, but those who hero-worship King refuse to accept it. They prefer romance to reality, so who am I to stop them? By definition, propaganda creates a world of illusions, but to a thoughtful person it leaves no room for any. However, there are few thoughtful people around, and therefore little cause for distress.

Q: *It's too bad you can't avail yourself of the comforts propaganda provides.*
Don't be sarcastic. Propaganda enslaves everyone, but most of all those who imagine themselves free from it. This is why I admire Jacques Ellul. Ellul understands that censoring propaganda automatically destroys democracy by denying free speech and subverting civil liberties. But tolerating it erodes and undermines democratic institutions, because every piece of propaganda weakens the resistance of the populace, prevents intelligent and informed debate, and lowers the quality of public discourse.[19] The result is triviality at best, mud-slinging at worst.[20]

Q: *Damned if you do, damned if you don't.*
You've got it. Ellul is also the only author I've ever encountered who doesn't exempt himself from the charge of spreading propaganda. He knows that what he is doing to expose and diagnose propaganda is propaganda, too, and that this paradox is unavoidable. He doesn't flinch, rationalize, or engage in special pleading. Nor does he conjugate verbs.

Q: *Conjugate verbs?*
You know: "I speak truth, you're partisan, (s)he's being paid." Or "I'm objective, you're biased, (s)he's a propagandist." Bertrand Russell [1872–1970] made up hundreds of them. They're miniature arguments that automatically shield you from criticism while freeing you to attack "vested interests" and be suspicious of people's motives. Now that's dirty pool.

Q: *Who lives by the sword, perishes by it. How dare you complain self-righteously about fallacies or object to a double standard?*
Oh, I'm not complaining. I can take care of myself. I'm just making an observation. If it's mud-slinging you want, I'll be happy to get in there and pitch with the best of them. But if it's after-hours and I'm cautiously letting my guard down over cocktails and dinner, I expect you to meet me half-way. That's my code of fairness: Take it or leave it. You see, only Ellul has the guts to admit that *every* attack on propaganda is itself propaganda, including his own. Without

that, there's no basis for further discussion. You might as well close up the bar and head home. But Ellul, he knows he's a scoundrel. That makes him different from everyone else. That's why I respect him. I might disagree with everything else he says, but I'll buy him a drink and talk with him until the wee hours.

Q: *Earlier you mentioned that propaganda calls forth its opposite.*
Yes, and I owe Ellul that insight, too.

Q: *But if everything we communicate is propaganda, how do we ever distinguish (in principle) between propaganda and nonpropaganda?*
I don't think we can. We've lost our innocence, if we ever had it.

Q: *But if propaganda is everywhere, then it's nowhere. You can't detect or describe it.*
It's ineffable, just like the Holy Spirit, or more accurately, the Demonic Spirit.

Q: *Then how can you use the word? Without solid criteria for identifying it, doesn't "propaganda" become gibberish, a contrastless concept, a meaningless label that you or anyone and everyone can apply to whatever they please? And isn't that the biggest propaganda hoax of all?*
So you do not trust me, eh?

Q: *Why should I? You haven't shown me what propaganda is. Maybe that's why you're such an authority on the subject—you know how to bluff. And that's all propaganda is, the art of bluffing. Well, I see through your bluff.*
Goethe was right: Verbal arguments are elegant but experience is green. Your problem is that you insist on deriving rational solutions to figure out an irrational universe. Then you wonder why words won't match up with facts. (Pause) Have you ever seen the film *The Stuff?*

Q: *Isn't that the new sci-fi spoof about a brand of yogurt that turns people into mindless robots and then makes them explode?*
Yes. But it's more than just a clever satire of futuristic horror films. It's also a "send-up" of advertising mania and of consumer product "hype" that knows no bounds. And what is "the stuff"? It's not just deadly yogurt. For it oozes everywhere, it swallows whole cities, it destroys everything in its path, while posing as harmless, bland, "pure," white, curdled health food. "The stuff" is a metaphor for propaganda itself: Colorless, odorless, tasteless, compatible with everyone's wishes and dreams, yet it inhibits thought and is ultimately poisonous. *The Stuff* is also an inside joke about the mass entertainment industry that produced and promoted it. Hence *The Stuff* loops back on itself, like [Rene] Magritte's *This Is Not a Pipe,* which is a painting of a pipe, or [M.C.] Escher's *Drawing Hands,* which is a drawing of two hands drawing each other.[21]

Q: *What logicians might call a "self-referential" artifact?*
Yes. *The Stuff* knows full well that it owes its existence to the propaganda machine that it ridicules. Thus the joke is on it as much as it is on the viewer

who is taken in by propaganda. *The Stuff* stubbornly refuses to distance itself from the phenomenon it studies or to claim some privileged relationship to it. It's the kind of film Ellul would appreciate, although the irony might be lost on him. What makes *The Stuff* so funny makes Ellul grim. He's out tilting at windmills, whereas *The Stuff* just laughs at the human predicament.

Q: *Including its own.*
Right. But there's no way to climb out of the propaganda net, so you might as well relax and have a good roll.

Q: *Does that entail that this conversation is also propaganda?*
You said it. Even "educational" discussions of propaganda exemplify the category they classify.[22] That's OK, provided you don't imagine you're in another category. That's just naive. We are all agents, not spectators, in the drama of existence. Today that includes bureaucratic rhetoric, academic jargon, and everything else we perform on the world stage.

Q: *But if you too are a propagandist, not a theorist who eschews propaganda, what is your object or goal?*
To warn those who flatly deplore propaganda to examine themselves before they criticize others. To advise those who reject all propaganda to beware of throwing stones from inside a glass skyscraper. And to remind those who are uncomfortable about propaganda that they are not alone, and that life offers no easy answers and no escape from ambiguity.

Q: *Aren't you afraid that disclosing these secrets will adversely affect the work you do here?*
No. Long ago P.T. Barnum said, "There's a sucker born every minute." Perhaps I am a sucker, too, but I'm convinced he was right. Even if I told people "this is propaganda, don't believe a word of it," they's still lap it up. In the last analysis, whether we're prudent and logical or hysterical and illogical makes no difference. Humans have a limitless appetite for self-deception. They're stupid and gullible. Orson Welles proved that inadvertently fifty years ago, and every day since then we've reconfirmed it. It's a law of nature, like greed and gravity. Desiderius Erasmus [(1466–1536), author of *In Praise of Folly*, 1509] knew well that we're all fools, and Jonathan Swift [(1667–1745), author of *Gulliver's Travels*, 1726] knew, but they were fools, too, because they thought others would heed their warnings and thus save the human race from its own idiocy. You see? We don't listen. We don't know how to listen. So whatever happens if OK. People deserve what's coming to them, even if it's a nuclear holocaust. After all, nobody forced them to build all those bombs. They did it themselves. So don't blame propaganda for your troubles, bud. It's your own fault. Actually, propaganda is superfluous, unnecessary. The trick is not to persuade the audience but to convince customers that they need propaganda to be effective. Metapropaganda is what keeps elites alive and in business. You don't need to brainwash the masses; they're already brainwashed. It's your cohorts and fellow workers who need to be charmed. That's why we're all fools. If we weren't we wouldn't be human, I guess.

Q: *You're just being modest.*

I'll prove it to you. Let's say the room is bugged. If anyone can overhear us, I'm sure they'll think, "Now I know all about propaganda, I'll never be cheated again." Then watch how quickly they're cheated! As Bishop Desmond Tutu [1931– , of South Africa] once said, the only thing we learn from history is that we never learn anything from history. We just repeat ourselves, relentlessly. Naturally, know-it-alls are supremely ignorant. As Socrates [470–400 B.C.] showed, the smarter you think you are, the dumber you really are. That's why people who think they know it all but are really ignorant are so easy to hoodwink. Ironically, so are those who do know it all.

Q: *Please explain.*

The easiest people to mislead aren't fools or dimwits but intellectuals and scholars. Even when (like Ellul) they sense that they too are propagandists, they all succumb to the same delusion. They equate life with thought, thus ruining both. That's why I never grant them interviews. What's the use of talking to someone who already has all the answers? They've propagandized themselves into a corner. Well, let them rot there. Of course, if they didn't believe in something, their tight mental world would crash and collapse, and then they'd be unable to function. So I suppose it's just as well. We are weak animals; we need props or crutches to sustain us.

Q: *Even you?*

Even me.

Q: *Thank you for your time, Dr. Binad.*

My pleasure. Don't forget to pay the secretary on your way out.

(At this point the tape breaks off abruptly.)

Questions for Reflection and Discussion

1. Why does Dr. Binad regard "propaganda" as indefinable? Is (s)he right? Why or why not?

2. What is Dr. Binad's view of human nature? Is it correct? How would you defend or refute it?

3. The essay portrays Dr. Binad as an "expert" on propaganda.
a. Is (s)he a propagandist, a propaganda theorist, or both?
b. Is it legitimate to appeal to authority to support a claim? If so, on what grounds? What might Dr. Binad say about that?

4. Does Dr. Binad regard propaganda as (1) a necessary evil, (2) morally justified, (3) amoral, being neither good nor evil? Which of these conceptions do you hold, and why?

5. Does this essay contain any propaganda? If so, identify and comment on it. Why do you think the author presents (or conceals) his thoughts in dialogue form?

Notes

1. This dialogue is a work of fiction. Any resemblance between the characters and persons living or dead is purely intentional.

2. Harold Lasswell and Abraham Kaplan, *Power and Society:* A Framework for Political Inquiry (New Haven, Conn.: Yale University Press, 1950), 111.

3. Leo Rosten, *The Joys of Yiddish* (New York: Washington Square Press, 1968), 348–349, 361.

4. Richard Schickel, *Intimate Strangers. The Culture of Celebrity* (Garden City, N.Y.: Doubleday, 1985), 192.

5. Michael Shudson, *Advertising: The Uneasy Persuasion. Its Dubious Impact on American Society* (New York: Basic Books, 1984), 75–76.

6. Erving Goffman, *Frame Analysis: An Essay on the Organization of Experience* (Cambridge, Mass.: Harvard University Press, 1974).

7. T.S. Kuhn, *The Structure of Scientific Revolution,* 2nd ed., enlarged (Chicago: University of Chicago Press, 1970).

8. Hadley Cantril, *The Invasion from Mars: A Study on the Psychology of Panic* (Princeton, N.J.: Princeton University Press, 1940).

9. Jacques Ellul, *Propaganda: The Formation of Men's Attitudes,* Trans. by Konrad Kellen and Jean Lerner (New York: Knopf, 1965), 155.

10. Walter Lippman, *Public Opinion* (first published 1922) (New York: Macmillan, 1960).

11. William Poindstore, *Big Secrets: The Uncensored Truth About All Sorts of Stuff You Are Never Supposed to Know* (New York: Quill, 1985), 200–218.

12. Richard Taylor, *Film Propaganda. Soviet Russia and Nazi Germany* (New York: Barnes and Noble, 1979), 189, quoting Leni Riefenstahl in 1965. (No relation to author of Good and Evil.)

13. Michael Arlen, *30 Seconds* (New York: Farrar, Straus, and Giroux, 1980).

14. Kuhn, *Structure of Scientific Revolution.*

15. William West, ed., *Orwell: The Lost Writings* (New York: Arbor House), 145.

16. Richard Taylor, *Good and Evil: A New Direction. A Forceful Attack on the Rationalistic Tradition in Ethics,* 2nd ed. (Buffalo, N.Y.: Prometheus Books, 1984), 255. (No relation to the author of *Film Propaganda.*)

17. Schickel, *Intimate Strangers,* 179.

18. Ibid.

19. Ellul, *Propaganda,* 237.

20. Neil Postman, *Amusing Ourselves to Death* (New York: Viking, 1985).

21. Douglas Hofstadter, *Goedel, Escher, Bach: An Eternal Golden Braid* (New York: Basic Books, 1979).

22. CBC Transcripts, "Propaganda," by Jan Fedorowicz, broadcast March 29–April 19, 1983.

8

What Is Bias?*

J. Anthony Blair

We have to distinguish three senses of the word "bias." Firstly, bias may be an unfair slanting of material, violating a norm of fair representation. This type of bias is harmful and avoidable. Secondly, bias also may be the selection of facts and aspects of reality from some particular point of view. This kind of bias is inevitable; it is neither avoidable nor harmful. Thirdly, a rare use of bias can be a good thing. In this sense, we speak of people as being biased toward the good or toward truth.

"It is a truism to observe that every author is biased in favor of the claim he is making. He wouldn't be writing otherwise," says Frederick Little in *Critical Thinking and Decision Making*.[1] "It's crucial to realize that bias and prejudice are forms of error," replies Michael Scriven in *Reasoning*.[2] If these writers are using the term "bias" in the same way, at least one of them must be wrong, because their claims are incompatible. Little would not agree that every author is in error, and Scriven would not hold that every author is biased. If they are using the term "bias" in two different senses, then they are not contradictory.

What are the two different senses, and why is one word used for both? Many people talk like Little: "Everyone is biased," they say. Others are inclined to speak like Scriven: "It does not make sense to call everyone biased. Bias is a fault, and calling someone biased is an accusation, distinguishing that person from those who are not biased."

The sorts of critical reaction that mark a person as a critical thinker seem to require certain habits of mind, prominent among which is—to put it controversially—a freedom from bias or—to put it noncontroversially—an ability to overcome or transcend either bias or at least harmful or unjustified bias. If in

---

*Used with permission of J. Anthony Blair.

some sense bias is a block to critical thinking, then there is good reason to understand what bias is and how it works. The need becomes the more urgent when we find people speaking in apparently contradictory ways about bias.

This essay looks at a number of examples of cases where people have said a bias is present (or where I would want to so classify it) and tries to generalize from them an accurate account of the concept of bias. The root idea of bias that emerges is that it is a slant, an angle, a leaning, or a limited perspective. This idea seems to appear in three types of cases: (1) bias that is bad and avoidable; (2) bias that is unavoidable, potentially dangerous, but for which one can compensate; and (3) bias that is contingent and good—or at least neutral. The term "bias" seems used most often in the first cases, but the other uses are significant too. A wide variety of things can be biased—people, actions or conduct, practices, judgments, terminology, choices, reports, presentations, and so forth. People can be blamed for their biased actions or choices particularly if these are self-conscious and deliberate or due to culpable ignorance. We can be more forgiving of bias due to self-deception or cultural prejudice, but since these can be guarded against, and to a degree overcome, culpability still exists. These points hold for the compensable effects of unavoidable bias as well as for bad and avoidable bias.

I do not think it is useful to dwell on the motives of those who display bias, because the effects are no less pernicious if the bias is unintentional than if it is deliberate. However we can attend to our own motives and thereby try to reduce the extent and harm of our own avoidable bias.

Bad and Avoidable Bias

Bias that is regarded as a bad thing and that can be avoided seems the most common. Some examples detail this concept of bias.

Example 1. In the Canadian province of Ontario there are three significant political parties, the Conservatives (who had been in power for forty-two years until 1985), the Liberals (the largest opposition party), and the New Democrats (who habitually get 20 percent to 30 percent of the popular vote). In an election in Spring 1985, the incumbent Conservatives failed to gain a majority of seats in the legislature, although they won a plurality. The Liberals and New Democrats agreed to form a loose coalition and to vote together to defeat the Conservative government after the election and before the legislature convened. In the Canadian political system, when such a situation occurs and the governing party is defeated in the legislature, the lieutenant-governor—who is an appointee with normally a purely ceremonial role as head of state, is not the head of the governing party, and is supposed to act, as the Queen's representative, in a completely nonpartisan manner—must decide whether to ask the party with the second-largest number of seats to form the government or to call another election. In the Ontario situation it was doubtful that another election would produce any change. But at the same time there was no precedent in provincial politics in Canada for a minority party's being asked to form a government. The Lieutenant-Governor Lincoln Alexander's decision would be precedent-setting.

During the period prior to the convening of the legislature, there was much speculation in the press. A political scientist at the University of Windsor was asked in a radio interview, "Since the lieutenant-governor earlier in his career and prior to his appointment was an active supporter of the Liberal Party, isn't he likely to be biased? Won't he ask the Liberals to form the government just because he is biased in favor of the Liberal Party?"

The interviewer was anticipating bias in a bad sense. The question was whether the lieutenant-governor would, wrongly, act from partisan interests, or whether he would or could act with the best interests of the province as a whole in mind. In general, in this sense you act (or choose) in a biased manner or with bias when you act to promote a narrow, private, sectarian, or partisan interest on an occasion when the ground or basis for that action ought to be wider, public, heterodoxical, or nonpartisan. A judge, a sports referee, a jury of a fine arts competition, and an arbitrator of a labor dispute are all supposed to be unbiased in this respect. Bias would be a violation of a norm of impartiality that applies in these cases.

(The lieutenant-governor made what almost universally was held to be the only reasonable decision in the circumstances. He asked the Liberals, the party with the second-largest number of seats and that had the promise of the New Democrats' support guaranteeing a majority, to form the government. No cry of "bias!" was raised, even by the outgoing Conservative government.)

Example 2. In 1983 a University of British Columbia professor made a formal complaint to the British Columbia Press Council (a voluntary-membership, self-disciplining body) alleging that *The Vancouver Sun* newspaper had shown "extraordinary bias" in its coverage of a rally by a coalition of unions and others, called Operation Solidarity, protesting the provincial government's wage and spending restraint legislation. The professor charged specifically that the newspaper had given the rally a "red smear" by publishing with the story about the rally a photograph of marchers carrying signs bearing the words "Communist Party of Canada." In charging bias, presumably his point was that the picture misrepresented the make-up and politics of the protesting groups by giving the false impression that they were Communists. (The B.C. Press Council dismissed the professor's complaint, yet added that a picture more broadly representative of the rally could have been used.)

There are two components of bias in the sense alleged here. There must be a particular unfavorable (or favorable) impression conveyed, and the unfavorable (or favorable) impression conveyed is not warranted, justified, or accurate. The newspaper is supposed to report objectively, accurately, and without any built-in advocacy or judgment pro or con. The alleged bias would be a violation of those norms. In the example, the professor claimed that the newspaper conveyed an unfairly unfavorable image of the protesters (given that Communists in Canada are generally viewed with hostility, if not horror). Other examples could readily be found that have the same structure as this one, but in which the bias would be a failure of objectivity resulting in an unduly favorable impression. Some newspapers, for instance, seem to have biased coverage favoring the hometown professional sports team.

What Is Bias? 95

Example 3. In Spring 1985, the R. J. Reynolds Tobacco Company ran a full-page ad in *Life* magazine under the heading, "The Second-Hand Smokescreen," in which Reynolds contended that the attack on second-hand smoke is really a disguised attack on smoking and said, "Many independent experts believe the scientific evidence on passive smoking is questionable." The copy of the ad continued:

> But a zealous group of anti-smokers are using this issue in their campaign against tobacco as if the claims were established scientific fact.
> We deplore the actions of those who try to manipulate public opinion through scare tactics . . .
> We are not ignoring the fact that cigarette smoke can be bothersome to many non-smokers. But we believe this problem is best solved not by governments but by individuals, not with more rhetoric but more common sense and courtesy . . .

(This is an excerpt from a 400-word text, so the cautious reader should check to be sure *I* have not distorted by selection.) Reynolds quotes Dr. H. Russell Fisher as a respected pathologist who has said that there is no proof of harm from "atmospheric tobacco smoke" and suggested that fear of second-hand smoke may be a "social problem" that itself might lead to medical problems.

I contend that there is bias in this ad. Notice that in the face of conflicting testimony, Russell's opinion alone does not establish that there is nothing to the case against second-hand smoke, so Reynolds has not sufficiently supported its claim that the attack on second-hand smoke is a "scare tactic" being used to "manipulate" public opinion. Nor has it sufficient basis for describing the case against second-hand smoke as "rhetoric" or for contrasting it with "common sense and courtesy." In using this terminology, however, Reynolds conveys an impression about those who attack second-hand smoke that tends to discredit them. After all, in everyday language, "zealotry" is excessive enthusiasm, "manipulation" is improper influence, "scare tactics" are substitutes for good reasons, and "rhetoric" is commonly understood as empty, unsubstantial persuasion. For these reasons I would argue that the language of the Reynolds ad is biased, and as a result the ad as a whole conveys a subtly biased message that the opposition to second-hand smoke is not responsible.

In the Reynolds example, the charge of bias implies that there is a misrepresentation of the opponent's position (in an adversary relationship) aimed at discrediting it. In such cases there is a violation of a norm of fairness or honesty that is expected to be honored in carrying on a dispute.

Example 4. In the June 1985 Newsletter of the International Society for Animal Rights (ISAR), there is a report about an American curriculum package called "Project Wild," sponsored by the Western Association of Fish and Wildlife Agencies and the Western Regional Environmental Education Council. It is not clear to me from the ISAR report just exactly what Project Wild is about, but it is clear that ISAR objects to it, and why. I quote from the newsletter:

While claiming to encourage students to make up their own decisions on such topics as hunting and wildlife management, the information presented is biased and leads to pro-hunting and trapping attitudes.

Two themes . . . evidence the slant of the material. Man is placed in the position of control and given the "responsibility" of managing wildlife. This management takes the form of hunting and trapping. A second idea . . . is that wildlife, "a renewable resource," has its value in the enjoyment it gives to man. According to the Project Wild literature all people have the right to pursue this pleasure in any way they choose, be it hunting or photography.[3]

I take ISAR's point to be that the conceptualization used in the Project Wild material—the way of thinking about wildlife, its terminology, presupposes, and entails—influences students to accept hunting and trapping as legitimate activities. If you speak in terms of "managing" wildlife, there have to be people who manage and acts of management: That is what "managing" implies. If wildlife is terms a "resource," it must serve some population and some purpose, for that is what we mean by a "resource." This conceptualization would not be classifiable as "bias" unless it were controversial and yet put forward, without any defense, as value-neutral. ISAR contends that the Project Wild material claims to be neutral and to leave students free to make up their own minds, thus disarming critical attention.

Once again the charge of bias is an allegation of misrepresentation. In this case there seems to be a violation of the norm that might be termed "respect for independent judgment." The Project Wild material is claimed not to advocate; ISAR contends that it in fact does—not directly, but by way of its built-in conceptual bias.

In each example there is alleged, as grounds for the charge of bias, a violation of some norm or expectation, respectively: of impartiality, fairness, neutrality, and nonadvocacy. The alleged bias is conveyed, or anticipated, in the first case, through an action, in the second by the juxtaposition of a photograph with a news report, in the third by the use of value-judgment-laden terminology, and in the fourth by concept-laden terminology.

Notice that the agents' intentions are really a minor consideration in these cases. Even if the lieutenant-governor were trying to remain neutral, if his sympathies for the Liberal party unconsciously swayed his judgment, the results might have been harmful. (As it happened, in this case, his sympathies could have in fact motivated his judgment without damage. He still would have made the correct judgment, even if for the wrong reasons.) Whether or not *The Vancouver Sun* was trying to associate the whole antigovernment Solidarity Movement with the tiny Canadian Communist Party, if its photograph had that effect, the bias occurred and the harm was done. The Reynolds Tobacco Company may have approved its ad copy in perfectly good faith, and the Project Wild sponsors may have been trying their hardest not to advocate any particular philosophy of wildlife treatment—the accusations of bias stand or fall independently. The only reason for considering motives is to pass judgment on the agents. Presumably deliberate bias in any of these four cases is more blameworthy, if no more harmful, than unintentional bias.

What Is Bias?

These four examples do not exhaust all the possible varieties of harmful bias, but they do, I hope, begin to fill in the picture. Before turning to some examples of unavoidable bias, I will comment briefly on a special type of bias in the bad sense, biased sampling and biased evaluation—what I call bias in the technical sense.

Technical Bias

When knowledgeable people speak of studies, statistics, surveys, or polls being biased, they are usually using "bias" in a clearly-defined technical sense, which if understood should cause no confusion. When a sample is selected in such a way that it systematically misrepresents the population it is supposed to reflect, it is a biased sample. It is bound to underemphasize or to overemphasize the characteristic of the population being studied.[4] Similarly, an evaluation procedure is said to be biased if its design is slanted in a way that may lead to errors. If the evaluators of a program have some ego-involvement with it or stand to gain income or career development if it gets a high grade, then the design of the evaluation procedure for that program is biased.[5] Such technical senses of bias are straightforward and need not detain us. Bias in these ways is misrepresentation that can cause error and is therefore harmful and to be avoided.

Unavoidable and Potentially Dangerous Bias

Consider the feature of news reports, whether in newspapers or on TV, that every report must have a certain organization or structure, must highlight some features of the story and downplay others, must restrict itself to a selection of the available information about the event, must choose words and, in the case of TV, also must select and edit film—in every case choices must be made that will affect the information and the impression about that information that the report conveys.[6] It would be accurate to say that every news report has a slant or bias. Yet this observation should not be understood as an accusation, as a pejorative comment. If there is no way to avoid presenting the news without some angle or other, criticism of the phenomenon seems misplaced. To object is to imply that the news could, somehow, be presented without any angle or bias. However, for the the sort of bias I am describing here—the unavoidable selection, ordering, and choice of information and of descriptive words and phrases of film segments and camera angles, which must of necessity preclude alternatives—there is no conceivable way to get around it. Here is a case of unavoidable, but not necessarily bad, bias.

The bias is not necessarily bad; it can be the case that the particular angle taken by a reporter is exactly the right one, or at least not at all objectionable. It can meet all the criteria we have for good reporting: completeness, accuracy, balance, depth, and so on.

In fact, the reason for pointing out that there is this particular sort of bias or slant to news reports is not to lament reporters' failure to produce reports that have no point of view whatever. On the contrary, it is to remind us that such reports will always have some point of view and that the ideal of a "neutral," God's-eye-view report of events is illusory and a myth—perhaps itself even an ideological prejudice. When we keep in mind the unavoidable bias or angle of news reports, we are then on our guard to assess critically the particular bias or angle the reporter or editor has employed. For what is unavoidable is only that news reports have *some* slant; there is no necessity that they exhibit or reflect one particular point of view rather than another. The recognition of the necessity of this kind of bias permits questions about alternative ways of describing the event reported, of weighing the relative significance of different elements of the story, and of judging the importance and implication of the event as a whole, independently of the judgments built into the point of view chosen by the reporter. Knowing that some bias must exist enables you to look at what was the actual bias and to decide whether it has any objectionable results or should be challenged in its application in the given case.

In contending that there is a sense in which the press may be biased unavoidably and unobjectionably, I am not at all saying or implying that the press cannot be biased in the sense in which bias is culpable. There are thus two senses of the word "bias" that can apply to one and the same person and piece of discourse. This is confusing, and I personally prefer to try to avoid the confusion by restricting the word bias to the first sense (bad and unavoidable) and using terms like "angle" or "point of view" for the second sense (unavoidable and potentially dangerous). However, many people use the word bias in the second sense, and apart from pointing out the dangers of confusing it with the use of the word in the first sense, it seems there is no basis for saying that they are wrong.

Those who point out that everyone inhabits and reflects some world view or other, and that this necessarily shapes our understanding of judgments about the world, are making a similar point. Having some cultural, historical, social (and so on) angle or slant on the world is an unavoidable feature of the human condition, and the mere having of a world view cannot be regarded as objectionable. As in the case of the unavoidable bias in journalism, however, recognizing that some world view is shaping a person's discourse permits the critical observer to raise questions about the legitimacy of that particular world view.

In my opinion, we can and may criticize world views. Most are enormous collections of quite varying kinds of beliefs, so that internal consistency is a major problem. Moreover, I believe there are standards—internal consistency, for one—that are world-view neutral, that is, which hold for all world views. Even if that belief is mistaken, it is hard to conceive how anyone could proceed to think except as if it were true. So the realization that a particular claim emanates from a world view permits you to wonder whether that world view may be inconsistent or mistaken. For example, thinking of undomesticated animals as a "manageable resource" seems to imply that these animals exist for human purposes and that they may be killed or protected from hunger and predators by humans for human ends. These beliefs do not seem to square with the theory of evolution or with certain strands of Old Testament theology. Yet the same people often embrace all of these beliefs. Those who do can be accused of inconsistency.

Not all who draw attention to the important influence of world views would agree with calling a world view a "bias," and I do not mean to saddle them with this position. My point is that it would not be incoherent to use the term bias in this connection. In both this case and the journalism case, to speak of bias is to speak of a slant, an angle, or a perspective that is one of a range of possible alternatives, some one of which it is necessary to occupy. This, then, would be unavoidable bias in a neutral sense.

Before leaving unavoidable bias, consider a distinct species that looks quite a lot like it but really is very different. On a great many issues of the day, nearly everyone has formed some opinion. Some people seem to have opinions about everything. In some cases, opinions are tentative, but often enough they are firm, strong, and even rigid. Perhaps on most well-publicized issues nearly everyone has some leaning—some initial inclination to be pro or con, to opt for this view over that one—though not necessarily anything even firm enough to be dubbed an opinion or a position. When it is said that everyone has a bias, it may be meant that everyone has an opinion or is at least disposed toward one position.

Some corrections and distinctions are in order. Firstly, it is perfectly possible to have no opinion and no leaning on an issue, even when you understand fully what is at stake. You genuinely can be torn between opposing considerations. Secondly, although having a leaning toward or standing behind one position on an issue legitimately might be called a bias, this could not be bias in the bad sense. This must be the neutral sense of bias—the leaning may be right-minded, or the opinion may be based on sound reasons and be the most defensible stand to take. Thirdly, having a strong conviction about an issue—although it might be called having a bias in the broad and neutral sense—should not be confused with being narrow-minded, close-minded, or biased in any bad sense. A person's strong conviction may be based on a careful, open-minded, and thorough consideration of the reasons for and against that position. The person may also be capable of giving up the conviction in question if faced with new evidence or arguments that refute it. Such a person might be said to "have a bias," but it does not allow that he or she must "be biased" in the sense that the commitment to the position blinds the person to evidence against it. Perhaps we confuse these reasonings because all-too-often those who "have a bias" in the sense that they have firm convictions are also people who "are biased" in the sense that they cannot be fair, impartial, or nonadversarial, and they distort and misrepresent in their reasoning. Such a combination is common; the crucial point is that it is not unavoidable.

Contingent But Neutral or Good Bias

So much for unavoidable bias in the neutral sense. It remains to be seen whether it can ever be either indifferent or positively good to have a bias or be biased in situations in which having the bias is a contingent matter.

The test is this: Are there any cases in which competent language users speak of someone's having a bias they could avoid or rid themselves of, and in speaking of such a bias mean either to convey no value judgment or else to praise or commend the person's bias?

If the *Oxford English Dictionary* may be regarded as authoritative, then we must admit at once that, at least historically, such uses of bias were quite acceptable. The following are some entries testifying to such uses:

> 1642 FULLER *Holy & Prof. State.* iv.iv.252 In his prime he [Wolsley] was the bias of the Christian world, drawing the bowl thereof to what side he pleased. 1660 W. SECKER *Nonsuch Prof.* 430 The love of God is the bias of a Volunteer. [In this use bias means an influence that sways someone or something.]
>
> 1829 SOUTHEY *Inscript.* xiv. My intellectual life received betimes The bias it had kept. [In this use bias means predilection, disposition, or inclination.]
>
> 1801 STRUTT *Sports & Past.* Introd. 4 Such exercises as . . . biased the mind to military pursuits. 1862 LYTTON *Str. Story.* I.216 Whether . . . it was the Latin Inscription . . . that had originally biased Sir Philip Derval's literary taste toward the mystic jargon. [In these uses, the verb to bias means "to incline to or toward, to cause to swerve."][9]

In all these uses, the noun or the verb either conveys no evaluative connotations or else—as in the case of Wolsley being called the bias of the Christian world, or the love of God being the bias of every volunteer—is used in a context in which the bias in question is considered good.

None of these meanings of bias is cited as obsolete in the *Oxford English Dictionary* but contemporary examples of this sort of use are hard to find. They do exist, however. One example comes from the exchange between the radio interviewer and the political scientist about the possible bias of the lieutenant-governor of Ontario in deciding whether to call on the provincial Liberal party to form a minority government. The radio reporter had asked whether the lieutenant-governor would be biased (in the avoidable and bad sense) as a result of his own long association with the Liberal party. To her question, the political scientist (a Liberal party supporter himself replied, "I hope the lieutenant-governor will be biased in favor of the best decision." The point is that, since the best decision is by definition good, it follows that a bias on the part of the lieutenant-governor in favor of the best decisions would be good. The bias spoken of here is contingent and good.

An Understanding of Bias

We are ready to summarize our findings. It seems that bias means a kind of leaning, or an inclination, or a predisposition. When this results in bad thinking— as when it consists of prejudice or pre-judgment, when it causes close-mindedness, or when it leads to distortion, misrepresentation, or unfairness—then it is bad. When it is an unavoidable feature of our thinking processes or of our methods of communication, then it is potentially dangerous but not necessarily harmful. When the influence of contingent bias is cause for neither praise nor condemnation, we regard it as innocent and value-neutral. And when it disposes us to right-mindedness, we regard it as good.

I would suggest that a lot of the confusion about bias and some of the contradictory assertions about it, such as those of Little and Scriven cited at the beginning of this article, are due to a failure to notice this range of senses or uses of the term or to a desire to raise one of them to a position of preeminence. Given the confusingly different uses of the word, someone committed to clarity might be tempted to bypass it altogether. Its value as a term of critical appraisal is certainly reduced by its variety of implications. We have seen that one cannot describe a person or an assertion as, simply and without qualification, biased and hoped to have communicated a single clear critical judgment.

On the other hand, the word is hard at work in the critical vocabulary of today's not-necessarily critical citizenry. In fact it seems to be one of those lazy man's words that is called on to bear much more of a load than it can carry comfortably. Together with everyday terms of critical appraisal such as "subjective," and "prejudiced," "biased" is used as a bludgeon to convey a sort of vague disapproval. Knowledge of the different uses of "bias" permits you to pick out different possible interpretatons of a clumsy speaker's or writer's critique.

An understanding of the meaning of "bias" seems necessary, in sum, to be able to fathom what a careless critic means and to permit the conscientious critic to supply the contextual elaboration needed to convey a precise sense of the word intended.[10]

Questions for Reflection and Discussion

1. If we said that everyone is biased because each person has his or her own background of culture and experience, which of Blair's senses of bias would we be using? Would such bias as this necessarily be bad, according to Blair? Do you agree?

2. If a paper referred to Republicans as "preservers of tradition" and to Democrats as "irresponsible radicals," would this be evidence of bias? If so, which of Blair's three types?

3. Could we be biased in favor of virtue, according to Blair? Do you think he is right about this? Why or why not?

4. Do you agree with Blair's judgment that the Reynolds Tobacco Company ad on the "second-hand smokescreen" is biased? Why or why not?

5. Does Blair's account give you suggestions as to how to detect bias in his first (avoidable, harmful) sense? If so, what are they?

Notes

1. Frederick Little, *Critical Thinking and Decision Making* (Toronto: Butterworths, 1980), 16.

2. Michael Scriven, *Reasoning* (New York: McGraw-Hill, 1976), 208.

3. International Society for Animal Rights, *Newsletter* (June 1985):4.

4. Trudy Govier, *A Practical Study of Argument* (Belmont, Calf.: Wadsworth, 1985), 293.

5. Michael Scriben, *Evaluation Thesaurus,* 3rd ed. (Inverness, Calif.: Edgepress, 1981), 15–16.

6. Edward Jay Epstein, *News from Nowhere* (New York: Random House, 1973).

7. Ralph Johnson and J. Anthony Blair, *Logical Self-Defense,* 2nd ed. (Toronto: McGraw-Hill Ryerson, 1983), ch. 10.

8. John Passmore, *Man's Responsibility for Nature* (New York: Charles Scribner's Sons, 1974), 12.

9. *Oxford English Dictionary,* S. V. "bias," vol. 1, 844–845.

10. This article is a revised version of a paper read at the Third International Conference on Critical Thinking and Educational Reform, Sonoma State University, Rohnert Park, California, July 20–23, 1985. I wish to thank Richard Paul, the conference director, for inviting me to speak. I also wish to thank the people, whose names I did not record, who attended my talk and engaged in an extremely fruitful discussion of the paper and of bias in general; their comments helped me in revising the paper. As well, Robert H. Ennis, David Hitchcock, Ian Wright, and Trudy Govier made comments and corrections on particular points, and I thank them for their help.

9

"Nuclear War" and Other Euphemisms*

J. J. MacIntosh

Words can impose on us—so much so that sometimes even talking in certain ways can be immoral. Language is not a private thing, it is a matter of public convention and understanding. Language provides a pre-conscious set of synonyms and associations for words, and these affect us without our even being aware of it. Cute, bland, or euphemistic language used in discussions of nuclear weapons and related policies is both immoral and dangerous. It misleads us, making us feel much too comfortable.

All of us use language immorally when discussing nuclear issues. In contrast with the horror involved in the possibility of the nuclear destruction of our planet, the immorality is a comparatively mild one. But since we ought to combat such a possibility at all levels, I make no further apology for the peripheral nature of this paper.

Words, if misused, can impose on us, a fact well known to politicians and advertising agencies. Further, speech acts are acts, and hence immoralities of omission and commission can be perpetrated verbally as well as in other ways. With these points in mind, I consider some of the ways in which these immoralities can occur, and argue, following a lead provided by Wasserstrom and others,[1] that when we talk about nuclear war we ourselves risk falling into such immorality.

The Immorality of Racist and Sexist Language

Let me begin with an analogy. It is clear that both racism and sexism are immoral and that, in consequence, we should eschew racist and sexist language:

---

*Used with permission of J. J. MacIntosh.

We should avoid, that is, racist and sexist vocabulary, idioms, turns of phrases, and assumptions.

I say, "as a consequence," but two points must be cleared up. Firstly, not everyone agrees—at least in practice—that this follows as a consequence. Following the well-known maxim, "Sticks and stones may break my bones, but words can never hurt me," some people argue that although what we *do* may be hurtful to others, what we *say* is somehow exempt from this, especially—so the claim goes—if the remarks in question are humorous.

This position (like the maxim that encapsulates it) is too obviously incorrect to warrant further discussion, but I mention it to remind us that what holds in the areas of sexism and racism holds, *mutatis mutandis,* in other areas as well.

Secondly, there is some disagreement over what counts as sexist or racist language. In Britain Sir Gerald Nabarro, a former member of Parliament, once claimed to have used the phrase "big, buck nigger" in a complimentary way. A relevantly similar claim is often heard about the use of the term "girls" to label adult females.

In much the same fashion, many people say, sometimes sincerely that they use terms such as "man" and "he" in a gender-neutral fashion. Now, of course it is impossible to use words in a particular way all on your own. Language is a team game, not an exercise for solitary players. So even if (and it is often a debatable *if*) the people who claim to be using such terms gender neutrally are genuinely trying to do so, they cannot succeed unless the audience hears their words as gender neutral.

The audience *cannot* hear them as gender neutral. It is interesting and, for our present purposes, instructive to investigate the reasons for this. I offer two reasons, at two different levels of explanation. There well may be others, but these two will suffice.

The Gricean Explanation

The first reason why terms like "he" cannot be used in a gender-neutral way and why it is immoral to miscall women "girls" comes from the fact, stressed by the English philosopher of language Paul Grice, that one of the strongest conventions of natural languages is their insistence on the provision of the maximum amount of relevant information available during the time of conversational space. If I remark that I have not seen my bank manager sober in the past three months, and it turns out that I have not seen her, drunk *or* sober, in the past three months, you have a right to feel that I have misled you.

Notice that I have not *lied*. A lie is a falsehood uttered with intent to deceive, and although the intent to deceive may have been present, my remark was *true*. It follows indeed, since $(P \& Q) \to Q$, from the fact that I have not seen her at all. Why then are you aggrieved? More importantly, why have you the right to feel aggrieved?

The Gricean suggestion is that my wrongdoing consists of my having contravened the maximal information principle. Since I easily could have given you the more embracing piece of information, you quite naturally find my behavior reprehensible.

Now let's apply such thinking to the case of the supposedly gender-neutral terms "man" and "he." Since it is always possible with a minimum of linguistic ingenuity, to find an alternative and genuinely neutral way of making the point in question, whatever it may be, the unthinking assumption must be that the terms are not being used neutrally. For if a neutral interpretation is intended, why not use a neutral formulation.

If I say, "Basically, what men really like is making love with other men," no native speaker of English can hear my remark neutrally. Yet the equally compact, "Basically, what people really like is making love with other people," raises no hackles at all. For after all, what is the alternative, sheep?

Similar considerations apply to the use of "girls" to refer to women. Women are sometimes asked at interviews, "How can a girl expect to do a job like this?" The point often is that, indeed, a girl could not be expected to succeed at it, even though a woman could. Of course, this is only a pair of central and well-known cases and represents only a few surface features of the sexist iceberg.

We cannot be consciously on our guard against such misuse of language every minute of every day, but—so strong is the convention—unless, and sometimes even if, we are consciously aware of the danger; we can still be misled.

But why are such misuses immoral? The fact that they violate Grice's maximal information principle and therefore mislead us is part of the explanation.

Before leaving this level of explanation, let me draw your attention to the fact that certain kinds of understatement and euphemism can themselves be immoral. For example, if someone were to describe a case of wife-battering by saying, "He gave her a few love taps," describing what happened in these terms would itself be an immoral act, even though the describing is not as immoral as the act described. The immorality would hold true even if the phrase were an accepted way of referring to wife-battering in the society in question. Why immoral? Well, once again, in part at least, because the euphemism takes up as much time as the correct description, and that being so, the audience, even when it knows what is going on, is consequently liable to underreact to the act under that description.

Preconscious Sorting Through in Language

The Gricean account is an account at the level of linguistic conventions, at the level of what philosophers call "implicature." The second level of explanation to consider is one to which, among others, Jerry Fodor has recently drawn our attention. In *Modularity of Mind: Faculty Psychology,* Fodor sketches a plausible top-down mechanism to account for a certain set of phenomena. But whether or not Fodor is right about the explanation—it is still a matter for further investigation—the phenomena themselves are clear and provide us with our second reason for the immorality of certain misuses of language.

The details of Fodor's account are fascinating, but it is only the bare bones of a small part of that account that we require here. Basically: when we are processing linguistic information there seems to be a considerable amount of *preconscious* sorting going on. And it seems, further, that the sorting is not being done by the cognitive system but by a system without any real pretensions to intelligent behavior, even though it usefully mimics such behavior on occasion. This system raises a whole network of synonyms and associations that go along with a given term.

The important point is that the tuning in of this associative network is preconscious. By the time we are aware of the word, the associations already have been made. Writing of the tendency to believe, on oversimple grounds, that what has happened in the past will happen in the same way in the future, Leibniz remarked, "That is why it is so easy for people to catch animals and so easy for empiricists to make mistakes." In this area it is easy for us all, empiricists and nonempiricists alike, to make mistakes; indeed it is almost inevitable that we should do so.

For example, think of the implications for the references—common among American politicians—of Caribbean and Latin American countries as being in the United States's "back yard." You *own* your back yard. And if that is the back yard, we all know what the front yard must be. You own your front yard as much as you do your back yard—you just keep it a bit tidier, that's all.

Perhaps the strongest convention of our language is that the information given be complete as well as correct. When things are mislabeled, our own associative networks already will have been called to mislead us before the word ever is heard consciously. If primitive peoples emphasize the power of names, as they are said to do, they are—from this point of view at least—absolutely correct. Moreover, as noted, the mislabeling itself may be an immoral act.

Abraham Lincoln was once asked, "If you call a dog's tail a leg, how many legs has a dog got?" He replied, "Four. Calling a dog's tail a leg does not make it one." But the truth is more Orwellian. If we did start calling a dog's tail a leg, we would all soon begin to think there was something slightly weird and unsavory about dogs. They would have too many legs, and one of their legs would be "abnormal."

The Immorality of Nuclear Terminology

The relevance to nuclear issues is obvious. Let's look at a few sample areas in which our language seriously distorts the issues involved. I begin with some of the uses that others try to foist upon us, all too successfully sometimes. It is a frequent and saddening occurrence to observe people at conferences on nuclear issues whole-heartedly adopting the militarist idiom.

Perhaps the most repellent uses in that idiom are the cutesy, game-playing terms, usually substantives. In this category we have, for example, the names given to the two bombs used against Hiroshima and Nagasaki in World War II: "Little Boy" and "Fat Man." We have President Ronald Reagan's use of the label "peacemaker" to refer to the MX ICBM that with ten 300kt MIRV warheads and a CEP of less than 130 meters is clearly a potential first strike weapon.[2] This sort of language is also to be found in assessing nuclear accidents where terms such as "dull sword," "bent spear," "broken arrow," and "nucflash" are used to signify increasingly dangerous accidents.

Then there are terms such as those used during the 1955 NATO Carte Blanche exercise, in which 335 so-called tactical nuclear explosions were simulated, and the estimate was that the 268 nuclear explosions simulated in West Germany would have killed 1.7 million Germans and "incapacitated" a further 3.5 million. Along with "incapacitated" are terms such as "collateral damage," which refers to the destruction of human beings and other nonmilitary targets. When you *really* intend to hit such targets, they are called "countervalue" targets or, sometimes, "soft" targets.

It sounds so much more soothing, of course, to say, "We are considering some countervalue targeting,"—rather than saying, "We are thinking about killing thousands and thousands of adults and children in ways that vary from the instantaneous to the lingeringly painful." Incidentally, if you kill fewer than 25 percent of the people in the country you are attacking or if *your* country has fewer than one in every four killed, this is known as "acceptable damage."

In this group of euphemisms we might include President Jimmy Carter administration's talk of "enduring" a nuclear war and President Ronald Reagan administration's talk of "prevailing" in one, with the use of what Reagan has called "protective hardware."

These euphemistic uses merge into simple lies: talk of "winning" a nuclear war, for example, or the doctrine of what Americans call "defense in depth." Unsurprisingly, West Germany has strenuously resisted "defense in depth" as a strategic possibility, realizing that if the United States defended the country in depth from a supposed attack by the Soviet Union, there would be no West Germany left to benefit from the "defense."

It is clear that the militarists themselves are aware of the danger of clear speaking. That is why we have terms such as MIRV, a label that is itself a euphemism: A reentry vehicle is a warhead. In this case there are ten of them, each with twenty to twenty-five times the destructive power of the bomb that destroyed Hiroshima. Sometimes the attempts to manipulate language are simply ridiculous, as in Edward Teller's claim that, "It's not an arms race. It's a competition in military technology.",[3] However, these attempts do succeed in muddying people's thinking. How else should we explain the following?

> Utica, N.Y.—In the event of a nuclear attack, Civil Defense officials here hope to order enough food from take-out restaurants and grocery stores to feed residents while they wait in the safety of shelters. Utica Civil Defense Director Joseph Pugliese Monday described this plan as ordering "1000 hamburgers and 1000 cups of coffee" for the people in the shelters—*Oneonta (N.Y.) Daily Star.*[4]

One could go on with the misleading and lying uses of language in which the militarists indulge. But the problem is wider. I think that not only is the language of the militarists misleading and strongly to be resisted, but that our language, too, is infected. Here are two clear examples.[5]

First consider the term "nuclear war." The term "war" has many connotations, different ones for different people, no doubt, but many in common for all of us.

Wars, for example, allow the exhibition of individual courage and heroism. They allow people to display loyalty, faith, and endurance. They allow the establishment of trust and comradeship. They have elements of tactics and of strategy; they can be looked on, without complete distortion, as games played with living, autonomous (or anyway semiautonomous) pieces.

They have winners and losers, nominally at least, and survivors, whose lot may or may not be improved. Moreover, wars require the support, even if only passive, of large numbers of the population of the belligerent countries. We might notice in passing that the nuclear destruction of the planet requires a very small number, a frighteningly small number, of strategically placed fanatics.

Wars allow people to exhibit and indulge in their competitive urges. They allow and encourage male bonding. They similarly allow and encourage xenophobia. Needless to say, these may also be causal factors in the production and continuation of wars. Wars take time. They last longer than a few hours.

Wars are, bizzare as it may seem, to some degree, *rule* governed. The individual killing, mutilation, and torture of the innocent, at short range, is still frowned on. The United States government, for example, though it continues to be willing to pay for such things to be done on its behalf in countries such as Nicaragua, claimed for a time to be distressed when it was revealed that Americans were doing the same things in Vietnam.

These are some of the features associated with war. I am not interested in evaluating their moral status, in or out of a military context. I merely want to draw attention to the fact that *none* of them are possible concomitants of the nuclear destruction of the planet, so we mislead ourselves by understatement, by culpable understatement, if we refer to such a possible destruction as a *war.* It is *wrong* to refer to a brutal assault by saying, "They roughed her up a bit." It is wrong in the same way and for the same reasons to speak of a nuclear "war." It is in the interests of the military fanatics that we should do so, but it is not in the interests of the planet.

Similarly, unless we are addicted to remarks like "a number of people passed away at Hiroshima," we should not speak of a nuclear "winter." If winter comes, spring *cannot* be far behind; contrapositively, if spring can never come, what we have got is *not* a winter.

These are merely two examples, and no doubt you readily will think of others. The point is the same throughout: We must not allow ourselves to use the terminology of understatement in this area for such understatement is itself immoral.

But aren't these points trivial compared to the real horror of nuclear destruction? Aren't they just about words? Yes, they are less important, just as calling people "niggers" is less important than lynching them. But both acts are immoral, even if not equally immoral, and part of the immorality of misused speech, of miscalling what is being done, lies in the fact that it makes the even more immoral direct act that much more acceptable.

To survive we must oppose nuclear folly at all levels, and one thing we all can do is not to play into the hands of the militarists by acquiescing in their understatement of the evil involved. So: *Do not* call the nuclear destruction of the planet a war: By comparison wars are cosy exercises in comradeship.[6]

Questions for Reflection and Discussion

1. What attitudes are assumed if United States citizens and policymakers refer to the Caribbean and Central America as "our backyard"? What is MacIntosh driving at with his reference here to the 'front yard'?

2. How does the convention that speakers should provide listeners with the maximum amount of information explain the fact that it is misleading to call a woman a girl? To say that you have not seen your bank manager sober in three months when you have not seen him or her at all?

3. Why, according to MacIntosh, is it misleading to call a series of nuclear explosions that might terminate human life on our planet a nuclear war?

4. In what way have the Civil Defense officials who plan to order food from take-out restaurants been misled about nuclear attack? How would language have contributed to their mistakes, according to MacIntosh? Do you tend to agree or disagree with his account here? Why?

Notes

1. Richard Wasserstrom, *Moral Issues of the Arms Race,* unpublished.
2. The jargon:

$$
\begin{aligned}
\text{kt} &= \text{the equivalent of 1000 tons of TNT} \\
\text{MX} &= \text{missile experimental} \\
\text{ICBM} &= \text{intercontinental ballistic missile} \\
\text{MIRV} &= \text{multiple independently targeted} \\
&\quad\ \text{reentry vehicle} \\
\text{CEP} &= \text{circular error probable}
\end{aligned}
$$

A reentry vehicle is a warhead. Circular error probably is "a measure of a missile's accuracy represented by the radius of a circle around a target point within which there is a 50 percent probability of the missile landing." (Michael Stephenson and John Weal, *Nuclear Dictionary* (New York: Longman, 1985). For comparison with the $10 \times 300 = 3000$ kt of the MX (the equivalent of three million tons of TNT), the bomb dropped on Hiroshima was in the 12 to 15 kt range.

3. Edward Teller, quoted in *The Observer* (London, 16 June 1985):9.

4. Quoted in the *New Yorker* (12 December 1983), from an Associated Press release in the *Oneonta (N.Y.) Daily Star.*

5. In what follows I am particularly indebted to the Wasserstrom, *Moral Issues of the Nuclear Arms Race.*

6. Conversations with Trudy Govier and Anton Colijn helped in writing this paper. Wasserstrom's *Moral Issues of the Nuclear Arms Race* was also very useful.

10

The Political Language of the Helping Professions*

Murray Edelman

Language is not merely a tool. Especially in social situations, language and reality shape each other. In helping professions, such as social work, psychiatry, and law enforcement, language serves a political role, without speakers and hearers always being explicitly aware of this. Professional labels categorize people and actions, rationalizing and perpetuating power relationships such as that between a nurse and a patient or a parole office and a juvenile delinquent. Designating poor children "pre-delinquent" will justify a considerable amount of professional restriction of their behavior, for instance. Language and roles thus reinforce each other. A special professional language helps to isolate actions and institutions from public criticism.

H ospital staff often deny or ignore the requests of angry mental patients because to grant them would "reinforce deviant behavior." Teachers sometimes use the same rationale to justify ignoring or punishing demanding students. The last two presidents of the United States have declared on occasion that they would pay no attention to peace demonstrators who resort to irritating or allegedly illegal methods. We commonly regard the last as a political act and the first two as therapeutic; but all of them are easily perceived as either political or therapeutic. How they are classified depends upon the assumptions of the observer, not upon the behavior being judged. Some psychologists reject the "reinforcement of deviant behavior" rationale on the ground that it pays no attention to all the special cognitive and symbolizing abilities of the human mind, equating people with rats; they believe such treatment too easily ignores reasonable grounds for anger and depresses the self

---

*"The Political Language of the Helping Professions" by Murray Edelman first appeared in *Politics and Society* Vol. 4 (Fall 1974), 295–310. © 1975, Geron-X, Inc. Reprinted with permission of Geron-X, Inc., Publishers.

esteem of people who already suffer from too little of it, contributing to further "deviance," not to health. In this view the "treatment" is self-serving political repression, rationalized as rehabilitative to salve the consciences of those in authority and of the public. Some psychiatrists, on the other hand, see political demonstrators or ghetto rioters as sick, calling for drugs or psychosurgery, not political negotiation, as the appropriate response; the Law Enforcement Assistance Administration has generously supported experiments based on that premise.

The language of "reinforcement" and "help" evokes in our minds a world in which the weak and the wayward need to be controlled for their own good. The language of "authority" and "repression" evokes a different reality, in which the rights of the powerless need to be protected against abuse by the powerful. Each linguistic form marshals public support for professional and governmental practices that have profound political consequences: for the status, the rights, and the freedom of professionals, of clients, and of the wider public as well; but we rarely have occasion to inhabit or examine both worlds at the same time.

Language is the distinctive characteristic of human beings. Without it we could not symbolize: reason, remember, anticipate, rationalize, distort, and evoke beliefs and perceptions about matters not immediately before us. With it we not only describe reality but create our own realities, which take forms that overlap with each other and may not be mutually consistent. When it suits us to see rationalization as reason , repression as help, distortion as creation, or the converse of any of these, language and mind can smoothly structure each other to do so. When it suits us to solve complicated problems of logic and mathematics, language and mind smoothly structure each other to do that as well. When the complicated problems involve social power and status, distortion and misperception are virtually certain to occur.

It is a commonplace of linguistic theory that language, thought, and action shape each other. Language is always an intrinsic part of some particular social situation; it is never an independent instrument or simply a tool for description. By naively perceiving it as a tool, we mask its profound part in creating social relationships and in evoking the roles and the "selves" of those involved in the relationships.

Because the helping professions define other people's statuses (and their own), the special terms they employ to categorize clients and justify restrictions of their physical movements and of their moral and intellectual influence are especially revealing of the political functions language performs and of the multiple realities it helps create. Just as any single numeral evokes the whole number scheme in our minds, so a term, a syntactic form, or a metaphor with political connotations can evoke and justify a power hierarchy in the person who used it and in the groups that respond to it.

Social scientists, and a large segment of the public, have grown sensitive and allergic to agitational political rhetoric and to the ambiguities of such labels as "democracy," "communist," and "law and order." The most fundamental and long-lasting influences upon political beliefs flow, however, from language that is not perceived as political at all, but nonetheless structures perceptions of status, authority, merit, deviance, and the causes of social problems. Here is a level of politics and analysis that conventional political science rarely touches, but one that explains a great deal of the overt political maneuvering and control upon which people normally focus.[1,2]

The special language of the helping professions, which we are socialized to see as professional and as nonpolitical, is a major example of this level of politics, though not the only one. Through devices I explore here, these professions create and reinforce popular beliefs about which kinds of people are worthy and which are unworthy; about who should be rewarded through governmental action and who controlled or repressed. Unexamined language and actions can help us understand more profoundly than legislative histories or administrative or judicial proceedings how we decide upon status, rewards, and controls for the wealthy, the poor, women, conformists, and nonconformists.

In this paper I examine such political uses of language in psychiatry, social work, psychiatric nursing, public school education, and law enforcement. My observations are based upon extensive (and depressing) reading in the textbooks and professional journals of these professions published in the last decade. I looked for covert as well as overt justifications for status differentials, power differentials, and authority. Once the subtle ways in which language serves power are recognized, the central function of language in all political interactions becomes clear, whether we call the interactions "government" or "professional."

Therapy and Power

To illustrate the subtle bearing of language on status and authority, consider a common usage that staff, clients, and the general public all accept as descriptive of a purely professional process: the term "therapy." In the journals, textbooks, and talk of the helping professions the term is repeatedly used as a suffix or qualifier. Mental patients do not hold dances; they have dance therapy. If they play volleyball, that is recreation therapy. If they engage in a group discussion, that is group therapy.

Even reading is "bibliotherapy"; and the professional literature warns that it may be advisable to restrict, supervise, or forbid reading on some subjects, especially politics and psychiatry. Because it is a polar example, such an assertion forces us to notice what we normally pass over. To label a common activity as though it were a medical one is to establish superior and subordinate roles, to make it clear who gives orders and who takes them, and to justify in advance the inhibitions placed upon the subordinate class. It does so without arousing resentment or resistance either in the subordinates or in outsiders sympathetic to them, for it superimposes a political relationship upon a medical one while still depicting it as medical.

Though the linguistic evocation of the political system is subtle, that very fact frees the participants to act out their political roles blatantly for they see themselves as helping, not as repressing. In consequence, assaults on people's freedom and dignity can be as polar and degrading as those typically occuring in authoritarian regimes, without qualms or protest by authorities, clients, or the public that hears about them. In this way a suffix or qualifier evokes a full-blown political system. No doubt it does so for most professionals who draw power from the system as persuasively and unobtrusively as it does for the clientele groups whom it helps induce to submit to authority and to accept the status of people who must let others decide how they should behave.

To call explicit attention to the political connotations of a term for power, on the other hand, is to rally opposition rather than support. To label an authority relationship "tyrannical" is an exhortation to oppose it, not a simple description. The chief function of any political term is to marshal public support or opposition. Some terms do so overtly, but the more potent ones, including those used by professionals, do so covertly, portraying a power relationship as a helping one. When the power of professionals over other people is at stake, the language employed implies that professionals have ways to ascertain who are dangerous, sick, or inadequate; that they know how to render them harmless, rehabilitate them, or both; and that the procedures for diagnosis and for treatment are too specialized for the lay public to understand or judge them. A patient with a sore throat is anxious for the doctor to exercise a certain amount of authority; but the diagnosis is easily checked, and the problem itself circumscribes the doctor's authority. When there is an allegation of mental illness, delinquency, or intellectual incapacity, neither the diagnosis nor the scope of authority is readily checked or limited, but its legitimacy is linguistically created and reinforced.

It is of course the ambiguity in the relationship and the ambivalence in the professional and in the client that give the linguistic usage its flexibility and potency. That is always true of symbolic evocations, and it radically distinguishes such evocations from simple deception. Many clients want help, virtually all professionals think they are providing it, and sometimes they do so. Just as the helping seems manifest until it is self-consciously questioned, and then it becomes problematic, so the political relationship seems nonexistent until it is self-consciously questioned, and then it becomes manifest.

The special language of the helping professions merges cognition and affect. The term "mental illness" and the names for specific deviant behaviors encourage the observer and the actor to condense and confound several facets of perception: helping the suffering sick person, repressing the dangerous nonconformist, sympathy for the former, fear of the latter, and so on. The terms carry all these connotations, and the actor-speaker-listener patterns them so as to utilize semantic ambiguity to cope with ambivalence.

We normally fail to recognize this catalytic capacity of language because we think of linguistic terms and syntactical structures as signals rather than as symbols. If a word is a name for a specific thing or action, then terms like "mental illness," "delinquency prone," or "schizophrenic" have narrowly circumscribed meanings. But if a word is a symbol that condenses and rearranges feelings, memories, perceptions, beliefs, and expectations, then it evokes a particular structuring of beliefs and emotions, a structuring that varies with people's social situations. Language as symbol catalyses a subjective world in which uncertainties are clarified and appropriate courses of action become clear. Yet this impressive process of symbolic creation is not self-conscious. On the contrary, our naive view holds that linguistic terms stand for particular objects or behaviors, and so we do not ordinarily recognize that elaborate cognitive structures are built upon them.

In the symbolic worlds evoked by the language of the helping professions, speculations and verified fact readily merge with each other. Language dispels the uncertainty in speculation, changes facts to make them serve status distinctions, and reinforces ideology. The names for forms of mental illness, forms of delinquency, and for educational capacities are the basic terms. Each of them normally involves a high degree of unreliability in diagnosis, in prognosis, and in the description of rehabilitative treatments; but they also entail unambiguous constraints upon clients, especially their confinement and subjection to the staff and the rules of a prison, school, or hospital. The confinement and constraints are converted into liberating and altruistic acts by defining them as education, therapy, rehabilitation, and by other linguistic forms to be examined shortly. The arbitrariness and speculation in the diagnosis and the prognosis, on the other hand are converted into clear and specific perceptions of the need for control. Regardless of the arbitrariness or technical unreliability of professional terms, their political utility is manifest; they marshal popular support for professional discretion, concentrating public attention upon procedures and rationalizing in advance any failures of the procedures to achieve their formal objectives.

Categorization is necessary to science and, indeed, to all perception. It is also a political tool, establishing status and power hierarchies. We ordinarily assume that a classification scheme is either scientific or political in character, but any category can serve either or both functions, depending on the interests of those who employ it rather than upon anything inherent in the term. The name for a category therefore confuses the two functions, consigning people to high or low status and power while drawing legitimacy from its scientific status.

Any categorization scheme that consigns people to niches according to their actual or potential accomplishments or behavior is bound to be political, no matter what its scientific function is. IQ's; psychiatric labels; typologies of talent, skills, or knowledge; employment statuses; criminal statuses; personality types— all exemplify the point. Regardless of their validity and reliability (which are notoriously low) or their analytic bases, such classifications rank people and determine degrees of status and of influence. The categorizations of the helping professions are pristine examples of the functions, and many of these categories carry over into the wider society. Once established, a categorization defines what is relevant about the people who are labeled. It encourages others to seek out data and interpret developments so as to confirm the label and to ignore, discount, or reinterpret counterevidence. As a civil rights lawyer recently noted, "While psychiatrists get angry, patients get aggressive; nurses daydream, but patients withdraw."[3] The eternal human search for meaning and for status can be counted on to fuel the interpretation.

The language of the helping professions reveals in an especially stark way that perception of the same act can range all the way from one pole to its opposite. Is an action punishment or is it help? The textbooks and psychiatric journals recommend actions that look like sadism to many and like therapy to many others; deprivation of food, bed, walks in the open air, visitors, mail, or telephone calls; solitary confinement; deprivation of reading or entertainment materials; immobilizing people by tying them into wet sheets and then exhibiting them to staff and other patients; other physical restraints on body movement; drugging the mind against the client's will; incarceration in locked wards; a range of public humiliations such as the prominent posting of alleged intentions to escape or commit suicide, the requirement of public confessions of misconduct or guilt, and public announcement of individual misdeeds and abnormalities.

The major psychiatric and nursing journals describe and prescribe all these practices and more repressive ones, repeatedly. The May 1973, issue of *Psychiatry* tells of a psychiatric ward in which a sobbing patient was required to scrub a shower room floor repeatedly with a toothbrush while two "psychiatric technicians" stood over her shouting directions, calling her stupid, and pouring dirty water on the floor.[4] Another recent professional article suggests withholding meals from noncompliant patients,[5] and a third recommends that cold, wet-sheet pack restraints be used more often, because they gratify the patient's dependency needs.[6]

To describe these practices in such everyday language evokes horror at the "treatments" in a person who takes the description naively, without the conditioning to the professional perspective to which everyone has in some degree been exposed. To the professionals and those who accept their perspective, on the other hand, it is the *language* rather than the actions that evokes horror, for they have been socialized to see these things only as procedures, as *means* to achieve rehabilitation, not as acts inflicted upon human beings. Language is consequently perceived as a distortion if it depicts what is observably *done* to clients rather than what ends the professional thinks the client should read into them and what the professional reads into them.

The professional's reaction to language of this kind exemplifies the reaction of powerful people in general to accounts of their dealings with those over whom they hold authority. Because the necessary condition of willing submission to authority is a belief that submission benefits the subordinate, it is crucial to the powerful that descriptions of their treatment of others highlight the benefit and not the physical, psychological, or economic costs of submission, as an unadorned factual description does. The revenue service deprives people of money, almost always involuntarily; the military draft imposes involuntary servitude; thousands of other agents of the state deprive people of forms of freedom. Usually the rationale for such restraints is an ambiguous abstraction: national security, the public welfare, law and order. We do not experience or name these ambiguous and abstract objectives as any different from goals that consist of concrete benefits such as traffic control and disease control. Linguistic ambiguity spreads the potent rationale of these latter types of benefits to justify far more severe constraints and deprivations (including death in war) in policy areas in which benefits are nondemonstrable and doubtless often nonexistent. We experience as radical rhetoric any factual description of authoritative actions that does not call attention to their alleged benefits to all citizens or to some, and authorities typically characterize such descriptions as subversive, radical, or treasonous. They are indeed subversive of ready submission and of political support.

The point becomes vivid if we restate the actions described previously from the professional's perspective: discouraging sick behavior and encouraging healthy behavior through the selective granting of rewards; the availability of seclusion, restraints, and closed wards to grant patients a respite from interaction with others and from making decisions and prevent harm to themselves or others; enabling them to think about their behavior, to cope with temptations to elope and succumb to depression, and to develop a sense of security; immobilizing patients to calm them, satisfy their dependency needs, give them the extra nursing attention they value, and enable them to benefit from peer confrontation; placing limits on their acting out; and teaching them that the staff cares.

The two accounts describe the same phenomena, but they occur in phenomenologically different worlds. Notice that the professional terms carry connotations about both physical conditions and the desires of clients that depict constraints as nonrestrictive. To speak of "elopement" rather than "escape," as psychiatrists and staff members do, is to evoke a picture of individual freedom to leave when you like (as eloping couples do) rather than of the locks, iron bars, and bureaucratic prohibitions against voluntary departure that actually exist. To speak of "seclusion" or "quiet room" rather than solitary confinement is again to suggest voluntary and enjoyable retirement from others and to mask the fact that patients are locked in against their will and typically resist and resent the incarceration. Such terms do in a craftsmanlike and nonobvious way what professionals also do directly to justify restrictions on inmates. They assert in textbooks, journals, and assurances to visitors that some patients feel more secure in locked wards and in locked rooms, that professionals know when this is the case, and that the patients' statements to the contrary cannot be taken at face value.

To speak of "limits" is to mask the fact of punishment for misbehavior and to perceive the patient as inherently irrational, thereby diverting attention from the manifest frustrations and aggravations that come from bureaucratic restrictions and from consignment to the lowest and most powerless status in the institution.

Many clients come in time to use the professional language and to adopt its perspective. To the staff, their adoption of the approved linguistic forms is evidence of insight and improvement. All clients probably do this in some degree, but for many the degree is so slight that the professional descriptions serve as irony or as mockery. They are repeatedly quoted ironically by students, patients, and prisoners.

In the institutions run by the helping professions, established roles and their special language create a world with its own imperatives. To recognize the power of language and roles to reinforce each other in this special setting is to understand the frequency with which good men and women in the larger society support governments that mortify, harass, torture, and kill large numbers of their citizens. To the outsider such behavior signals sadism and self-serving evil, and it is impossible to identify with it. To the people who avidly act out their roles inside that special world, motives, actions, and consequences of acts are radically different. Theirs is a work of purification: of ridding the inherently or ideologically contaminated of their blight or of ridding the world of the contamination they embody.

It is no accident that governments intent on repression of liberties and lives are consistently puritanical; just as helping professionals exhibit few qualms about exterminating resistance to their therapies in people they have labeled dangerous and in need of help. To the inhabitants of other worlds, the repression is a mask for naked power, but to those who wield authority, power is a means to serve the public good. Social scientists cannot explain such phenomena as long as they place the cause inside people's psyches rather than in the social evocation of roles. To attribute evil or merit to the psyche is a political act rather than a scientific one, for it justifies repression or exaltation, while minimizing observation. To explore phenomenological diversity in people's worlds and roles is to begin to recognize the full range of politics.

Class or status differences may also entail wide differences in the labelings of identical behaviors. The teacher's underachiever may be the epitome of the "cool" student who refuses to "brownnose." The middle class's criminal or thief may be a "political prisoner" to the black poor. Such labels with contrasting connotations occur when a deprived population sees the system as unresponsive to its needs and organized rebellion as impossible. In these circumstances only individual nonconformity remains as a way to maintain self-respect. To the deprived the nonconformity is a political act. To the beneficiaries of the system it is individual pathology. Each labels it accordingly.

The term "juvenile delinquent" historically served the political function of forcing the assimilation of Catholic immigrants into the WASP culture of late nineteenth- and early twentieth-century America. This new category defined as "criminal" youthful behaviors handled informally among the urban Catholics and not perceived by them as crime at all: staying out late, drinking, smoking, reading comic books, truancy, and disobedience. Now, however, the definition of prevailing urban norms as "delinquency" justified the authorities in getting the Irish children away from their "bigoted" advisers, the priests.[7] The language of individual pathology was part of an effort to repress a distinctive culture and a religion, but the language that described it masked its political consequences while rationalizing it in terms of its motivation of salvaging youth from crime.

Some professionals reject the professional perspective, and all, no doubt, retain some skepticism about it and some ability to see things from the perspective of the client and the lay public. In these cases the ambivalence is typically resolved in more militant, decisive, and institutionalized forms than is true of ambivalent clients; for status, self-conception, and perhaps income hinge upon how it is resolved. In consequence professionals adopt radical therapy, existentialist, or Szaszian views, or they attack these dissidents as unprofessional and unscientific.

The lay public by and large adopts the professional perspective; for its major concern is to believe that others can be trusted to handle the problem, which is potentially threatening to them but not a part of everyday lives. This public reaction is the politically crucial one, for it confers power upon professionals and legitimizes their norms for society generally. The public reaction, in turn, is a response to the language of the professionals and to the social milieu that gives that language its authoritative meaning. When status and self-concept are reciprocal for two groups, it is natural that one group's "repression" should be another's "therapy." Through ambiguous language forms, professionals, clients, and outsiders manage to adjust to each other and to themselves and to establish and maintain status hierarchies.

Professional Imperialism

The special language of the helping professions extends and enlarges authority as well as defining and maintaining it. It accomplishes this by defining the deviance of one individual as necessarily involving others as well, by seeing the absence of deviant behaviors as evidence of *incipient* deviance, and by defining as deviant forms of behavior that laymen regard as normal.

Because man is a social animal, deviance by definition involves others as well. In the helping professions this truism serves as a reason to multiply the range of people over whom the professional psychiatrist, school psychologist, social worker, or law enforcement officer has authority. The "multiproblem family" needs counseling or therapy as much as its emotionally disturbed member. People who adopt a nonmiddle class norm need help even if they do not want it; and professionals have an obligation to "reach out" or engage in "case finding." These phrases and approaches place a particular interpretation upon the sense in which deviance is social in character; namely, that because other people are involved, they also need the ministrations of the professional. By the same token they mask an alternative interpretation: That it is the conditions of deviants' lives, their environments, and their opportunities that primarily need change, not the state of mind of their families and associates. Manifestly, both interpretations and approaches are appropriate. The professional interpretation, whatever its clinical uses, also serves the political function of extending authority over those not yet subject to it and the more far-reaching political function of shaping public perceptions so as to mask the appropriateness of change in economic and social institutions.

The more sweeping professional forays into alien territory rely upon lack of evidence to prove the need for treatment. Consider one of the favorite terms of social work literature: the "pre-delinquent"; or corresponding psychiatric terms, like the "pre-psychotic." On their face such terms imply that the reference is to all who have not yet misbehaved, and that is certainly one of their connotations, one that would appear to give the professional *carte blanche* to assert authority over everybody who has not yet committed a crime or displayed signs of disturbance.

Though they do permit a wide range of arbitrary action, the terms usually have a considerably narrower connotation in practice, for social workers, teachers, psychiatrists, and law enforcement officials apply them largely to the poor and usually to children. Affluent adults are often in fact "pre-delinquent" or "pre-psychotic"; but it is not actual behavior that governs the connotations of these terms, but rather the statistical chances for a group and the belief that poor children are high risks, especially if they come from broken homes. They are indeed high statistical risks: partly because their labeling as pre-delinquents and the extra surveillance are certain to yield a fair number of offenders, just as they would in a wealthy population; and partly because poverty does not encourage adherence to middle class behavior.

In a program to treat "pre-delinquents" in a middle class neighborhood of Cambridge-Somerville, Massachusetts, the "treated" group more often became delinquent than a control group, due, apparently to the effects on the labeled people of their stigmatization. In a similar experiment in a slum neighborhood this result did not appear, apparently due to the fact that stigmatization was not significantly different from the demeaning labels routinely applied to slum residents.[8]

The term "pre-delinquent" nonetheless focuses the mind on its user and of the audience upon the need for preventive surveillance and control and diverts the mind from the appropriateness of social change. The term also evokes public confidence in the professionals' ability to distinguish those who will commit crimes in the future from those who will not. Once again we have an illustration of the power of an unobtrusive symbol to evoke a structured world and to direct perception and norms accordingly.

Still another form of extension of authority through the pessimistic interpretation of normal behavior is exemplified in the psychiatric phrase, "escape to health." Here the linguistic term again draws its connotation from the disposition to interpret behavior according to the status of the person engaging in it. If psychiatric patients show no pathological symptoms, the professional can designate the phenomenon as "escape to health," implying that the healthy behavior is itself a sign that the patients are still sick, possibly worse than before, but intent now on deceiving themselves and the staff. The consequence is continued control over them.

The term epitomizes an attitude common to authorities who know or suspect that their charges would prefer to escape their supervision rather than "behave themselves." The student typed as a trouble-maker or unreliable excites as much suspicion when quiet as when active. Parole boards have their choice of interpreting an inmate's conformist prison behavior as reform or as cunning deception. Anxious public officials in all historical eras have feared both passivity and peaceful demonstrations among the discontented as the groundwork for rebellion. Always, there are metaphoric phrases to focus such anxieties and arouse them in the general public: underground subversion, plotting, the calm before the storm, quiet desperation, escape to health. Always, they point to an internal psychological state or a physical allegation not susceptible to empirical observation.

In the schools, other phrases emphasize student nonactions, discount their observable actions, and so justify special staff controls over them. Especially common are "underachiever" and "overachiever." The former implies that the student is lazy, the latter that the student is neurotic. "Overachiever" is an especially revealing case, for it offers a rationale for treating achievement as deviance. The helping professions are often suspicious of people who display talents beyond the "norm," as they must be in view of their veiled equation of the norm with health. Textbooks in "special education" and "learning disabilities" group gifted or exceptionally able students with the retarded and the emotionally disturbed as special students and advocate separating these "special" students from the normal ones. They urge that the gifted be required to do extra work ("enrichment"). This may or may not mean they learn more or learn faster. It certainly means that they are kept busy and so discouraged either from making demands on the teacher's time or intelligence or from pointing up the stultifying character of the curriculum through restiveness or rebelliousness.

At least as common is the view that the poor require treatment and control whether or not they display any pathological symptoms. Though this belief is manifestly political and class based, the language social workers use to justify surveillance and regulation of the poor is psychological in character. Here are some examples from social work and psychiatric journals and textbooks.

Regarding a preschool nursery in a slum area:

> The children did not have any diagnosed pathology, but as a result of existing in an atmosphere of cultural deprivation, they were vulnerable to many psychosocial problems.[9]

An article in *Social Work* suggests devices through which a social caseworker can induce the poor to come for counseling or treatment by deceiving them into thinking they are only accompanying their children or only attending a party or social meeting:

> Cognitive deficiency . . . broadly refers to the lacks many people suffer in the normal development of their thinking processes. For the most part, though not exclusively, such deficits occur among the poor regardless of nationality or race.[10]

The same article quotes a memorandum issued by the Family Service Association of Nassau County: "Culturally deprived adults seem to be impaired in concepts of causality and time."[11] This last sentence very likely means that the poor are likely to attribute their poverty to inadequate pay or unemployment rather than to personal defects (causality) and are not punctual in keeping appointments with caseworkers (time). It is bound to be based upon a limited set of observations that have powerful implications for the professional observer's own status and authority. The quotation is an example of one of the most common linguistic devices for connoting pathology from specific behaviors equally open to alternative interpretatons that make them seem natural and normal. One of several concrete acts becomes a generalization about an "impairment." To those who do not know the basis for the generalization, it is *prima facie* scientific. To the professionals who have already been socialized into the view the generalization connotes, it is persuasive and profound. To those who meet neither of these conditions, it is a political exhortation rather than a scientific generalization. These people are inclined to treat it as problematic and controversial rather than as established by authoritative procedures.

Still another psychiatric convention legitimizes surveillance over people without symptoms: the inhibition against describing any former patient as cured. To use the word "cured" is to demonstrate naiveté and an unprofessional stance. The approved term in the professional literature is "improved."

Vacuous language serves several functions. Because it is a special vocabulary, it marks off the insiders from the outsiders and defines the former as authoritative and professional. It helps insiders to legitimize social and political biases. They are not prejudiced against the poor but against cognitive deficiencies, not against women but against impulsive-hysterics, not against political radicals but against paranoids, not against homosexuals but against deviants. They are not in favor of punishing, stigmatizing, humiliating, or imprisoning people, but rather of meeting dependency needs, security needs, and of rehabilitation.

It is not chance that the groups constrained by these rationales are also the groups repressed by society at large or that the "treatment" consists of either restoring conformist behavior or removing political offenders from the sight, the consciences, and the career competition of the conventional. Those who become clients have experienced problems either because they have acted unconventionally or because they belong to a category (the young, the poor, women, blacks) whose behavior is largely assessed because of who they are rather than because of what they do. As long as they define their function as winning acceptance for deviants in the existing social structure, the helping professions can only promote conventionality. An alternative is to embrace an explicitly political role as well as a professional one: to promote change in the social structure and to promote the extermination of extant definitions of acceptable behaviors and acceptable social groups. Some helping professionals have adopted this role, fully or partially.

"Helping" as a Political Symbol

The ambiguity of "helping" is pointed out when we examine the contrasting ways in which society "helps" elites and nonelites. Subsidies from the public treasury to businesspeople are not justified as help to individuals but as promotion of a popularly supported goal: defense, agriculture, transportation, and so on. The abstractions are not personified in the people who get generous depletion allowances, cost-plus contracts, tax write-offs, or free government services. To see the expenditure as a subsidy to real people would portray it as a blatant inequity in public policy. The word "help" is not used in this context, though these policies make people rich and substantially augment the wealth of the already rich. Nor is there a dependency relationship or a direct personal relationship between a recipient and a grantor with discretion to withhold benefits. The grantor wields no power over the administrators who carry out the law; for there are always legislators and executives eager to penalize bureaucrats who call attention to the subsidy aspect of the program; and some of the more cooperative administrators can look forward to lucrative employment in the industries they come to know as dispensers of governmental benefits.

When "help" is given to the poor or the unconventional, a wholly different set of role relationships and benefits appears. Now it is the beneficiaries who are sharply personified and brought into focus. They are individuals living off the taxpayer or flouting conventionality. What they personify is poverty, delinquency, dependency, or other forms of deviance. They are in need of help, but help in money, in status, and in autonomy must be sharply limited so as to avoid malingering. One of the consistent characteristics of the "helping" institutions is their care to *limit* forms of help that would make clients autonomous: money for the poor, liberating education and freedom for children of the poor or for "criminals", physical and intellectual autonomy. The limit is enforced in practice while denied in rhetoric.

The "help" for nonelite recipients of the largesse of the state that draws ready political support is control of their deviant tendencies: laziness, mental illness, criminality, nonconformity. They are taught to tolerate indignity and powerlessness when employed, poverty when unemployed, and the family and social stresses flowing from these conditions without unconventional modes of complaint or resistance and without making too many demands on society.

In at least one of the worlds elites and professionals create for themselves and for a wider public, the help is real and the need for it is manifest. So manifest that it must be given even if it is not wanted. So manifest that failure to want it becomes evidence that it is needed and that it should be forced on recipients involuntarily and through incarceration if necessary.

When a helping relationship of this kind is established, it is likely to dominate the self-conception and the world view of those on both sides of the relationship. When a doctor sets a patient's broken arm, neither doctor nor patient lets the relationship significantly influence the doctor's conception or view of function in society. When a public official tests an applicant for a driver's license or a radio license, this relationship is also just one more among many for both parties. But the psychiatrist who defines a patient as psychopathic or paranoid, or the teacher who defines a student as a slow learner or a genius, creates a relationship that is far more fundamental and influential for both professional and client. It tells them both who they are and so fundamentally creates their social worlds that they resist evidence that the professional competence of the one or the stigmatizing or exalting label of the other may be unwarranted. For both, the label tends to become a self-fulfilling prophecy and sometimes immune to falsifying evidence.

In consequence the professionals and the public officials whose function it is to "help" the inadequate, the powerless, or the deviant are willing and eager to play the role, equipped with a built-in reason to discount or reinterpret qualms, role conflicts, and disturbing facts. To comfort, to subsidize, to limit, to repress, to imprison, even to kill are all sometimes necessary to protect the client and society, and conscientious professionals of political authorities play the role to be true to themselves.

As any society grows more frustrating and more alienating for a larger proportion of its inhabitants, more behaviors are inevitably labeled deviant and more people have good reason to experience themselves as unfulfilled and repressed. Such a society can survive and maintain its frustrating institutions only so long as it is possible to manipulate the discontented into conformity and docility and to isolate or incarcerate those who refuse to be "rehabilitated." The helping professions are the most effective contemporary agents of social conformity and isolation. In playing this political role they undergird the entire political structure, yet are largely spared from self-criticism, from political criticism, and even from political observation through a special symbolic language.[12]

Questions for Reflection and Discussion

1.   Why does Edelman think it would be naive to regard language merely as a tool?

2.   What is implied if a person in a psychiatric institution has a habit of reading and the reading is called "bibliotherapy"? What power relationships are implied by this term?

3.   Why does Edelman think that any categorization scheme that sorts people according to their accomplishments or behavior is bound to be political as well as scientific? Do you agree with him? Why or why not?

4.   What is implied by the label "overachiever"? Do you think this label could be used in a harmless, nonpolitical way? Why or why not?

Notes

1. Murray Edelman, *The Symbolic Uses of Politics* (Urbana, Ill.: University of Illinois, 1964), ch. 6, 7, and 8.

2. Murray Edelman, *Politics As Symbolic Action* (Chicago: Markham, 1971), ch. 5.

3. Daniel Oran, "Judges and Psychiatrists Lock Up Too Many People," *Psychology Today.* 7 (August 1973): 22.

4. D. L. Staunard, "Ideological Conflict on a Psychiatric Ward," *Psychiatry.* 36 (May 1973): 143–156.

5. Carl Carlson, Michael Hersen, and Richard Eisler, "Token Economy Programs in the Treatment of Hospitalized Adult Psychiatric Patients," *Mental Health Digest.* 4 (December 1972): 21–27.

6. Rose Kilgalen, "Hydrotherapy—Is It All Washed Up?," *Journal of Psychiatric Nursing.* 10 (November-December 1972): 3–7.

7. *Struggle for Justice.* Prepared for the American Friends Service Committee (Philadelphia: Hill and Wang, 1971), 112.

8. Jackson Toby, "An Evaluation of Early Identification and Intensive Treatment Programs for Predelinquents," *Social Problems.* 13 (Fall 1965): 160–175. David Harris, "On Differential Stigmatization for Predelinquents." *Social Problems.* 15 (Spring 1978): 507–508.

9. Evelyn McElroy and Anita Narciso, "Clinical Specialist in the Community Mental Health Program," *Journal of Psychiatric Nursing.* 9 (January-February 1971): 19.

10. Robert Sunley, "New Dimensions in Reaching-Out Casework," *Social Work.* 13 (April 1968): 64–74.

11. *Ibid.:* 73.

12. This research was supported in part by funds granted to the Institute for Research on Poverty at the University of Wisconsin-Madison by the Office of Economic Opportunity pursuant to the Economic Opportunity Act of 1964. The opinions expressed are those of the author.

11

Relying on Experts*

John Hardwig

We all believe more things than we can possibly have independent evidence
for. Our beliefs often depend on the evidence and understanding that other
people have. Sometimes it is rational not to think for ourselves but rather to
rely on experts for evidence for our beliefs. To do this rationally, we need
not fully understand their evidence and reasoning. We do need to know that
experts are competent, so we can trust them. Even experts must defer at
some stages to other experts. In ignoring the dependency of people on each
other for their evidence and beliefs, the traditional theory of knowledge has
been falsely individualistic.

I find myself believing all sorts of things for which I do not possess evidence:
that smoking cigarettes causes lung cancer, that my car keeps stalling
because the carburetor needs to be rebuilt, that mass media threaten
democracy, that slums cause emotional disorders, that my irregular heart
beat is premature ventricular contraction, that students' grades are not correlated
with success in the nonacademic world, that nuclear power plants are not safe
(enough) . . . The list of things I believe, though I have no evidence for the
truth of them, is, if not infinite, virtually endless. And I am finite. Though I
can readily imagine what I would have to do to obtain the evidence that would
support any one of my beliefs, I cannot imagine being able to do this for *all* of
my beliefs. I believe too much; there is too much relevant evidence (much of it
available only after extensive, specialized training); intellect is too small and life
too short.

What are we to say about all these beliefs? If I, without the available evidence,
still believe a proposition, am I irrational to believe it in these circumstances?

---

*"Relying on Experts" by John Hardwig is an adaptation of "Epistemic Dependence",
published in *The Journal of Philosophy* Vol.LXXXII, No. 7 (July 1985), 335–349. Alterations
were made by Trudy Govier, with permission of the author. The material is republished with
permission of *The Journal of Philosophy* and the author.

Is my belief a mere belief without any adequate justification on the basis of evidence? If not, why not? Perhaps there are other good reasons for believing propositions, reasons that are not direct evidence for the truth of those propositions. If this were so, what would these reasons look like?

In this essay, I consider the idea of intellectual authority, concentrating on the intellectual authority of experts. I want to explore the logic of appeals to intellectual authority and the way in which such appeals give us justification for believing and knowing.

The essay has three parts:

1. A person can have good reasons for believing a proposition because other people have good reasons to believe it. This can be called indirect evidence—unlike more standard evidence, it is based on the evidence other people have.

2. Because nonexperts, or laypeople, are the inferiors of experts with regard to their special subjects, nonexperts are sometimes rational in refusing to think for themselves on these subjects. Contrary to what is often thought and said, rationality sometimes consists in refusing to think for oneself.

3. These results can be applied to the concept of knowledge. Scholars and scientists often can be knowers only because they have deferred and continue to defer to other experts in their pursuit of knowledge. Thus modern knowledge is often possible only through a complex network of appeals to the authority of experts.

If I am correct, appeals to epistemic authority are an essential part of much of our knowledge. Appeals to the authority of experts often provide justification for claims to know and for claims that beliefs have a rational basis. Because experts are superior in their areas of knowledge, they have a kind of authority over laypersons, and over experts in other areas as well—an epistemic authority. This situation means that often we are not independent in our quests or knowledge. Because of this epistemic dependence, laypersons and even experts lack full rational autonomy.

Most theories of knowledge are individualistic. They hold that people can seek knowledge and critically evaluate evidence independently, without relying on other people. My arguments here indicate that this individualism cannot be entirely correct; it is too simple-minded in ignoring the role of experts. This fact has important implications for our understanding of knowledge and persons who know, and for our understanding of rationality.

Part One

Consider a proposition for which people could have evidence. One simple example of such a proposition is "There is no vaccine against chicken pox." Usually we think of evidence as the sort of thing that would count toward establishing that that proposition is true. Evidence in this sense could include sound arguments as well as factual information. Evidence may exist even though some people who are interested in whether the proposition is true do not know about that evidence. Many parents of young children may be interested in the question of whether there is a vaccine against chicken pox, and there is good evidence that no such vaccine exists. However, though doctors are familiar with this evidence, it is not known to many parents.

Let's suppose that Smith, a doctor, has good evidence that there is no vaccine for chicken pox, but that Jones, a parent, does not. Suppose, however, that Jones does have reasons to believe that Smith has good evidence that there is no such vaccine. Can Jones have indirect evidence for that proposition, based on what she thinks Smith knows or believes? If Jones could get reasons for her beliefs indirectly from Smith, in such a case, then we could say that Jones has a kind of epistemic basis for her belief that comes from Smith's authority.

Perhaps we can say that in this case and other similar ones, a person has good reasons for a belief, but those reasons are based on trust or confidence in the evidence somebody else has. If so, the dependent person would still have evidence for the beliefs, and these beliefs would be more than mere opinions. They would be backed up by evidence, a kind of indirect evidence.

This, I think, is an attractive sort of theory. However, it is odd in a way, because the evidence that the dependent person (the parent in this example) has is not evidence that counts directly for the truth of the proposition. What Jones knows about her doctor has nothing to do directly with chicken pox and vaccines. (It has to do with Smith's competence and what Smith knows and believes.) If people can build up evidence by depending on each other in this sort of way, eventually there will have to be persons like Smith, who do have evidence directly bearing on the issue itself.

The question arises as to how Jones as a parent can have good reason to believe that Smith as a doctor knows about chicken pox vaccines, when she herself does not know about it. The answer is that Jones and persons in similar epistemically-dependent positions have good reasons to think that Smith and persons in similar authoritative positions have conducted those sorts of inquiries necessary to provide evidence for such claims.

In fact, sometimes the necessary inquiry is very simple. When this happens one person may base a belief on evidence another person has, even though the nondependent person is not somebody we would call an expert. For example, if the service station attendant who checks my oil says it is all right, I would believe him, but I would not call him an expert. However, the more interesting and complicated cases are those in which expertise is involved. These are cases in which laypersons believe that others are experts on the basis of sustained, prolonged, and systemic inquiries.[1]

I have been emphasizing that laypeople may be intellectually dependent on an expert and epistemically inferior to the expert on the matters where the expert has expertise. Sometimes laypeople's inferiority and dependence are so radical that they would need extensive training and special competence before they could even begin to conduct the necessary inquiry that the expert can conduct. When this happens, laypeople may not even understand the expert's reasons for a particular belief, or they may not be able to appreciate why these are good reasons.

Michael Polanyi and Harry Prosch put the first part of this point dramatically, taking their examples from the physical sciences:[2]

> The popular conception of science says that science is a collection of observable facts that anybody can verify for himself. We have seen this is not true in the case of expert knowledge, like that needed in diagnosing a disease. Moreover, it is not true in the physical sciences. In the first place, for instance, a layman cannot possibly get hold of the equipment for testing a statement of fact in astronomy or in chemistry. Even supposing that he could somehow get the use of an observatory or a chemical laboratory, he would not know how to use the instruments he found there and might very well damage them beyond repair before he had ever made a single observation; and if he should succeed in carrying out an observation to check up on a statement of science and found a result that contradicted it, he could rightly assume that he had made a mistake, as students do in a laboratory when they are learning to use its equipment.

Moreover, the training and resultant competence to conduct a required inquiry are often accessible only to those with certain talents and abilities. Sometimes, Jones is dependent on Smith, and Jones might not even be able, ever, to obtain the evidence Smith has for a certain proposition about which he is an expert. If my own desperate and losing struggle with freshman calculus is a reliable indicator, I might never be able to obtain the evidence for my belief that relativity physics is correct, no matter how much time and effort I devoted to the enterprise. I simply may lack the mathematical ability to possess that evidence.

But extensive training and special competence may be necessary before a person can assess or even understand an expert's reason for some particular proposition. Although I might be able to understand studies about the impact of mass media on voters, I am not competent to assess the merits of these studies, because I am not knowledgeable about the issues that surround the social scientific research methods used. Lacking the required mathematical training and ability, I cannot even read the books and articles that directly could support my belief that relativity physics is correct.

Suppose that all the following conditions hold true of a layperson (Jones) who would like to know whether a particular proposition (*p*) is true:

a. Jones has not performed any inquiry that would provide evidence for a belief that *p* is true.

b. Jones is not competent and perhaps could not even become competent to perform such an inquiry.

c. Jones is not able to assess the merits of evidence that an expert's inquiry may provide, relevant to *p*.

d. Jones may not even be able to understand the evidence experts have for *p* and how that evidence can support the expert's belief that *p* is true.

Given all these conditions, could we still say that Jones may be able to have good reasons to believe that *p* is true? Yes. We should acknowledge that Jones's belief in such a case, where she relies on an expert, is more solidly based than beliefs that are just irrational or based on no evidence at all.

Many people would reject this conclusion, because it is so different from what we usually think about the nature of rational belief. But I think we must say that Jones's belief in such a case can be rationally justified.

If we do not allow this, we will have to conclude that a large percentage of beliefs in any complex culture are simply, and unavoidably, irrational. If they are not irrational, they are nonrational—that is, evidence and logic have no bearing on them at all. In complex cultures, far more is known that is relevant to the truth of any person's beliefs than any one person could know alone. Surely it would be paradoxical to maintain that the more that is known in a culture, the less rational are the beliefs of individuals in that culture!

Part Two

Nevertheless, epistemological individualism may still seem to many people to be correct. Following such individualism, a critic of my position might suggest that responsible and rational laypeople have to develop an appropriate stance to experts. If they cannot understand why the expert's reasons for a proposition are good reasons, then they cannot check the accuracy of the expert. A tempting suggestion, to support individualism, would be that any layperson who has the required ability should become informed so as to be able to assess the reliability of the expert's reports. In this way, a layperson could escape dependence on experts and regain intellectual autonomy, or independence.

The idea behind this suggestion lies at the heart of one model of what it means to be an intellectually responsible and rational person, a model which is nicely captured by Kant's statement that one of the three basic rules or maxims for avoiding error in thinking is to "think for *oneself.*"[3] This is, I think, an extremely pervasive model of rationality—it underlies Descartes's methodological doubt; it is implicit in most epistemologies; it colors the way we have thought about knowledge. On this view, the very core of rationality consists in preserving and adhering to your own independent judgment; for how can you be sure you are being informed, not misinformed, if you relinquish your independence?

But I submit that this model provides us with a romantic ideal that is thoroughly unrealistic and that, in practice, results in less rational belief and judgment. I could, indeed, escape epistemic dependence on *some* experts; perhaps, if I am talented enough, I could escape reliance on any given expert. I can and do choose where to establish my intellectual autonomy. But if I were to pursue epistemic autonomy across the board, I would succeed only in holding relatively uninformed, unreliable, crude, untested, and therefore *irrational* beliefs. If I would be rational, I can never avoid some epistemic dependence on experts, owing to the fact that I believe more than I can become fully informed about.

Once more, then: If I am not in a position to know what the expert's good reasons for believing that *p* are and why these are good reasons, what stance should I take in relation to the expert? If I do not know these things, I am also in no position to determine whether the person really is an expert.[4] By asking the right questions, I might be able to spot a few quacks, phonies, or incompetents, but only the more obvious ones. For example, I may suspect that my doctor is incompetent, but generally I would have to know what doctors know to confirm or dispel my suspicion.

This checking and ranking of experts could be expressed in a kind of formula. Person *B* has good reasons, we might say, for believing that person *C* has good reasons for believing that person *A* has good reasons for believing that a particular proposition is true. In this way, a person might appeal to a kind of hierarchy of experts. But by such an appeal, the layperson does not regain epistemic independence. Dependence has merely been extended and refined. Nor could a person regain epistemic autonomy in all cases without believing things on the basis of relatively crude and untested reasons.

Granted also, if I do not know and have no way of finding out who the experts are, I will have no way to appeal to the chain of authority. I will then not know who has good reasons for the belief, to whom to defer, or whose opinion (if any) can give me good reasons for a belief. This sometimes happens, and when it does, I cannot find even indirect support for a belief, from experts. Generally, however, I can find someone whose opinion is more informed than mine and who can refer me to someone who is knowledgeable about a matter. Even if a layperson, because of a relative inability to discriminate between more and less reliable experts, ends up appealing to a lesser instead of a greater expert, the lesser expert's opinion will still be better than the layperson's.[5]

A layperson may believe a claim either on direct evidence, on vicarious evidence from one expert, or by relying on a hierarchy of experts. But in any case, the layperson remains a kind of subordinate of the experts. Even if the layperson raises a logically important objection to the view the experts hold, it is up to those experts to make an accurate assessment of the significance of that objection. Only the experts fully understand what is involved in the methods, techniques, premises, and basis of their training and inquiry, and how these bear on an issue.

The layman can, in other words, propose criticisms and alternatives but rationally must allow the expert to dispose of them, for in a conversation with an expert (as opposed to a dialogue among equals),[6] the final court of rational appeal belongs solely to one party, by virtue of that party's greater competence for and commitment to inquiry into the relevant subject matter. Rational laypeople recognize that their own judgment, uninformed by training and inquiry, is *rationally inferior* to that of the expert (and the community of experts for whom the expert usually speaks) and consequently always can be *rationally* overruled. Recognizing that the highest court of rational appeal lies outside of themselves, laypeople simply may have to accept the fact that their objections are not good ones, even though they still seem good to them.

There are a number of ways in which the layperson rationally can refuse to defer to the expert's opinion. These can be called *ad hominem,* because they are based on criticisms of the personal reliability of the expert. The layman can assert that the experts are not disinterested, neutral witnesses; that their interest in the outcome of the discussion prejudices their testimony; that they are not operating in good faith—that they are lying, for example, or refusing to acknowledge a mistake in their views because to do so would tend to undermine their claim to special competence; or that they are covering for peers or knuckling under to social pressure from others in the field; and so on. Such ad hominems are not always fallacious, and they sometimes do ground the rational refusal to defer to the statements of experts. But one interesting feature of such ad hominems is that they seem and perhaps are much more admissible, important, and damning in a layman's discussions with experts than they are in dialogues among peers. It does not matter so much if your peers are biased or operating in bad faith; they will be found out. The merits of their arguments can be tested and evaluated rather than just accepted.

With the exception—often an important exception—of such ad hominems, I see no way to avoid the conclusion I have proposed: that rational laypeople will recognize that, in matters about which there is good reasons to believe that there is expert opinion, they ought (methodologically) not to make up their own minds. Their stance on these matters usually will—if they are rational—be rational deference to the epistemic authority of the expert.

Sometimes expert opinion is divided. A layperson will have no way of determining what the belief should be. Still, the layperson cannot resolve the issue alone in such a case. A layperson only can conduct a relatively crude and casual inquiry. The layperson will face a dilemma: either suspend judgment about the matter or arrive at a position on a nonrational basis. It also must be admitted that laypeople can go wrong when they rely on experts. Sometimes they are misled by phony or mistaken claims to expertise, even though they carefully attempt to determine that a supposed expert is genuine. In addition, even the most careful and respected experts sometimes are not correct.

Despite these limitations of the view that laypeople must depend on experts, such lack of autonomy in nonexperts is a fact of modern life. It does seem odd to allow that it is sometimes irrational to think for yourself and that rationality sometimes consists in deferring to epistemic authority, and thereby passively and uncritically accepting what we are given to believe. These ideas go against our models of rationality, which depict the solitary independent thinker, appraising evidence alone. But such models do not fit modern life, where dependence on experts is real and unavoidable.

Part Three

So far I have not spoken about knowledge. The standard model of knowledge is:

> A person, A, knows a proposition, p, to be true if the following conditions are met:
> a. A believes p.
> b. A has good reasons to believe p.
> c. p is true.

Many people worry about the difficulty in determining that a proposition, *p*, is true.

I suggest that we turn our attention to part b in this model. It is reasonable to think that better reasons are required to know something than are required merely to believe it. For instance, if I am said to know that there is no vaccine for chicken pox, I need very good evidence, whereas if I am said reasonably to believe this claim, weaker evidence will suffice. It is natural to think that there is a kind of progression in evidence from what we have for mere belief, to what we have for rational belief, to what we have for knowledge.

In the model of epistemic dependence which I am developing, we have to allow for evidence that comes from the evidence and expertise of other people. This raises the issue of whether there can be vicarious knowledge. Can knowledge, as well as rational belief, be based on an appeal to epistemic authority?

Suppose someone tells me something that is true without giving me evidence for its truth. Perhaps a man, Achinstein, tells me that laetrile does not cure cancer and does not give me the studies that prove this, much less the concrete data on which those studies are based. Suppose I have good reasons to believe that Achinstein is an authority in the field of cancer research, and so I believe what he tells me. Do I then know that laetrile does not cure cancer? Or have I achieved something much less than knowledge—perhaps only right opinion, or rational belief? If I can acquire knowledge on the basis of Achinstein's evidence and understanding, then it is possible for me to know that laetrile does not cure cancer without having any evidence that bears directly on the effects of laetrile on cancer. That seems quite paradoxical!

We insist that evidence is relevant to establishing knowledge, but then we allow that I might have knowledge even though I have no direct evidence. It is a real question whether my belief should count as knowledge in such circumstances as these.

Much of what people count as knowledge, in modern societies, does rest on structures of epistemic dependence. Scientists, researchers, and scholars are, sometimes at least, knowers, and all of these knowers stand on each other's shoulders. You know only because others have direct evidence.[7]

These knowers could not do their work without presupposing the validity of many other inquiries that they cannot (for reasons of competence as well as time) validate for themselves. Scientists, for example, simply do not repeat the experiments of other scientists unless the experiment is important and something seems fishy about it. It would, moreover, be impossible to get to the research front in, say, physics or psychology, if you relied only on the results of your own inquiry or insisted on assessing for yourself the evidence behind all the beliefs accepted in the field. Thus, if scientists, researchers, and scholars are knowers, the layperson-expert relationship is also present *within* the structure of knowledge, and the expert is an expert partially because the expert so often takes the role of the layperson *within the expert's own field.*

Moreover, research in many fields is increasingly done by teams rather than individuals. For example, it is not uncommon for the title of an article reporting experimental results in particle physics to look like this:

Charm Photoproduction Cross Section at 20 GeV

K. Abe, T. C. Bacon, J. Ballam, L. Berny, A. V. Bevan, H. H. Bingham, J. E. Brau, K. Braune,
D. Brick, W. M. Bugg, J. Butler, W. Cameron, J. T. Carroll, C. V. Cautis, J. S. Chima, H. O. Cohn,
D. C. Colley, G. T. Condo, S. Dado, R. Diamond, P. J. Dornan, R. Erickson, T. Fieguth,
R. C. Field, L. Fortney, B. Franek, N. Fujiwara, R. Gearhart, T. Glanzman, J. J. Goldberg,
G. P. Gopal, A. T. Goshaw, E. S. Hafen, V. Hagopian, G. Hall, E. R. Hancock, T. Handler,
H. J. Hargis, E. L. Hart, P. Haridas, K. Hasegawa, T. Hayashino, D. Q. Huang, [a] R. L. Hulsizer,
S. Isaacson, M. Jobes, G. E. Kalmus, D. P. Kelsey, J. Kent, T. Kitagaki, J. Lannutti, A. Levy,
P. W. Lucas, M. MacDermott, W. A. Mann, T. Maruyama, R. Merenyl, R. Milburn, C. Milstene,
K. C. Moffett, J. J. Murray, A. Napier, S. Noguchi, F. Ochiai, S. O'Neal, A. P. T. Palounek,
I. A. Pless, M. Rabin, P. Rankin, W. J. Robertson, A. H. Rogers, E. Ronat, H. Rudnicka, T. Sato,
J. Schneps, S. J. Sewell, J. Shank, A. M. Shapiro, C. K. Sinclair, R. Sugahara, A. Suzuki,
K. Takahashi, K. Tamai, S. Tanaka, S. Tether, H. B. Wald, W. D. Walker, M. Widgoff,
C. G. Wilkins, S. Wolbers, C. A. Woods, Y. Wu, A. Yamaguchi, R. K. Yamamoto, S. Yamashita,
G. Yekutieli, Y. Yoshimura, G. P. Yost, and H. Yuta

*Birmingham University, Birmingham B152TT, England, and Brown University, Providence, Rhode
Island 02912, and Duke University, Durham, North Carolina 27706, and Florida State University,
Tallahassee, Florida 32306, and Imperial College, London SW72BZ. England, and National Laboratory
for High Energy Physics (KEK), 37830, and Rutherford Appleton Laboratory, Didcot, Oxon OX11
0QX, England, and Stanford Linear Accelerator Center, Stanford University, Stanford California 94306,
and Technion-Israel Institute of Technology, Haifa 32000, Israel, and Tokoku University, Sendai 980,
Japan, and Tufts University, Medford, Massachusetts 02155, and University of California, Berkeley,
California 94720, and University of Tel Aviv, Tel Aviv, Israel, and University of Tennessee, Knoxville,
Tennessee 37916, and Weismann Institute, Rehoval, Israel*

Stanford Linear Accelerator Center Hybrid Facility Photon Collaboration)

(Received 2 May 1983)

Forty-seven charm events have been observed in an exposure of the SLAC Hybrid
Facility bubble chamber to a 20-GeV backward-scattered laser beam. Thirty-seven
events survive all the necessary cuts imposed. Based on this number the total charm
cross section is calculated to be 63: ???

PACS numbers: 13.60 Le, 13.60.Rj

In this Letter we present results on the charm
photoproduction cross section in an experiment
using the SLAC Hybrid Facility. Results on life-
times of charmed particles based on part of the
data were published earlier.[1]

The SLAC 1-m hydrogen bubble chamber was
exposed to a 20-GeV photon beam produced by
Compton scattering of laser light by the 30-GeV
electron beam. it was collimated to 3 mm in
diameter. The photon beam energy spectrum is
shown in Fig. 1. It peaks at 20 GeV with a full
width at half maximum of 2 GeV. Most of the
data were taken at photon intensities of 20-30 γ/
pulse. In order to detect decays of charmed particles, a fourth camera with high-resolution optics
having a resolution of 55 μm over a depth of field
$\pm$ 6 mm was used. The cameras were triggered
either on the passage of a charged particle
through three multiwire proportional chambers
and pointing back to the fiducial volume of

the bubble chamber or on a sufficient energy
deposition in an array of lead-glass blocks. Particle identification was provided by ionization mea-
surements in the bubble chamber and light
detection in two large-aperture Cherenkov
counters. More details of the experimental setup
and trigger are given in Ref. 1.

The results presented here are based on
270,000 hadronic interactions found in a restricted fiducial volume. All hadronic events were
closely examined for the decays of short-lived
particles within 1 cm of the production vertex.
When such a decay was found, the following cuts
were applied to ensure that the decays which
survived were genuine charm decays: (a) Decays
with less than two charged products were rejected. (b) Two-prong decays consistent with
either photon conversions or strange-particle hypotheses were rejected. To eliminate K° decays,
the two-body (assumed to be as) invariant

156

William Bugg, professor of physics at the University of Tennessee, Knoxville,
and a participant in this experiment, explained how such an experiment is done.
This experiment, which recorded charm events and measured the lifespan of

Relying on Experts   **133**

the charmed particles, was one of a series of experiments costing perhaps $10 million. After it was funded, about fifty man-years were spent making the needed equipment and the necessary improvements in the Stanford University Linear Accelerator. Then approximately fifty physicists worked perhaps fifty man-years collecting the data for the experiment. When the data were in, the experimenters divided into five geographic groups to analyze the data, a process that involved looking at 2.5 million pictures, making measurements on 300,000 interesting events, and running the results through computers to isolate and measure 47 charm events. The "West Coast group" that analyzed about a third of the data included forty physicists and technicians who spent about sixty man-years on its analysis.

Obviously, no one person could have done this experiment—in fact, Bugg reports that no one university or national laboratory could have done it—and many of the authors of an article like this will not even know how a given number in the article was arrived at.[8] Furthermore, even if one person could know enough and live long enough to do such an experiment, there would be absolutely no point in attempting to do so, for the results would have become obsolete long before the experiment was completed. Although Bugg expresses confidence that the team's measurement of the lifespan of charmed particles is a good one, he estimates that within three years some other group will have come up with another technique that will give considerably better results. He consequently expects that within five years the paper will no longer be of general interest.

Finally, Bugg notes that the article's ninety-nine authors represent different specializations within particle physics, but all are experimentalists. None would be able to undertake the theoretical revisions that might be required as a result of this experiment and that provide a large part of the rationale for doing it. On the other hand most theoreticians would not be competent to conduct the experiment—and neither the experimentalists nor the theoreticians are competent to design, build, and maintain the equipment without which the experiment could not be run at all.

Obviously, this is an extreme example, though not all that extreme in the realm of particle physics.[9] However, we can see how dependence on other experts pervades any complex field of research when we recognize that most footnotes that cite references are appeals to authority. And when these footnotes are used to establish premises for the study, they involve the author in layperson-expert relationships even encompassing the author's own pursuit of knowledge. Moreover, the horror that sweeps through the scientific community when a fraudulent researcher is uncovered is instructive. What is at stake is more than public confidence. Rather, researchers also are forced to acknowledge the extent to which their own work rests on the work of others—work that they have not and could not (if only for reasons of time and expense) verify.

Thus in many cases, a complex network of appeals to the authority of various experts clearly exists. The resulting knowledge could not have been achieved by any one person. We could represent it with the following sort of model, where A, B, C, D, and E are different persons, and m, n, o, and p are different propositions.

A knows that *m* is true.
B knows that *n* is true.
C knows that A knows that *m* is true and that, if *m* is true, *o* is true.
D knows that B knows that *n* is true, and that C knows that *o* is true,
and that if *n* and *o* are both true, then *p* is true.
E knows that D knows that *p* is true.

In complicated contexts, such as that of particle physics, some such model may very well represent the only way anybody could come to know a particular claim, *p*. It might well happen that no one person knows all the claims (*m, n,* and *o*) that provide evidence for *p*—except vicariously, by knowing that others know them.

Such a situation raises the question of whether anybody knows that *p*. We may say that most of our scientific research and scholarship can never result in knowledge, because results are obtained by cooperative methods. This is not a plausible conclusion. If we say that cooperative research produces knowledge, then we have to allow that, in such cases as the preceding, the proposition resulting from various persons' evidence is known. This means that we have to grant that vicarious knowledge is real knowledge. Granting this requires changes in many of our common ideas about what knowledge is.

If this conclusion is unacceptable, another one is possible. We might say that no individual, among A, B, C, D, E, knows the resulting proposition, *p*, but that instead there is a community of investigators, and the community knows *p*. The community, then, would be understood to be something over and above these individuals. The early twentieth-century American philosopher C.S. Peirce claimed that the community of inquirers is the primary knower and that individual knowledge is derivative from that of the community. Perhaps this model of collective pursuit of knowledge is similar to what Peirce had in mind.

We must either allow that individuals can know things vicariously, or we must cease to see individuals as the primary knowers and attribute knowledge to communities of investigators. In either case, epistemic individualism is undermined.

These results will seem deeply disturbing to some people. They reveal the extent to which even our rationality rests on trust. In addition, they threaten some of our most cherished values—individual autonomy and responsibility, equality, and democracy.

If you accept the arguments of this essay, some basic changes in epistemologies are required. We must revise our conception of what it means for beliefs and persons to be rational. We also either must agree that people can know without possessing direct supporting evidence or accept the idea that there is knowledge that belongs to a community and not to any individual.[10]

Questions for Reflection and Discussion

1. Hardwig says that he believes that smoking causes lung cancer, but he possesses no evidence for this. Do you believe it? What is your evidence?

2. What would follow from Hardwig's position if we were to assume that many people identified in our society as experts are not reliable sources of knowledge? What do you think about the reliability of experts or so-called experts? What is the basis for your belief?

3. What may be indicated about the individual knowledge even of experts themselves when a technical paper has as many as ninety-nine authors? Do you think that errors are more likely or less likely when a piece of research or academic paper has ten or more authors, as opposed to two or less? What reasons would you give for your estimation?

4. Why does Hardwig think that the maxim "Think for yourself" embodies a romantic ideal? What is implied by the term "romantic", as he uses it?

5. Why are ad hominems (refusals to give credibility to claims or unreliability of a supposed expert) on the grounds of the nonneutrality more significant in dialogues between experts and laypersons than in dialogues between experts?

Notes

1. I assume that we can all agree that there are experts, but I have not attempted in this paper to offer a precise definition of "expert" or to delineate the range of possible expertise (beyond the introductory proviso that this paper is restricted to belief in and knowledge of propositions for which there is evidence). If the theses of this paper are correct, however, it will become crucial for epistemologists to argue about the definition of "expert" and the range of actual and possible expertise.
   One observation about my use of "expert" is in order: It does not presuppose or entail the truth of the expert's views. If one defines "expert" in terms of the *truth* of views (as Plato's Gorgias and Thrasymachus do), it is often impossible in principle to say who is an expert—even if you are an expert yourself!—since it is often impossible to say whose view is coincident with the truth. But I submit that it is not similarly impossible to say what constitutes sustained, relevant inquiry and to ascertain who is engaged in it (though there will sometimes be very real problems in making this judgment). And whenever sustained inquiry is both necessary for and efficacious with respect to determining whether or not *p*, the expert's views are less likely to be mistaken and likely to be less mistaken than an inexpert opinion. Thus, in my use of "expert," the connection between truth and the views of the expert is not completely severed, though that connection is neither necessary nor simple.

2. Michael Polanyi and Harry Prosch, *Meaning* (Chicago: University of Chicago Press, 1977), 184.

3. J. H. Bernard, tr., *Critique of Judgment* (New York: Hafner, 1951), 136; Kant's emphasis. Kant repeats this statement in the *Anthropologie*, 118, and in the *Logik*, 371, both (Berlin: Cassier, 1932).

4. In a series of recent articles, Keith Lehrer has explored the issues concerning the ranking of experts and the opinions of various experts and, consequently, the way to handle the problem of disagreement among experts, all with much more rigor and precision that I can muster here. For example, see "Social Information," *Monist*, 50, no. 4 (October 1977): 473–487, and also the articles Lehrer refers to in his footnotes to this article.

5. Of course, a more detailed account of the whole issue of identifying relevant experts would have to distinguish among (1) *B* merely believing that *A* has good reasons to believe that *p*, (2) *B* having some reason to believe that *A* has good reasons to believe that *p*, and (3) *B* having

good reasons to believe that *A* has good reasons to believe that *p*. And none of this resolves the often excruciating practical problem of identifying who the real or best experts are—what is the patient faced with conflicting medical opinions to do? But these are logically posterior issues and problems; the argument here is that in any case, the patient should *not* make the diagnosis nor even read a little about the problem and then make the diagnosis.

6. I have attempted to explicate the logic of dialogue among presumed epistemic equals in the area of moral reasoning in John Hardwig, "The Achievement of Moral Rationality," *Philosophy and Rhetoric*, 6, no. 3 (Summer 1973): 171–185.

7. This strategy for approaching these issues will mean, of course, that it remains open to a courageous enough epistemologist to avoid my conclusion by embracing the view that the achievements of scientists, researchers, and scholars are not and could not be *knowledge* whenever these achievements are based on cooperative methodologies. This option does not seem attractive to me.

8. Of course, only a few people actually write the article, but it does not follow that these people are masterminds for the whole procedure or that they completely understand the experiment and the analysis of the data. According to Bugg, although a few persons—"the persons most actively involved in working on the data and who therefore understand most about it"—wrote up the experiment (this article is three-and-one-half journal pages long), they really only prepared a draft for revisions and corrections by the other authors. The team then met to argue substantive points about the techniques for analyzing the data and how the article should be presented to enable other physicists to understand it best.

9. Of the forty-two articles on elementary particles and fields published by *Physical Review Letters* during April 25 to July 18, 1983, eleven listed more than ten authors, nine listed more than twenty authors, and five listed more than forty authors. In the same period only five articles were by single authors.

10. In a paper about epistemic dependence, it is fitting that I acknowledge my own debts. Helpful comments and criticisms of earlier versions of this paper provided by William R. Carter, members of the philosophy departments at the University of Tennessee and East Tennessee State University, and Mary Read English. My dependence on William Bugg, professor of physics at the University of Tennessee, for discussion of a central example is evident.

12

Making Reasonable Decisions as an Amateur in a World of Experts*

Jerry Cederblom and David Paulsen

Modern dependence on experts poses a dilemma. On the one hand, we cannot avoid relying on them. Yet if we do not know enough to select the right experts and decide what to do when experts disagree, we are not even capable of relying on experts. We need, in addition, to limit the influence of experts, because they may have a vested interest in one outcome or another or a limited perspective due to specialization. Relativism—assuming that any opinion is as good as any other—is no solution. Nor is embracing a so-called "true belief"—an all-encompassing theory of the world such as Marxism or fundamentalist Christianity. A better strategy is to develop your own arguments and theories, at least tentatively, and use these to be more than a passive recipient of expert opinions.

Ours is an age of specialization. Technical or engineering backgrounds are rewarded by high salaries, public policy debate calls upon the testimony of experts, and colleges and universities encourage students to declare a major at an increasingly early point in their academic careers. Given this trend, is it not reasonable to simply endorse the opinions of experts rather than relying on judgments, arguments, and theories of your own? But what then do we believe if experts disagree? How should we react when expert judgment turns out to be wrong? Should we become skeptics who use the critical reasoning procedures we have discussed to discredit the arguments and theories of others without advancing creative alternatives of our own? We

*"Making Reasonable Decisions as an Amateur in a World of Specialists" by Jerry Cederblom and David Paulsen is taken from Chapter 11 of their text, *Critical Reasoning*. (Belmont, CA: Wadsworth, 1986, Second Edition.) It is reprinted with the permission of the authors and the publisher.

will now consider some strategies for making reasonable decisions as amateurs in a world of specialists.

Unfortunately, we are faced with a very serious dilemma. We need to understand the world, but we can't understand what the experts say about it. If we try to figure things out for ourselves, it is very likely that we will be wrong. But if we simply leave things to the experts without understanding their theories, we have difficulty in deciding who the experts are, in determining what to believe if the experts disagree, and in limiting the influence of experts to its proper domain.

This dilemma is extremely difficult to resolve—neither alternative is completely satisfactory. But we maintain that in the face of this difficulty it is important not to hide from the problem—not to take the view that it doesn't matter what you believe since all opinions are uncertain, or the view that in order to escape the uncertainty of rational processes it is necessary to rely on faith. It is crucial to continue to pursue reasonable belief, even if such belief is never certain, because belief is connected to action. Responsibility for our beliefs stems from responsibility for our actions.

When we say certain people are "experts," we are not assuming that society is divided into two groups—those who understand the world and the masses who do not. Even if you are an expert in one area, there are many other areas of which you are uninformed. We are not all equal in our general knowledge or in the breadth of our expertise, but we can consider each of us to be in the position of an amateur in a world of specialization.

Leaving It to the Experts

What do you really know about nuclear energy, the balance of trade, or the most effective ways of combating crime? Chances are you have expressed opinions on some of these issues in casual conversation, and you probably think that some views on these issues are *not* correct (such as, there are no dangers involved in nuclear energy; a trade deficit, i.e., buying from abroad more than we are selling, is good for the economy; crime will stop by itself). You are probably quick to acknowledge, however, that there are people who know more about these issues than you do. Why not, then, simply leave opinions on these matters to people who *do* know more—who have made it their business to learn all they can about areas such as these? You could say that for each issue on which you might need to express an opinion, you will just wait until the occasion arises and then try to find out what the experts think about it and adopt their advice. Surely you would then have a greater chance of being right about each issue than if you spread out your time trying to learn a little about everything; and by leaving things to the experts you will have more time to do the things you really enjoy. What could be more sensible?

Let us imagine that we have adopted this policy of leaving things to the experts—what problems might we encounter?

Who Are the Experts?

Our first problem would be to determine who the experts are, so we could know whom to ask about the views we should adopt. Suppose the issue is how dangerous are nuclear power plants. As a starting point we might go to various professors of physics and of engineering and ask them who the best experts are on this issue. If there were some consensus as to who the experts are, and these experts all had about the same story concerning the major risks in nuclear power plants and the extent these risks could be minimized, then we would probably feel confident that our strategy of leaving it to the experts had been successful. But what might go wrong in this process?

We might pick the wrong fields of study in our search for experts. Perhaps the biggest risks involving nuclear power don't have to do with science and engineering but with politics. Perhaps the technical problems of protecting against radiation leaks can be easily solved, but a revolutionary political group who wanted to gain power could get access to and control of nuclear power plants. How would we know this in advance when we began looking for experts? Perhaps the physicists and engineers we consulted would see the problem of political security and send us to the right experts on this part of the issue, but there is nothing to guarantee it. It is important to see that it would be helpful to know something about the dangers of nuclear power before we began looking for experts.

What If the Experts Disagree?

Second, we have a problem if the experts themselves disagree. Suppose the issue is what to do about the trade deficit—what causes it, how it might be reduced. Since this issue is an economic one, we would try to find out who the leading economists in the country are and consult them. As a matter of fact, the answers we would get on this issue would be particularly varied, but this issue is hardly unique. Suppose we get three different answers from three widely renowned economists: How do we decide what to believe? We can ask for reasons to support the varying points of view, but the reasons will probably be imbedded in three different broad economic theories. We might need to learn the theories even to evaluate the particular views on inflation.

Both of these problems—determining in which field an issue lies and deciding among conflicting expert opinions—are related to a third, more difficult problem. If a supposed expert states a number of views on an issue, how can we tell which of these are based on expertise and which are based on personal political or moral preferences? That is, how do we prevent technical expertise from expanding into political power?

How Can We Control the Influence of Experts?

Consider the issue of the most effective means of controlling crime. We might go to a famous criminologist who has studied carefully the variation of crime rates with different kinds of punishments, rehabilitation programs, police procedures, social conditions, and so on. But this criminologist also happens to believe that no one should ever be punished because all actions are socially caused and no one should be blamed for an act that is socially caused. Now this view about punishment is not one that is based on criminological investigation; it just reflects our "experts' " view about the way things should be. But on the basis of this political opinion, the criminologist might alter the answer he gives us about the most efficient way to control crime, because he wants to influence political opinion in a direction he would approve of. We might have the same problem with physicists and engineers generally *wanting* nuclear production, and certain economic experts wanting inflation controlled in one way rather than another because of views they hold about the desirability of, say, a free market economy. And in each case, by relying on expert opinion, we as a society might be setting experts up so that they have things the way they want them— no longer will they just be giving us factual advice and letting us decide how we want things to be.

The *National Enquirer* Syndrome

The mentality of "leaving it to the experts" has further unhappy side effects. As the areas of expert knowledge become more specialized and more technical, the gap between the theories of experts and what the common person can understand becomes wider and wider. Many people lose contact entirely with the science of the day, and yet they want to understand why things happen. In this light, we can understand the immense popularity of newspapers like the *National Enquirer.* As you go through the checkstand at the supermarket, where these tabloids are usually placed, notice the headlines. You might find that all the political assassinations in the past two decades were a result of a single conspiracy, that a recent disaster was caused by visitors from outer space, that some common substance can cure cancer, that supernatural forces caused a plane crash, and so on. The upshot of all these theories is that you can understand what happens in the world without understanding all of the complicated and technical theories of the "experts."

Although the tabloid readers have, in a sense, "left things to the experts," they have not deferred to the judgment of experts out of respect. Rather, they have *abandoned* any attempt to comprehend specialized, technical theories. In most cases, the *National Enquirer* type of explanation is either one which is very simple—such as a single conspiracy accounting for many assassinations—

or one which goes beyond science in a way that tells you, "You understand what is going on as well as anyone does, *because no one really understands.*" That is, the "explanation" is supernatural; it has to do with ESP, demonic forces, and so on.

We doubt that many theories of the *National Enquirer* type would withstand critical tests. The contrast between these theories, which are so popular, and the sophisticated theories of modern science, which have become so inaccessible, is striking evidence of the problem of the amateur in a world of specialization.

The Dilemma

The dilemma, then, is this: If we try to create our own arguments and theories without relying on experts, we will very likely be wrong. If we just leave things to the experts to figure out, thinking that we will adopt their opinions as our own, we have difficulty in knowing who the experts are, in deciding who is right when the experts disagree, and in controlling the influence of the experts on whom we rely. In addition, simply leaving things to the experts means neglecting the development of our own ideas so that we may find we fall back on explanations of the *National Enquirer* type in our understanding of the world.

If, by adopting the opinions of experts, we came to understand all that the experts understand, our dilemma would be resolved. However, when we spoke of "leaving things to the experts" we assumed that no one really has the time, energy, and intellectual ability to actually acquire more than a tiny fraction of the knowledge you would need to make expert opinions yourself. In this age of specialization it is a rare scholar who can keep up with the major developments in just one discipline such as psychology or physics. It is because of the rapid proliferation of knowledge that we run into the problems of determining who the experts are, resolving their disagreements, and so forth. We are forced to make these decisions in the absence of direct knowledge of the area in which we are seeking expert help.

How then are we to resolve this dilemma?

Two Ways of Not Facing the Dilemma

Relativism. A kind of disillusionment strikes many people as they come to realize how easily most opinions can be doubted. The fact that there is widespread disagreement, even among experts, on almost any issue of importance is unsettling. Perhaps this situation is grounds for a kind of skepticism— that is, we should be guarded in our claims to knowledge and realize how many of our beliefs are uncertain. But it is tempting to go from skepticism to a more extreme point of view: that one opinion is as good as another and it doesn't really matter what you believe. It simply doesn't follow from the fact that people disagree that no one's opinion is more reasonable. And even if we granted that all of our beliefs are uncertain, it doesn't follow that all our beliefs are equally uncertain.

Often, the kind of complete relativism to which we are objecting comes out when someone is challenged about the truth of an opinion. A common reply is that some things are "true for me," and other things are "true for you," but no one can say what is *really* true. This may be an appealing point of view as long as the discussion remains abstract. But most if not all of the particular opinions we hold have implications for how we shall act. If you are riding in a car and you are of the opinion that it is heading for a cliff, but the driver doesn't share this opinion, it is doubtful that you will be satisfied to say that it is *true for you* that the car is headed for a cliff, but it isn't *true for the driver,* and that no one can tell what is really true in this case. Leaving aside questions of absolute certainty, one opinion is probably much more reasonable to hold than the other in this case, and it obviously makes a big difference which opinion you do hold. The consequences of many opinions are less direct and less drastic. But the fact that your beliefs determine your actions should be reason enough to reject the view that it doesn't really matter what you believe.

The "True Believer." A second attitude is also commonly held in reaction to the uncertainty of most opinions. This is the attitude of the "true believer," who wants some firm doctrine to hang onto, does not find it through ordinary rational processes, and turns instead to faith. It is typical of the true believer that the doctrine picked explains anything and everything. And once accepted, the true believer is blind to any weaknesses. Whether the doctrine is Marxism, religious fundamentalism, laissez-faire capitalism, or astrology, the true believer holds it so ardently that no conceivable argument will diminish the belief. We are not claiming that a person who holds any of the beliefs just listed is irrational and is a "true believer." We are concerned about the *way* in which the true believer maintains the doctrine. Perhaps the true believer will undergo some personal change and suddenly withdraw faith in one doctrine and put it equally wholeheartedly into another, but this will not be the result of hearing a good argument.

Two tendencies, both partly the result of the difficult situation of the amateur in a world of specialization, contribute to the true-believer syndrome. One is an insecurity resulting from the very tentative nature of belief based on science. With experts disagreeing, one theory succeeding another, and most theories only partly understandable by the common person, many people feel they lack a satisfying system of beliefs. It is comforting to put your faith in a single, understandable doctrine that will explain a great many things and will tell you where you stand in the scheme of things. But the fact that such a doctrine is comforting is not evidence that it is true.

The second tendency that contributes to the true-believer syndrome is the tendency to see faith as parallel to and in competition with reason. This idea is especially attractive to the religious dogmatist who sees the uncertainty of belief, which we have been discussing, as a weakness of reason, a weakness that can be remedied by choosing faith instead. We do not maintain that faith has no justifiable role in our lives, but it is a mistake to see faith and reason as competing paths to knowledge. The true believer who sees faith as a path to knowledge is at a loss to answer one crucial question: Why have faith in one doctrine rather than another? The answer cannot be produced from within faith itself; it must be produced from within reason. Or if it isn't, it must be granted that the decision is arbitrary. It is not as though reason might choose one set of beliefs and faith another; faith does not choose.

Furthermore, the same point can be made against the true believer as was made against the relativist: Your beliefs form the basis for action, and as such you have a responsibility to choose them reasonably. Both relativism and the true-believer syndrome may be understandable reactions to the dilemma of the amateur in a world of specialization, but this does not make them justifiable reactions.

Coping with the Dilemma

The first part of the dilemma we have presented is that if you try to figure things out for yourself you will probably be mistaken. Let's explore this half of the dilemma first, to see whether some of the problems associated with such a course can be remedied.

When we spoke loosely about "figuring things out for yourself," we had in mind developing your own arguments and theories. We did not suppose you would do this in a vacuum, with no help from other people and their writings. But even with this help, the arguments and theories you would develop would very likely be inadequate compared with those of experts in the different fields.

But even if your arguments and theories are inferior to those of experts, what is wrong with developing these inadequate opinions? The main drawback is that your opinions form the basis for actions, so you want to acquire opinions with the greatest chance of being correct. But is it *necessary* for us to use the opinions we develop on our own as a basis for action? Can't we develop our own arguments and theories and maintain them tentatively, allowing them to be overridden by expert opinion when we decide that this is wise?

Developing Opinions Without Acting on Them

Consider some examples. Suppose you were to read and think about physical health and how it should be maintained. You might adopt some theories of nutrition that you read about and came to understand; you might develop some opinions about exercise, based both on the theories of others and on your own experience and experimentation. You might form some ideas concerning your own ailments: what causes them, and how they should be treated. You could do all this and yet, when it came to diagnosing a certain ailment and providing treatment for it, you *could* decide to let one of your own beliefs be overridden by that of a doctor.

Suppose you read and thought about certain questions in the field of economics. You might read magazine articles on the nation's economy, discuss economic questions with other people, take a course or two in economics at a university, and read some books in the area. You could come to understand and adopt certain theories you read or heard about, and you could develop certain variations of these theories yourself. You might acquire your own unique overview of economics, while hardly considering yourself an expert. And throughout this development of your own ideas you would probably remain ready to defer to someone whom you thought knew more about a certain issue than you did. If it came to giving investment advice or even to voting for a political candidate who held an economic ideology quite different from yours, you might put your own opinions aside in favor of an expert's.

It seems clear, then, that it is possible to develop your own opinions in any area and still refrain from acting upon them. But what would be gained from doing so? Is there a way we can fit this possibility into a strategy for coping with the dilemma that confronts us?

A Proposed Strategy

There are two things to be gained from developing your own opinions, even though you probably won't act on them. First, self-realization is important to any person. And developing your own ideas, your own understanding of the world, is an important part of self-realization. There is a satisfaction—a feeling of autonomy—in taking the task of understanding the world into your own hands. This does not mean shutting out the opinions of others, but it means actively engaging in understanding rather than being a passive receptor of opinion. In the process, you will develop your mental abilities more fully.

Secondly, you reduce the problems involved in relying on experts. This point brings us, now, to what we see as the best strategy for coping with the dilemma of leaving things to the experts or figuring them out for ourselves. The strategy is to combine both practices. This is not a complete resolution of the dilemma because it leaves problems unsolved. But it does allow for self-realization while reducing the problems that arise from leaving things to the experts.

The more understanding you have, the better chance you have of minimizing the problems involved in relying on experts. The three major problems we anticipate are determining who the experts are, deciding what to do when the experts disagree, and controlling the influence of experts. Of these, the problem of disagreement among experts is probably the most difficult to overcome by gaining a limited understanding of the area in question.

Still a Problem: The Disagreement of Experts

When experts disagree, considerations beyond the credibility of the competing opinions may give us grounds for making a choice. If one physician advises that you have an operation but a second physician advises against it, there is an obvious reason for accepting the second opinion. It may also be possible to test competing opinions by putting each into practice for a trial period. A president, for example, might try one economic policy for a certain period and then shift to another. But the results of such trials are often difficult for the amateur to assess and there is not always time to experiment. Furthermore, a disagreement among experts may be such that you would need to understand both competing theories as well as the experts themselves do in order to make a reasoned choice between them. The other two problems, however, do not seem no intractable.

Creating Arguments and Theories and Determining Who Are the Experts

One fringe benefit of creating your own arguments and theories is that in the process of gaining background knowledge upon which to base them, you can become acquainted with a large number of areas. You can begin to understand how various academic disciplines, professions, and specialized occupations deal with the different sciences and their branches. This is precisely the kind of knowledge that is crucial in the age of specialization. Furthermore, by actually developing arguments and theories, you have a better chance of seeing the many different areas of expertise that apply to this issue.

There is a broad tendency to see generals as the experts on national defense issues, doctors as the experts on medical care issues, police chiefs as the experts on crime issues, and so on. In fact, all these issues have political, economic, and technological aspects that could be addressed by experts from dozens of fields. By attempting to develop your own ideas on these issues, you have a greater chance of seeing how diverse they are.

Creating Arguments and Theories and Controlling the Experts

The point that many different areas of expertise usually apply to a single issue is an important one when it comes to determining how to control the influence of experts. This is one of the few considerations that should give amateurs confidence when considering their status in comparison to that of the experts. Very often, *no one* is an expert when it comes to seeing how the expert opinions from various fields should all be brought together to form a policy. And this is precisely the point at which the influence of experts can and should be controlled. At this point, the amateur who has tried to create arguments and theories concerning a broad issue need not defer to someone who is an expert on only one facet of the issue.

Furthermore, the relation between certain areas of expertise and their application to real world issues might be very indirect. Many academic disciplines develop abstract, technical theories and models whose relation to the real world may be poorly understood even by experts within the discipline. It is too often assumed that any behavioral psychologist can give you advice on child rearing, that an economist can help you with your investments, or even that a mathematical logician can help you evaluate an argument from a piece of informal prose.

It is important that you see as best you can the limitations of each area of supposed expertise. The experts will not be anxious to limit their own influence— they might attempt to run a bluff, hoping that the amateur will be too meek to challenge them. The more you have adopted the habit of leaving things to the experts rather than developing your own arguments and theories, the greater the chance that such a bluff will succeed.

The Strategy and Its Prospects

The strategy we have recommended for the amateur in a world of specialization is one that combines creating your own arguments and theories with selectively and cautiously relying on experts. As we have stated, we are not entirely optimistic about the outcome of this strategy. The number of problems and issues to study and the number of areas of expertise to monitor are overwhelming. Perhaps it is possible to gain back a significant degree of control over experts who affect you most directly and personally—your doctor, your mechanic. But the *social* effects that a single individual can have by carrying out this strategy are practically negligible. What must be hoped for, as specialization increases, is an increased intellectual activism on the part of a significant portion of the population.

But this point—that *one* person can't do much to guard against the dangers of relying on experts—brings into focus an aspect of our dilemma about which we have said very little so far. That is, the dilemma we have presented is *not* simply that of a *single individual* who wonders how to best attain knowledge. Neither, however, is it a matter of bringing together the knowledge of all the individuals of society. There is no repository for such an aggregation—society as a whole has no mind. If there were such a collective repository, it would be easy to combine the opinions of many experts to form a more complete and adequate body of knowledge than that which any single individual possesses. But in reality, *each* person must try to combine the opinions of experts from a position of relative ignorance. We each must to some extent *guess* which experts to trust. The problem becomes in part political, that is, power and influence become issues. How can each of us muster a picture of the world that has the best chance of accuracy, but also of not being biased in favor of the personal preferences of experts?

The Contemporary Problem of Knowledge

Through much of history, the problem of knowledge and the problem of the good society have been dealt with separately. A division of philosophy called epistemology attempts to answer the question of what knowledge is and how it can be attained. Political philosophy and social philosophy, on the other hand, deal with such problems as: How can a group of individuals combine to form a good or just society? In the modern world of specialization, the problem of how to attain knowledge becomes in part a social one.

In ancient philosophy, for example, Plato's *The Republic* stresses the connection between knowledge and the "good society." For him, true belief and knowledge could be ranked in levels depending in part on how specialized they were. A technician who assembled, for example, an electronic listening device (a "bug") would have more limited and specialized information than the electrical engineer who designed it and who could compare it with other devices having a similar function.[1] For Plato, knowledge about what might have counted as a "good" electronic listening device would not have been restricted to electrical engineering. An essential, more general question would have to be asked about whether, or in what form, such a device would exist in a good society.

Similarly, a "good computer" or a "good nuclear power plant" or a "good space station" would be ones that would exist in a good society. We are not accustomed to asking this general question about most of the objects, institutions, and policies that confront us. We don't typically move from a discussion about what is a good car (for us or for U.S. car manufacturers) to questions about whether a transportation system relying on a private auto is part of a good society. The problem, of course, with such a move is that it raises the difficult question of how to gain knowledge about the "good society."

Plato solved the dilemma by envisioning a class of super-specialists who sought knowledge about the good society. In the society Plato describes, knowledge was concentrated in a few individuals, and ruling was included among the specialized roles. In contemporary society, knowledge is at best spread among many specialists, and no one specializes in ruling—at least that is not seen as the ideal. Specialization, however, is compromised by an attempt at democracy. To put it pessimistically: For Plato, a few had knowledge and they would rule; for us, no one has very much knowledge, but everyone must try to rule.

It is doubtful that many of us would want to transform our society into the one Plato envisioned. It is difficult for us to part with the ideal of democracy, and we are justifiably suspicious of the "knowledge" of those who would rule. But to give our society the best chance of persisting, we must cope with its problems. Not the least of these is the problem of reasoning as well as we can from limited perspectives as amateurs in a world of specialization—reasoning both critically and creatively.

Questions for Reflection and Discussion

---

1. To what academic disciplines might you turn to find experts on the following questions?

a. the safety of research into genetic engineering

b. the question as to whether a person is dead when the heart stops beating

c. an estimation as to what the risk is of getting into a nuclear war by accident

d. the safety of regular use of marijuana, so far as preserving your alert mental faculties is concerned

If you have difficulty saying what qualifications a person would need to be an expert on one or more of the preceding, what does this difficulty indicate, according to Cederblom and Paulsen?

2. What is the *National Enquirer* syndrome, according to these authors? Do you think that people who read the *National Enquirer* really believe what they read there? What is the basis for your estimation? How, if at all, could you find out whether it is correct?

3. Why is relativism inadequate?

4. Why is the true-believer approach inadequate?

5. Can you see any problems in employing the strategy Cederblom and Paulsen recommend to deal with the dilemma of our dependence on experts? If so, what are they?

Note

---

1. Plato saw the "craftsman" as having only very limited skills; thus, technicians need retraining for each new project.

13

Heavy Question Arguments

Carl Cohen

"Heavy questions" smuggle many unwarranted assumptions and
implications into a debate. Compound questions, using loaded
language, and presuming unwarranted suppositions can be called heavy
questions. Some critics of DNA research, including even some very
respected scientists, have resorted repeatedly to the use of heavy
questions in public discussions of whether research into new life forms
and genetic engineering should be prohibited. Heavy questions often
have been used in conjunction with appeals to ignorance—the
implication being that because we are not sure that terrible effects will
not occur, research ought to be prohibited. Neither the use of heavy
questions nor the appeal to ignorance is a proper way to defend points
of view.

B y "heavy question arguments" I refer to a somewhat heterogeneous
class of arguments, put in ponderous interrogative form, that serves to
impede rather than to facilitate rational dialogue. As directed against
research with recombinant DNA, these heavy questions are so framed
as to be either unanswerable, yet effective in surrounding the research with the
aroma of catastrophe, or to be literally answerable, but only upon the supposition
of the truth of unfounded allegations that are never plainly stated or defended.
If arguments in this form had been proposed only by irrational persons,
motivated perhaps by ideological enthusiasm or the thirst for personal advancement, they could be dismissed summarily. In fact, the most reputable of scientific
critics of research with recombinant DNA have grounded their most fundamental
reservations on heavy questions of precisely this kind.

"Heavy Question Arguments" by Carl Cohen is an abridgment of his "The Dangers of Inquiry
and the Burden of Proof," Southern California Law Review, Vol. 54, 1081–1113 (1985).
Reprinted with the permission of the Southern California Law Review and the author.

Concrete illustrations, from leading essays on this vexed subject, are in order. Foremost among the practitioners of the heavy-question argument is Erwin Chargaff, professor emeritus of biochemistry at Columbia University. In a now famous letter to *Science,* Professor Chargaff asks:

1. If Dr. Frankenstein must go on producing his little biological monsters . . . [h]ow can we be sure what would happen once the little beasts escaped from the laboratory?

Further in the same letter he writes:

2. [T]he principal question to be answered is whether we have the right to put an additional fearful load on generations that are not yet born.

And again:

3. Is there anything more far-reaching than the creation of new forms of life?

And yet again:

4. Are we wise in getting ready to mix up what nature has kept apart, namely the genomes of eukaryotic [higher] and prokaryotic [lower] cells?

And still again:

5. Have we the right to counteract, irreversibly, the evolutionary wisdom of millions of years in order to satisfy the ambition and the curiosity of a few scientists?[1]

These are exercises in rhetorical flourish, one might say, designed to call attention to what might otherwise be ignored. Perhaps. But the suggestion that without such rhetoric there would have been no attention to ethical aspects of this research is simply false; the moral issues had been carefully addressed long before the matter had become a public sensation.[2] Whatever their original purposes, these questions are designed so that they may be asked repeatedly, with mounting evocative consequences, no matter the care with which moral concerns had been previously addressed. They are devised as argumentative weapons shielded from rational response.

Professor Chargaff is a master of the technique, but far from its only practitioner. Clifford Grobstein, professor of biology and vice-chancellor for University Relations at the University of California, San Diego, presents a series of ethical, social, and political issues about which "substantial concern has been expressed" and which "remain to be evaluated." The following are examples of Grobstein's use of the heavy question technique of argument:

6. Are there some kinds of knowledge, even though they offer health benefits, for which the price in other values is too high?

7. Is it safe, in the present state of our society, to provide means to intervene in the very essence of human individuality, even to achieve humanitarian ends?

8. Can genetic destiny, whether of human or other species, wisely be governed by human decision?

9. Will genetic engineering widen or close the existing gap between knowledge-rich and knowledge-poor cultures and nations?

10. Will [genetic engineering] provide a new club in the hands of terrorists or dictatorial regimes?

11. Will [genetic engineering] render still more turbulent the currents of national and international power conflict?[3]

Frances R. Simring, writing to *Science* as a representative of the Committee for Genetics, Friends of the Earth, applies the heavy question technique to the narrower issue of laboratory containment.

12. What scientist would claim that complete laboratory containment is possible and that accident due to human fallibility and technical failures will not inevitably occur?[4]

Liebe F. Cavalieri, professor of biochemistry at the Cornell University Graduate School of Medicine, directs his heavy question at any efforts to develop weakened strains of host bacteria that will be unable to survive outside of the laboratory. He asks:

13. [H]ow can all the possible bacterial growth conditions outside the laboratory be simulated for the test?[5]

Professor Robert L. Sinsheimer, chairman, Division of Biology at the California Institute of Technology, uses heavy questions in several differing argumentative contexts.[6] His heaviest queries appear in his essay, *Troubled Dawn for Genetic Engineering:*

14. How far will we want to develop genetic engineering?

15. Do we want to assume the basic responsibility for life on this planet—to develop new living forms for our own purposes?

16. Shall we take into our hands our own future evolution?[7]

Some two years later, at a forum conducted by the National Academy of Sciences in Washington, D.C., Professor Sinsheimer sharpened and reapplied the heavy question method of argument:

17. Does anyone imagine that the roster of carcinogens or mutagens has been completed?

18. Could their ingredients [that is, those of slow viruses] lurk in these random bits of genome we now juggle?

19. Are there really no evolutionary booby traps for unwary species?[8]

George Wald, Nobel Laureate and Higgins Professor of Biology at Harvard University, helped to fuel the politicized disputes over DNA research in the City Council of Cambridge, Massachusetts.[9] Later, at the Academy Forum in Washington,[10] Wald had some difficulty meeting the arguments of Paul Berg, Wilson Professor of Biochemistry at Stanford University Medical Center, concerning the potential benefits of increased understanding of the regulatory mechanisms of animal genes. Wald responded with a heavy question:

20. I think the central problem before use in this direction is how many normal, healthy persons to put at risk in order to achieve the possibility, not at all clear, of eventually proceeding to cures.[11]

The absence of real answers—answers that, as the questioners themselves sometimes admit, are impossible or nearly impossible to give—encourages heavy questions at the metalevel. Why don't they answer our questions? Might not the answers be fearsome? Jonathan King, assistant professor of biology at the Massachusetts Institute of Technology, provides an example of this escalation:

21. Now I ask you, what is going to happen if by some chance, by some small chance, the Walds, and the Hubbards [Ruth Hubbard, professor of biology at Harvard University], and the Cargaffs, and the Cavalieris are right; the experiment is done, and we get the answer—a disaster. Where will we be?[12]

The list of illustrations need not be extended. What I shall say about this pattern of argument will refer exclusively to its use by major critics of recombinant DNA research, those cited previously who all bear fine scientific reputations. It is important to realize, however, that after persons of high repute have indulged publicly in this mode of discourse, an excited bandwagon quickly forms. The argument is taken up by serious, but much less knowledgeable persons. It is they—some representatives of public interest groups,[13] some journalists,[14] and some political figures[15]—who are most effective in reaching large audiences. When it is also widely held that the issues of restriction or continuation of such research should be decided in the political forum, by an informed public, the instruments of public information come to be of crucial importance.[16] With the example of Professors Chargaff, Sinsheimer, and others before them, some political persons find the temptation of the heavy question too strong to resist.

Arguments by heavy question are disturbing. The instances cited herein are at different levels of sophistication, obviously; but they are registered seriously, with practical argumentative purpose, by able scientists whose leads have been widely followed. I emphasize that heavy questions are not peripheral to the scientists' positions, or merely incidental to them. To the contrary, such questions serve as the pillars upon which the attack has rested. Coming from reputable scholars, the questions have been quoted and requoted as putative profound critiques of recombinant DNA research. Both the forms of these arguments and their substance, therefore, must be carefully examined.

Questions—and heavy questions very clearly—*do not assert anything*. This is an obvious but fundamental point. Whatever may be suggested by a question, or implied by the terms used in it, or inferred by the hearer from the attitude of the person doing the asking, the interrogative does not express any proposition whatever. It cannot, therefore, be true or false. Precisely for this reason, the questioner need not accept any responsibility for any claims that the question may suggest. If, in reply to the questioner, one points out that some suggestion implicit in the question is mistaken, the questioner may always, and sometimes honestly, reply, "But I never asserted that!" Quite so. The questioner asserts nothing; the utterance, therefore, cannot serve even as the premise of an argument.

Some of these interrogatives are textbook examples of the common fallacy of the compound question.[17] What color is the president's beard? Interrogatives may be so framed—or loaded—as to permit response only upon the assumption of the truth of some related claims that are implied but are not asserted.[18] It is difficult to grapple with some of these because the related propositions whose truth they assume are not always easy to formulate. When they can be formulated, they turn out to be either (1) very probably false, (2) quite uncertain and highly debatable, or (3) entirely unverifiable. Such related propositions are often mixed, by this interrogative form, with matters that are capable of rational disposition. The resultant brew is pungent.

Look more closely at some of the preceding illustrations. Before answering whether "we have the right to put an additional fearful load on generations that are not yet born,"[19] one is obliged to assume both that the inquiry in view will put a "load" on future generations and that it will be a "fearful" one. In the sense that every acquisition of knowledge leaves its inheritors with the task of deciding how it is to be used, all science puts a load on future generations— although we may find the noun "load" to be loaded in the context. Whether, in this case, the "load" will be "fearful" is, in fact, precisely what is at issue—but assumed in a question whose covering suggestion, wholly unsupported, is that some people are doing what they have no *right* to do. How is one to deal with such an argument? To reject one or more of the implicit assumptions, one cannot simply respond to the questioner, who did not assert them, but must address some apparently neutral third party. And even to formulate that rejection appears to give substance to the insinuations without their ever having been defended or even straightforwardly advanced.

Consider the logical difficulties in responding to the question, "Have we the right to counteract, irreversibly, the evolutionary wisdom of millions of years, in order to satisfy the ambition and curiosity of a few scientists?"[20]

Just to take the question apart requires much effort and more space than the answerer is normally given. Irreversibility of results is an important and an interesting matter. Defending some research we might wish to deny that it has irreversible effects. Or we might agree that its effects are indeed irreversible, but only in the same sense that the effects of any important experiments are irreversible. Experiments with many drugs on humans are not reversible; neither are experiments with a nuclear reactor. What is objected to as "irreversible" may in fact be troubling to the critic not because it is that, but because the effects have, the critic believes, an unmanageable scope. The question obliges the assumption by responder both that evolution over millions of years has been "profoundly wise," and that the research in question will "counteract" it. These are doubtful propositions, to say the least. In response to the first of these assumptions, a leading microbiologist and DNA researcher, Stanley Cohen, professor of medicine at Stanford University, replies for much of the scientific community:

> I would like to point out that this so-called evolutionary "wisdom" has given us bubonic plague, and smallpox, and yellow fever, and typhoid, and diabetes, and cancer. The search for and the use of virtually all biological and medical knowledge represents a continual and intentional assault on what Dr. Chargaff considers to be evolutionary wisdom. Most post-Darwin biologists believe that there is no wisdom in evolution, only chance occurrences. Do we really desire to glorify chance evolutionary occurrences as "wisdom" and to accept without protest or countervening action the diseases and plagues that such "wisdom" has bestowed on mankind? I would suspect that most of us are not prepared to simply endure whatever nature may have in store. Thus science continues to search for new ways to influence the "wisdom" of evolution.[21]

Such responses are bypassed, however, foreclosed by the suggestions implicit in the Chargaff question, whose ostensible thrust is that terrible things are being done "in order to satisfy the ambition and the curiosity of a few scientists."[22] There is no doubt that the results sought in this sphere wold satisfy the ambition and curiosity of some scientists. All this criticism simply obscures what is at issue here, however, because these motivations, even if their role could be ascertained, might only help to account for the personal efforts expended— while the matter before us is the justifiability of the research itself, or its restriction. That is a subject entirely separate from the motivation of those who may pursue it.

It is at best awkward to sort all this out before getting to the question—which was what? It was about rights! "Do we have the right to . . . "[23] Answering that question supposes a framework of moral theory not even hinted at by the questioner. Were such a framework put forward in response, it is doubtful that it wold be accepted. The point of the question, I submit, is not to inquire about rights, but in seeming to do so, to insert a set of allegations about the imagined consequences of the research and the character of the researchers—so folded into one another that the answerer must drown in words while extricating himself. If the effort to extricate is made, it is almost certain to go unheard in the circles for which the impact of the question was intended. Anyway, the rejoinder is easy: Repeat the question in a different but similar form.

Some of these compound questions have the effect of attaching certain descriptive predicates to recombinant DNA research in the hearer's mind, without the questioner having to take responsibility for asserting their applicability. For example, Grobstein has asked, "Will [genetic engineering] provide a new club in the hands of terrorists or dictatorial regimes?"[24] How to respond? No one can deny that any new, powerful instrument may someday be used by bad people. Because terrorists and dictators need instruments that pose immediate threat of pain or disaster, the vast array of clubs already at hand seem more suitable to their purpose than any uses—even far-fetched uses—of recombined DNA. But the association has been made; our imaginations have been set to work; no answer can erase the smirch.

Consider the impact on the audience of the following heavy questions: "Does anyone imagine that the roster of carcinogens or mutagens has been completed?"[25] "Could their ingredients [that is, those of slow viruses] lurk in these random bits of genome we now juggle?"[26] Zap! Pow! No matter what responses are calmly given or what the evaluation of these responses is in the light of fullest knowledge, the damage has been done: "carcinogens," "mutagens," "lurk," "juggle." The very process of replying to such questions, or even of trying to reframe them so as to be able to reply fairly, obliges the researcher to crawl into the net thrown.

Again, when the mayor of Cambridge (Massachusetts) brings to the legislative process a discussion of things "crawling out of the laboratories into the sewers,"[27] that is not different in tone from the query of a distinguished professor of biochemistry who asks, "If Dr. Frankenstein must go on producing his little biological monsters . . . [h]ow can we be sure what would happen once the little beasts escaped from the laboratory?"[28] The only appropriate response to questions emotionally loaded in this way is the exhibition of their character.

Some of the questions are purely rhetorical, of course: their answers being either perfectly obvious or totally inaccessible. One professor asks what happens if the outcome of some experiment is disaster?[29] "Where will we be?"[30] in a disastrous situation, clearly. "Is there anything more far-reaching than the creation of new forms of life?"[31] Who can say? The destruction of all or much life might prove much more far-reaching. But rational responses are not really sought by such questions. Although in the form of questions, these utterances function in discourse more like expletives or intensifiers. Because we respect the authors' honest feelings of concern, and may share them, we are tempted to nod our heads to the question—acquiescing inadvertently to the suggestions embedded within them.

In the debate over DNA research, two sides are in deep disagreement. One side, the researchers, would move ahead with inquiries using recombinant DNA; the other side, their critics, raises heavy questions with which they hope to stop, delay, or otherwise restrict such inquiries. We need to determine whether the burden of proof, with respect to the matters raised in these questions, rests on the researchers or on their critics. We need to decide whether there should be freedom to advance until restriction has been justified or restraint in advancement until freedom has been justified.

It is true, of course, that there is a world of knowledge about genetic molecules, their role in evolution and the effects of their recombination, that we do not have. Many very awful things are logically *possible*. We do not know, and probably will not ever be certain, that these awful outcomes cannot transpire. When Sinsheimer asks whether the ingredients of slow viruses *could* "lurk in these random bits of genome we now juggle," the only rational answer is yes. When Chargaff asks, "How can we be sure what would happen once the little beasts escaped form the laboratory?," the only rational answer is that we cannot be sure—either that they are beasts, or that they will escape, or what would happen were those events to transpire. But nothing of consequence for the argument may properly be inferred from such ignorance. The future events we cannot be sure about are literally numberless. No argument against advancing on some line of scientific inquiry can be rationally grounded on the sheer possibility of misadventure. It is a truism that possible misadventures "lurk" in every sphere, even in the business of everyday life and certainly in the conduct of political affairs. If heavy questions like these must be answered before the inquiry is allowed to proceed, then advance on virtually every research frontier, in chemistry, physics, and biology, not to mention every bold political venture, is subject to the same blockage. Some inquiries, now critical in climatology, in high-energy physics, and elsewhere, are far more vulnerable to such gloomy speculations than those in microbiology. Possible dangers are certainly worth thinking about—but the sheer possibility of them cannot be taken as a serious argument for restriction.

"But," the critic replies, "the dangers upon which I speculate are more than sheer possibilities. There is some probability that they will be realized if this research goes forward. My heavy questions oblige you to consider the substantial weight of these factors before proceeding."

This objection is only superficially reasonable. It is, in fact, virtually impossible to weight the "danger factors" suggested in these heavy questions. Any such weighing would presuppose both (1) some moderately specific description of the catastrophic eventuality envisaged, *and* (2) some reasonable estimate of the probability of that outcome. In any calculation of the advantages and disadvantages of following or not following some line of conduct, it is the product of a given result multiplied by the likelihood of that result that is required. Logically conceivable outcomes for which no such product can be rationally estimated cannot be serious considerations in appraising conduct. Most of the outcomes intimated in the heavy questions of the critics cannot be described at all. Some are not even identified but are left for the imagination to conjure up. Not one of the "danger factors" alluded to approaches the degree of specificity that would be required to estimate in the roughest way—much less calculate—its probability on present evidence. The thoroughly amorphous quality of the dangers suggested disqualifies them as serious "probabilities" to be weighed.

For those imagined outcomes having some very vague description, the task of estimating the likelihood of their occurrence remains. Consider Grobstein's question, "Are there some kinds of knowledge, even though they offer health benefits, for which the price in other values is too high?" How can one answer such a question? What are the prices paid in values? How are they estimated or compared? Is this a calculation we are seriously expected to undertake? Perhaps the questioner may respond as follows, "Well, it *is* a hard question. But that's the point. We don't know. We cannot even guess what the price of knowledge in this sphere will be. Ought not we try to find out?'' No one will object to that exhortation. Any guidance we can get on the prices of knowledge, in whatever currency we can identify, will help us to decide whether we are prepared to pay for that knowledge.

Unanswerable questions cannot prove points. Professor Cavalieri, after asking how "all the possible growth conditions outside the laboratory can be simulated'' for the development of new bacterial strains, and after speculating upon eventualities he himself calls "far-fetched,'' undoes his own argument with his own clincher, "There are no objective answers to these questions." Just so. That is why asking them has no probative force in support of restriction.

"But,'' the critics may rejoin, "you fail to appreciate the magnitude of the disasters we are asking about. It's true we can't describe them. We can just imagine them—great plagues, or blights, or the like. It's true also that we haven't any sound estimate of their likelihood. But suppose the likelihood is small—even very, very small. Won't you agree that the product of a catastrophe of enormous dimensions, multiplied even by a very small probability fraction, yields a significant danger factor? And doesn't that serve as a proper consideration in deciding whether to go ahead now?''

Some arguments of this kind, I submit, underlie many of the almost inchoate questions that have been put before us. It embodies two serious mistakes. First, the application of a probability calculus to such states of affairs is spurious. We may talk as though the event in question has a certain probability, although it is very small. In fact, we do not have any real event in mind, and we do not have any serious estimate of its likelihood, even that it is infinitesimal. The whole enterprise is one of wildest conjecture. It is, as mentioned previously, a variety of conjecture that can go on with respect to almost any form of human activity. The more vivid our imagination and the more cautious our souls, the less likely we will be to undertake any inquiry or any enterprise of any kind that could, with any degree of probability, yield the outcomes imagined. This game of frightening speculation can be played with respect to far-fetched outcomes of not acting, as well as of acting. As easily as we can dream up catastrophes flowing from the malevolent future uses of recombinant DNA technology, we can imagine scenarios in which changes in our natural environment will require, for the very survival of the human species, a capacity to control genetic codes that is just now becoming possible. Extinction, or other disaster, *could* be the result of failing to develop that control. Science fiction can be written in many ways.

Arguments from ignorance really must, in this case, be turned back upon their proponents. The critic asks whether there may be some very small probability of some very great disaster flowing from recombinant DNA research; the researcher is as fully entitled to ask whether there may be some very small probability of some very great and wonderful boon for human kind flowing from that research. Might we soon eliminate all genetic diseases and malfunctions? Might we greatly increase, perhaps double, the length of productive life for all humans? Might we learn how wisely to stabilize the population of the globe, and through the mastery of genetic codes to eliminate hunger forever? Might we learn how to open new realms of human consciousness? It would be irresponsible to argue that the hope of accomplishing these ends in the foreseeable future through the recombination of DNA and allied research *justifies* anything. It is fair to say, however, that because some of these outcomes may in fact become actual research objectives, the likelihood of their occurrence may be as great or greater than that of imagined superdisasters. If the game of multiplying conjectured states of affairs by wholly conjectural quantities is taken as a serious enterprise on the one side, it can be taken as seriously on the other. Against some unspecified but profound evolutionary disruption multiplied by its conjectured probability, let us put on the scales the elimination of all cancers and genetic diseases, multiplied by its conjectured probability. Both parties may find some satisfaction in the manufacture of descriptions and numbers. Neither, surely, will have proved anything.

But if such speculations can be taken seriously, one is probably better advised to stake bets on the imaginative researchers than on the imaginative critics, not because the researchers' powers of clairvoyance are stronger, but because they have the advantage of being able to say, with some degree of concreteness, where they intend to go, and to push when pushing is possible, in that direction. The researchers at least have good reasons to want to reach their envisaged destinations.

Both sides in these disputes are pained by their ignorance; indeed, dismayed by it. It is precisely ignorance that we seek to overcome. Professor Sinsheimer expresses this dismay most poignantly:

> Can we predict the consequences? Except in the most general terms we are ignorant of the broad principles of evolution, of the factors that govern its rate and directions. We have no general theorems to account for the spectrum of organisms that we see and the gaps in between . . . We simply do not know.
>
> We are ignorant of the relative importance of the various factors we currently perceive to participate in the evolutionary process . . .
>
> We are ignorant of any absolute measure of adaptation. We are ignorant of the depth of security of our own environmental niche . . . We do not know.

All profoundly true. But the inferences from such ignorance must be carefully drawn. If the resultant admonition is simply to be cautious, as Sinsheimer appears to conclude in some contexts, no one will decry his wisdom. If sharp restriction upon inquiry is admonished, the argument is very different indeed. Premises that may support caution will not support anything close to prohibition.

Heavy questions seem persuasive because they play on our ignorance. But ignorance of the kind they rely on does not shift to any legitimate scientist the burden of proving inquiries danger-free. Presenting the indeterminable possibility of some barely describable outcomes of some research cannot serve as an argument for restricting or prohibiting that research.

Questions for Reflection and Discussion

1. What makes "Is there anything more far-reaching than the creation of new forms of life?" a heavy question?

2. Think of heavy questions that might be used in public debates on the following issues:
a. whether capital punishment serves to deter murder
b. whether there should be state-supported dental services for schoolchildren
c. whether all college students should be required to take and pass at least one course in computer science

3. If you were in a debate and a heavy question were used against you by someone else, what would be an efficient and effective way to respond?

4. How does Cohen argue that arguments from ignorance can be turned back on their proponents"?

5. Is it possible, even assuming that everything Cohen says in this essay is correct, that there are other good reasons for restricting DNA research? Why or why not? If you think that there are such reasons, state them.

Notes

1. Erwin Chargaff, "Letter to the Editor," reprint in *Science* 192 (1976):938–940.

2. See, for example, Report of the Working Party on the Experimental Manipulation of the Genetic Composition of Micro-Organisms, cmnd. no. 5880, 3 (1975). Presented to Parliament by the secretary of state for education and science. This document is widely known as the Ashby report, after Chairman of the Working Party, Lord Eric Ashby.

3. Clifford Grobstein, "Recombinant DNA Research: Beyond the NIH Guidelines," *Science* 194 (1976):1134.

4. Francine Simring, "Letter to the Editor," reprint in *Science* 192 (1976):940.

5. Liebe Cavalieri, "New Strains of Life—or Death," *New York Times Magazine* (22 August 1976):8, 67.

6. Research on the aging process, on techniques to determine the sex of children before birth, on isotope separation, and on efforts to contact extraterrestrial intelligences are also the targets of Professor Sinsheimer's heavy questions. See Robert Sinsheimer, "Inquiring into Inquiry: Two Opposing Views," *Hastings Center Report* (August 1976):18.

7. Sinsheimer, "Troubled Dawn for Genetic Engineering," *New Scientist* 168 (1975):148, 150.

8. Sinsheimer, "Potential Risks," *National Academy of Sciences, Research with Recombinant DNA* (1977); 74–76. An Academy forum funded by the National Institutes of Health.

9. See June Goodfield, *Playing God* (New York: Random House, 1977), 187.

10. The three-day forum, March 7–9, 1977, was sponsored by the National Academy of Sciences. Participants discussed the future of research with recombinant DNA

11. *Research with Recombinant DNA,* 82–83. Wald's discussion of Sinsheimer, "Potential Risks," 74. Questions such as the one propounded by Wald incorrectly assume that the burden of proof on the dangers of this research lies with the researchers.

12. *Research with Recombinant DNA,* 40. King's discussion of Callahan, "The Involvement of the Public," 31.

13. Jeremy Rifkin, a representative of the People's Business Commission, presented the following variants of the heavy question, arguing fervidly at the opening sssion of the National Academy of Sciences Forum (March 1977):20–21.

> How many scientists and corporate executives from the pharmaceutical companies in this room believe that they have a moral right and an authority to proceed on this experimental path before the American people, all 200 million, and are fully informed about all, good and bad, of the long-range implications of this research? . . . What do you think the American public would say if they heard Abbott, Upjohn, Pfizer, Hoffmann-LaRoche, Lilly, say to the American public, we companies have a right to patent new forms of life? . . . What does that [the patent on a new form of life] mean twenty years from now?

Rifkin's discussion of Hamburg, "Priorities for Day I," 17–18.

14. Caryl Rivers, an associate professor at the School of Public Communication at Boston University, in an article in a national magazine, confuses recombinant DNA techniques with a wholly different process of cell fusion. She compounds new and heavier questions: "What if some 'genetic stew' escaped—could it turn into a 'Doomsday Bug'?" Caryl Rivers, "Genetic Engineers—Now That They Have Gone Too Far, Can They Stop?" *Ms.* (June 1976):116. The title of the piece itself involves the heavy question technique.

15. The introduction of heavy questions into the legislative process was inevitable. It would be unfair to condemn the Mayor of Cambridge, Massachusetts, Alfred E. Vellucci, for translating the words and spirit of his more sophisticated mentors into terms the members of his city council could react to viscerally. "I want to know about these things that may come crawling out of the laboratories into the sewers . . . " See Goodfield, *Playing God,* 187.

16. The Democratic Party of Washtenaw County, Michigan (home of the University of Michigan), in plenary session, February 1978, faced the following resolution:

> Whereas the debate in the scientific community concerning the hazards of recombinant DNA research continues,
>   Whereas some biologists of the highest standing in their profession believe that a public health or environment catastrophe might result from recombinant DNA research,
>   Whereas no one has given a rigorous demonstration that the risks are small,
>   Whereas the people of the world have not given their "informed consent" to recombinant DNA experiments which risk their health,
>   Be it resolved that recombinant DNA research be prohibited and that this prohibition be rescinded only if the people of the world freely and democratically give their consent to recombinant DNA research. *Ann Arbor News* (20 February 1978):sect. A, 10.

17. See Monroe Beardsley, *Practical Logic* (Englewood Cliffs, N.J.: Prentice-Hall, 1950), 525–526; Irving Copi, *Introduction to Logic,* 5th ed., (New York: Macmillan, 1978), 98–100.

18. "Genetic Engineers—Now That They've Gone Too Far, Can They Stop?" and "Is Harvard the Proper Place for Frankenstein Tinkering?" are crude examples of this form of heavy question as used in the mass media. The same compound structure is manifest in some more subtle efforts.

19. *Ibid.*

20. *Ibid.*

21. *Research with Recombinant DNA.* See Cohen's discussion of Chargaff's "Potential Risks" and Nathan's "Potential Benefits."

22. Chargaff, "Letter to the Editor."

23. *Ibid.*

24. Grobstein, "Recombinant DNA Research."

25. Sinsheimer, "Potential Risks."

26. *Ibid.*

27. See note 15.

28. Chargaff, "Letter to the Editor."

29. *Research with Recombinant DNA,* 40. King's discussion of Callahan, "The Involvement of the Public," 31.

30. *Ibid.*

31. Chargaff, "Letter to the Editor."

14

Poll-ution: Coping with Surveys and Polls*

Ralph Johnson

Polls are often reported and are increasingly significant in political life. We need to know how to assess reports of polls. Crucial information such as the nature of the sample and the precise question asked is often not reported. No matter how accurate sampling techniques are, a poll cannot provide valuable information if its question is misleading or loaded. The use of polls has certain dangers for democratic politics: Governments may time and exploit polls for their own purposes; politicians may resort to relatively uninformed opinion instead of working out their own substantive views, as representative democracy requires. In some circumstances polls may even help to create the phenomena they purport to describe.

P olls have become an increasingly prominent feature in the political and social lives of North Americans. It is difficult to open a daily newspaper without seeing a poll about which candidate is leading in the next election or a survey of how people feel about restrictions on pornography or about the death penalty. Unless average citizens know how to process the "information" contained in these reports, then they are ill-prepared to confront surveys and polls in a critical way. It would be ideal if everyone had some form of training in both the quantitative and qualitative aspects of survey research. But until then, individuals need guidelines for dealing with polls or surveys.

The guidelines I propose require no knowledge of statistics or probability theory but only the capacity to ask intelligent questions in nontechnical language. As always, the difficulty is in deciding which question is relevant in a given instance. The term "poll-ution" is not meant to denigrate the practice of sampling or polling, but rather it is meant to call attention to some real and potential abuses of polling and sampling and to the lamentable state of news reports of polls.

---

*Used with permission of Ralph H. Johnson.

The Basic Concepts

The following is a quick introduction to the vocabulary we will use. Some of it is no doubt already familiar. A *sample* is drawn from a *population* (or collection of things) and is *tested* for a specified property (sometimes referred to as the *target property*). The results are then *projected back* onto the population.

To take the simplest sort of example, suppose that you were making soup and you wondered whether or not you had put enough thyme in it. You probably first would stir the batch of soup well (the batch is the population) and test a portion that has been well-mixed and hence is a good indicator of the whole batch. In doing this, you would be acknowledging the fundamental principle of sampling, which we will discuss shortly. Next you would select a spoonful of it (the sample), test it (by tasting it) and—based on your perception—project that property back into the population: "There should be more thyme," you might say.

When you stirred the soup, it was to make as sure as you could that your sample was typical of the whole batch. The key feature in construction of a sample is that it be *representative*. However, notice that even if your sample is a good one, it will be of little use unless you get accurate information from it. Thus if you had a cold and could not taste, then no matter how well you had stirred your sample, the information gained from it would not be reliable. It is fair to say that most of the problems in survey research and polling come more from the difficulties in eliciting accurate information from the sample than from problems in its construction. The technical part of survey research (drawing the sample) is fairly routine; designing the input—the questions and how to ask them—is not. An article in (Toronto) *The Globe and Mail* titled "The Delicate Art of Polling the Public" states, "Writing and arranging the questions is the art of the public-opinion pollster; drawing the sample to survey is the science, the science of random selection."[1]

Suppose that information was desired about how people are going to vote in an upcoming federal election in Canada. A polling organization might construct a sample of about 1800 individuals, who will then be contacted (either in person or by telephone) and asked a series of questions; the results will be tabulated and an extrapolation made projecting those results onto the entire voting population. When the sample is representative and when the input into the sample is unbiased, then the projection will have a high, specifically-assignable, degree of probability.

However, in sampling, it must be remembered that we are dealing with probabilities. It is always possible that the sample may be properly designed, the questions may be phrased appropriately, and yet the true result may be different than the projection. If there are 100 socks in the drawer and ninety-nine are red and one is blue, your chances of picking a red sock are very high—99 percent; but there is only a slight chance that you will pick the blue sock—1 percent. Hence no matter how well the pollster does the job, there is always the chance of going wrong in the projection.

Reports of Polls

With this rudimentary introduction to vocabulary and the practice of polling, we ask what information does the average person need to interpret news reports of polls intelligently and to avoid being misinformed or misled by them?

Our original question has undergone a slight reformulation as it is now phrased in terms of *reports* of polls. The reason is that most of us have access to public opinion polls only through newspaper reports. Very few of us will ever see the research itself; and fewer still would understand it.

In my experience, newspapers by and large do not do a satisfactory job of reporting polls. The standards I am applying are those that the American Association of Public Opinion Research established at its 1967 conference as the minimum amount of information that should be presented in a newspaper account. Eight essential points were enumerated as requirements:

1. who sponsored the survey

2. the exact wording of the question asked

3. a definition of the population actually sampled

4. the sample size (for mail surveys, include both the number of question-naires mailed out and the number returned)

5. an indication of what allowance should be made for sampling error

6. which results are based on part of the sample rather than the total sample

7. whether interviewing was done personally, by mail, or on street corners

8. the timing of the interviewing in relation to the events

The Association went on to say:

> We strongly urge the news media to ask for and include ALL the above information when preparing final copy for publication or broadcast.[2]

In other words, these knowledgeable people are telling us that deprived of such information we are not going to be in much of a position to judge the poll. My experience (a sample, of course) suggests that very few newspapers comply with these guidelines. They frequently omit crucial information such as the margin of error or the wording of the question.

By way of an example, examine this news article taken from a recent issue of *The Windsor (Ontario) Star:*

> MONTREAL (CP)—Support for the federal Liberals among decided voters has increased by six percentage points to 45 percent, the party's best showing since the 1984 election, a new Gallup poll indicates.

Conducted Dec. 3–6, just after the Liberal national convention that reaffirmed John Turner's leadership, the poll says support for the governing Progressive Conservatives has dropped by one point to 30 percent since the previous Gallup survey Nov. 6–8.

The New Democratic Party has dropped four points to 25 percent. The level of undecided voters dipped to 25 percent from 29.

Clara Hatton, Gallup's research director, said the rise in Liberal popularity is partly due to the party's convention, in which 76.3 percent of delegates gave Turner a vote of confidence.

The survey's Quebec results contradict a Dec. 3–7 poll, conducted by Angus Reid Associates, which said NDP support in the province has risen to 32 percent.

Gallup indicated only about 16 percent of decided Quebecers support the NDP.

The Liberals are favored by slightly more than half of decided Quebec voters, with about a third backing the Conservatives.

Notice the gap between what was reported and what should have been reported.

To explain further these prerequisites for the intelligent reading of a poll, let me present that information under two headings: the design of the sample and the input into the sample.

The Design of the Sample

How samples are designed (or "drawn") is dictated by the theory of probability. We cannot go into the labyrinth of probability theory here, but the following are some pointers to keep in mind.

Sample Size

About sample size: Intuitions (if yours are like most people's) will conflict. On the one hand, you probably think that the bigger the sample is, the more likely it is to mirror or represent the population it is drawn from and the less likely the chance that eccentricities will be overrepresented. On the other hand, you probably also believe that the larger the population of interest, the larger our sample must be. Intuition tells us that the relationship between population and sample size is *linear.* It is important to understand why that intuition is incorrect.

Firstly, let's return to our soup, still simmering on the stove. Assume that two batches are in different size cauldrons: One pot is a five-gallon pot and the other holds one quart. Do you need to take a bigger spoonful of the bigger batch? Would you? Probably not. You are likely to use the same spoon and the same size sample for the bigger as for the smaller pot. Even though the pots are of different sizes, a spoonful of soup taken from a properly stirred pot could well provide an accurate sample in both instances.

The second way to defuse that intuition requires a bit of background information. In Canada, a sample for a federal election would typically consist of about 1800 people. The voting population of the United States is about ten times that of Canada. If you follow your intuition, you would reason that a similar sample for the United States should be 18,000 people (that is, ten times the size of the Canadian sample). However, a Gallup poll taken in the United States to test voters' preferences in national elections would typically constitute 1800—about the same sample size as is found in Canada.

Obtaining Representative Samples

Various ways exist of trying to make sure that a sample is representative. Ideally, we would take a *random* sample. But when you understand what the term "random" means here, you will see that in connection with large populations (where this technique is most useful) the process of randomizing would be too costly. A sample is random only if every member of the population has an equal possibility of being chosen for the sample. To randomize the voting population, some way of assigning a number to all eligible voters would have to be found. Randomizing telephone numbers comes pretty close, though we thereby exclude that 7 percent of the population without telephones, a small enough risk to be acceptable to most polling organizations for most purposes.[3]

Still, randomizing is expensive, thus alternative techniques have been developed. I mention a few without trying to explain how they are carried out: cluster sampling, interval sampling, stratified, stratified random. Unless you enjoy the technicalities of sampling, knowing which process was used is not much help in deciding whether or not the sample is representative.

The point about cost warrants amplification. Surveys and polls cost. Someone has to pay. It might be the politician who commissions a poll; it might be a government department that wants reaction to a policy; sometimes the polling organization does the survey itself for public relations. You could always get better and better samples by increasing size, but only by increasing the cost. So sample design must balance size, cost, degree of accuracy, depth of penetration, and so on.

Occasionally, by paying careful attention to the description of the sample, you will be able to judge that the sample is flawed by being not representative. Consider the following excerpt from an article titled "Govt. Cuts Threatened B.C. Universities, Says Public in a Faculty-Sponsored Poll." It appeared in the *CAUT Bulletin,* November 1985:

> University administrators and faculty at British Columbia's universities are cautiously optimistic about the results of a recent public opinion poll that indicates there is a wider scale of support for universities among Lower Mainland residents than was originally thought.
>
> The survey conducted in August clearly showed that attitudes were strongly favorable toward universities, regardless of people's educational background or work.

Only 33% of the 506 respondents had university educations, another 10.5% had completed technical school, and another 9.5% had finished college. Some 45.5% had finished high school.

Comment: Unless these figures replicate the distribution of the levels of education in the entire lower mainland population, then the sample is unrepresentative.

62% of those polled were employed. Of those who were employed, 47% held blue-collar jobs, 35% held white-collar jobs, and a further 11.3% were homemakers or students.

Comment: If only 62 percent were employed, then 38 percent would be unemployed? That figure seems much higher than you would expect for that area. If so, then the poll overrepresents the unemployed.

57% of the respondents were female and 42.5% were male.

Comment: Aside from wondering about the sexual identity of the one-half percent unaccounted for, there is reason to suspect that this sample overrepresents females, unless they comprise 57 percent of the population of that area.

On the issue of government funding, 40% of the respondents "strongly agreed" with the statement "some have said that the quality of education is being threatened as a result of the present government cutbacks," 27% said they "somewhat agreed" with the statement, and 32% disagreed.

Comment: Later we will return to this report to note what has not been said and also to reflect on the adequacy of the input into the sample. For the present, note that sufficient evidence exists of unrepresentativeness for us to withhold confidence in the poll and not draw any firm conclusion from it.

Two kinds of surveys often turn up in news reports and are inherently unreliable in their representativeness.

The "Man on the Street." Surveys of "the man on the street" are not representative samples. No matter where the sample is taken it will represent too many of one group and not enough of another. Suppose you go to a major intersection of your downtown at, say, 11:30 A.M. on a weekday and ask people "at random" who they think should be the next Prime Minister. If you do this during the school year, you are going to underrepresent people involved in schooling at all levels (they are in school), factory workers (they are in the factory) white-collar workers (they are in their offices), and farmers (they are on the farm), and so on. Just plunking yourself down in some location and questioning people who wander by is not a random procedure and will not produce a representative sample. Remember that a sample has to be constructed, produced, and drawn—not left to chance.

The Self-Selecting Sample. When your elected representative sends out a questionnaire and you respond, no doubt you are providing important feedback. Keep in mind that the sample that results, though often large, is not representative because the individuals select themselves for inclusion. Those who have strong opinions are likely to respond, and those who are only moderately interested in the issues may not.

Margin of Error and Confidence Factor

Suppose that the sample you are reading seems representative. There are other things to look for: *margin of error* and (related) *confidence factor.* Every sample carries with it a margin of error (sampling error) and a degree of confidence (confidence level). These are determined by the size of the sample. In political polls conducted in Canada, a polling organization will typically draw a sample of about 1800 that will yield a margin of error of +/− 3 percent at a 95-percent confidence level. This information is extremely important to you as a consumer, provided you know what it means.

A margin of error is necessary because we are dealing with probabilities. When, for example, a survey reports that 50 percent of those sampled would vote for one party, the inference is then drawn that this same result could be obtained in the entire population. But that inference will be qualified by a margin of error of, say, 3 percent, which means that the result achieved by actually contacting the entire population would fall within three percentage points either way of the predicted value. The result could be low as 47 percent or as high as 53 percent.

The 95 percent confidence factor means that nineteen times out of twenty, the actual results will be as predicted—that is, they will fall within the range indicated by the margin of error. But there is always the possibility—one in twenty, or 5 percent—that the actual result will fall outside the predicted range— not because of human error but rather because of the nature of probabilistic inference.

We can illustrate the importance of having this information by using a simple, hypothetical example. Suppose that in a local election, a survey reported the following:

Candidate A: 36%
Candidate B: 34%

Although some people might be tempted to infer that A was leading, in fact the 2 percent difference would be swallowed up if the margin of error were 3 percent or more—a likely situation. A reputable polling organization (like Gallup) would say, "The result is too close to call." But many newspapers are not so scrupulous and might say, "A still ahead by a nose!"

Consider again the survey about attitudes toward funding of higher education in British Columbia. The information given was as follows:

Strongly Agreed   40%
Somewhat Agreed   27%
Disagreed   32%

Firstly, we were not given any margin of error of confidence level. Hence we have been deprived of crucial information. But suppose that the margin of error were 4 percent. Then the "strongly agreed" could be anywhere in the 36–44 percent range, the "somewhat agreed" anywhere in the 23–31 percent range, and the "disagreed" anywhere from 28–36 percent. Thus, it is conceivable that as many disagreed as strongly agreed and the total of those in the disagreed and somewhat agreed could be 67 percent. In other words, it might be that only one out of every three persons strongly agrees with the statement they were asked to respond to. Put in this context, the information creates quite a different impression.[4]

The moral is that it is important to have the information necessary to interpret a poll properly. Since all reputable polling organizations provide such information as a matter of course, if that information is not included in the news report, it is most likely the fault of the newspaper.

"Reputable Polling Organizations"

Most of us do not have the savvy to be able to read the fine details and make judgments about, for example, sample design. Precisely for that reason, the intelligent consumer must know who did the survey, and also who sponsored it, if the two are different. Since credibility is at issue here, an important factor in assessing any poll involves a judgment on the reliability of the organization doing the survey. If the company has a solid reputation, that lends weight to their findings. An organization with a good track record, like Gallup in the United States or Decima Research, CROP, or Martin Goldfarb and Associates in Canada, is generally more credible than a relatively unknown organization. It is therefore absolutely essential that the identity of the organization be made known. Then if you want to check the record of that organization you can do so.

We also should be told who sponsored the poll. I am not suggesting that because a poll is sponsored by Candidate A that it is unreliable if it shows A ahead. But because the person who sponsors the poll is the person ultimately who has the decision of whether or not to release the information, we are better off knowing the identity of the sponsor as well as that of the organization. There is, by the way, no law that says a person must make the results of a poll public, nor is there any law that mandates that the paper print the poll if it is made public.

Problems Regarding Input into Sample

So far we have spoken of the problems and the considerations governing the design of the sample. However, the general consensus among survey researchers is that the statistical part of their task is virtually straightforward. The harder part is getting accurate input into the sample. Eliciting information and opinions from those who constitute the sample is the most treacherous aspect of the science of survey research.

A cartoon in a recent issue of *The New Yorker* shows one newsman talking (on camera) to another: "Glad you brought that up Jim. The latest research on polls has turned up some interesting variables. It turns out, for example, that people will tell you any old thing that pops into their heads." The situation is probably not quite that bad, but at least three factors complicate this aspect of sampling.

1. People are often reluctant to reveal their true opinions, either because they fear reprisal or criticism. People are so accustomed to masking their beliefs and attitudes—especially those that are controversial—that it may be quite difficult to divulge them to a complete stranger. This problem is lessened but not eliminated by the use of the telephone.

2. People will often say what they think others want or expect to hear rather than what they actually believe. This is related to the first point. It is a human tendency to want to please others and to be well thought of by them. Pollsters are aware of this. Martin Goldfarb, president of Martin Goldfarb and Associates, said, "You've got to ask questions in a way that doesn't intimidate the people you're interviewing, that doesn't get them to say something just because they think they should."[5]

A classic illustration is the anecdote about the man taking a poll about what magazines Americans like to read. (The way I heard this story, the pollster is standing in front of a bookstore in New York during the 1950s.) The survey requires that the pollster question passersby about what is their favorite magazine. Perhaps because they want to seem informed and well-read, the people give such names as the *Atlantic Monthly* or *Harper's*—magazines known for their intellectual quality. Then the pollster says, "As our way of thanking you for taking part in this survey, you can select any magazine you would like from inside the store." What do people select? *Harpers?* No. *Atlantic Monthly?* No. They take *Photoplay* or *True Detective* or *Life*. People will often say what they think will sound good or please the pollster or will make them look intelligent or savvy.

3. People may be ignorant of their own beliefs and mental processes, including their reasons for selecting from among possible choices. Some psychological evidence exists that people are often either ignorant or mistaken about their own mental processes. In one experiment subjects were asked to choose from among nightgowns identical in quality the one they thought was the best quality:

> After they had made their choice, they were asked why. Subjects chose the nightgown on the right most frequently. Yet when asked why, not one mentioned its position as a reason. When they were directly questioned about the possible effect of position on their choice, they not only denied it as a reason but showed through a gesture that perhaps they had misunderstood the questioner or that the questioner was a "madman."[6]

These three factors make it difficult for the pollster to get accurate feedback; that is, questions must be worded to allow people to express their real opinions and must scrupulously avoid using any terms or any wording that would prompt the participant to respond one way rather than another. A question that is *loaded* in any direction may well compromise the reliability of the poll, except in those instances where the respondent is asked to agree or disagree with a set of loaded statements. These reflections testify to the importance of knowing the exact wording of the questions asked. Sometimes we will be able to detect bias in the wording of the question; once bias is suspected, any inference from the sample is jeopardized.

Loaded Questions

A few examples of questions illustrate loaded questions. For instance, in March 1983, Jerry Falwell, the leader of the so-called Moral Majority in the United States, took out a full-page advertisement in many papers asking readers to respond to a set of questions, among them this one:

> Are you willing to trust the survival of America to a nuclear freeze agreement with the Soviet Union, a nation which rejects on-site inspection of military facilities to ensure compliance?[7]

The question is hardly worded in such a way as to get an honest response. The reason for saying "No" is conveniently provided in the wording of the question— The Soviet Union rejects on-site inspection, and so on. If it were true that the Soviets reject on-site inspection, that may well be an excellent argument for not adopting a pro-freeze position, but it is hardly a question that will elicit an uncued and honest response.

In March 1982, the Progressive Conservative Party was boycotting the Canadian Parliament to protest the Liberal government's attempt to introduce a complex piece of legislation on energy. On March 10, 1982, an article appeared in the *Windsor (Ontario) Star,* reporting a Southan News survey. The question asked of respondents was:

> The Progressive Conservatives have been boycotting Parliament since last Tuesday to protest the Liberal government's refusal to split the controversial energy bill into smaller separate bills. Do you support the Conservative tactics?[8]

This question is worded in a biased way. The phrases "protest the . . . refusal to split" and "controversial" incline the respondent toward an affirmative answer.

However you view these last two instances, the point is that a poll can be skewed by the input. For us to have any chance of making such a judgment, we must know the exact wording of the question asked.

An interesting case was a survey done about Canadian attitudes toward President Ronald Reagan's Strategic Defense Initiative—"Star Wars"—carried out by *The Globe and Mail* and CROP. As reported in *The Globe and Mail:*

> A majority of Canadians favors Canada's participation in the U.S. Star Wars research program and the proposition increases to almost two-thirds if participation means more jobs.

In the column accompanying the poll we are given the relevant information about the poll, as well as the questions asked:

> As you may know, U.S. President Reagan is currently promoting a research program to find new methods of defending North America against nuclear attack. It's called the Strategic Defense Initiative or Star Wars:
> Do you think that Canada should or should not participate in research for the Star Wars defense plan?
> Would you be in favor of Canada participating in the Star Wars research if it meant more jobs for Canadians?[9]

One reader wrote to take exception to wording of the questions:

> . . . Reading the questions, it became clear why a majority of Canadians appears to support Canadian participation in Star Wars. What did these questions suggest? That U.S. President Reagan is currently promoting a research program to find new methods of defending North America against nuclear attack, and second, that participation would mean jobs for Canadians. These questions are dishonest and deceptive and have no relationship to the reality of Star Wars. Star Wars is neither a research nor a defense program; nor is it a job creator, except for a few Canadians.[10]

The writer's point is that the wording of the questions tended to encourage a yes response. The writer went on to make another important point about polling: timing. The time the poll is conducted may influence people's answers. In connection with the Star Wars example, the writer also said (not cited) the survey seemed to have been timed to coincide with the government's agenda.

Timing is also crucial in political polling before elections. If polling occurs too far in advance of the election, it may fail to detect last-minute shifts in the electorate. In the 1948 United States presidential race, most pollsters predicted victory for Governor Tom Dewey of New York. (One paper in fact had published an edition with the headline "Dewey Wins.") But Harry Truman won and one of the morals derived from that sad (for the pollsters) experience was that they stopped their polling too early and failed to detect last-minute shifts to Truman.

The Impact of Survey Research and Polling on Society

A host of questions surrounds the role of survey research in our society. Limited space permits only the briefest consideration of a few.

In Politics and Government

It is fairly well known that surveys are used in planning and decision making at the highest levels. Governments use them to discover how voters might react to policies. Political parties use them to find out how they are perceived and what issues are most important to voters in an upcoming election. You might argue that in a democracy, where the people are supposed to be the sovereign, that surveys and polls are the perfect instruments of decision making.

Objections to this view can be only touched on here. Firstly, we have already seen how fragile the process of sampling is. Finding out what people think about an issue or a policy may depend as much on how the question is put to them:

> A classic example is a question first posed by Elmo Roper in a 1940 survey. When asked, "Do you think the United States should forbid public speeches against democracy?" about half of the interviewees said yes. But when asked "Do you think the United States should allow public speeches against democracy?" three-quarters said no. Nobody knows why it happened . . . but one explanation is that the word "allow" may conjure up the idea of promoting speeches against democracy.

A government can use polling results for its own ends.

Secondly, ours is a representative democracy, which means that we elect representatives to govern and make decisions in our name and then hold them accountable at regular intervals in elections. A government unwilling to risk the discontent of the voters by taking an unpopular course of action would not be true to the ideals of democratic government.

The Influence of Polls

There is a widespread belief that polls can and do influence the outcomes of elections:

> One of the most-heard criticisms of public opinion polling is that it tends to foster a bandwagon effect—that predicting victory for a political candidate inclines people to vote for that candidate, to side with a winner. On the other hand, some people might tend to support the underdog. Clara Hatton [vice-president and director of Canadian Gallup Poll Ltd.] disputes such criticism, maintaining that if either of the above scenarios held true, "we would be wrong 100% of the time."[12]

This belief concerns more the television reporting of elections (chiefly the use of what is called the exit-poll) than it does polling itself. There may be some truth to this belief, but to the best of my knowledge no reliable study has turned up any evidence of significant influence on the outcome of elections.[13] There are competing intuitions about what the effects would be. In the 1980 presidential election, the network news shows predicted very early in the evening a victory for Ronald Reagan. The polls had not yet closed in California and many believed that discouraged by this prediction some Democrats decided not to vote at all, even for local candidates and issues. However, no substantive evidence of this hypothesis was ever presented. Indeed another point of view—the underdog syndrome—also is involved. That is, since many people like to support the underdog, it is possible that reports showing one candidate leading may cause some to vote for the opponent. No single view has been shown to be true.

Possible Objections to Polls

There are several objections to the use of polls. The first is that polls will sometimes treat informed opinion as of equal value to uninformed opinion and ignorance. If you volunteer to take part in the poll, you may find yourself asked to answer questions about which you have no opinion. A friend who recently took part in a survey complained that the questions were "quite absurd and they just insisted on a response even if you said you didn't know and had no basis for judgment. For example, they wanted [John] Turner graded for leftness-rightness on a one-to-ten scale, and the same done for [Brian] Mulroney, [Jean] Chretien, and [Ed] Broadbent."[14] Being forced to have an opinion when you have no opinion, it could be argued, walks a very thin line between sampling public opinion and creating it. To be sure, "no opinion" responses are often allowed for and should always be reported somewhere. Also many polls do attempt to control for levels of information with screen questions such as "Have you ever heard of . . . ?" or for intensity of opinion with questions such as "How strongly do you feel about . . . ?" However no pollster can control for the quality of thoughtfulness (or lack of it) that goes into an opinion. In that sense, the pollster cannot judge the quality of opinion, only quantity.

Polls cannot discriminate between the thoughtful and the unreflective response. If Mr. Smith has not been following events in Nicaragua (and does not even know where Nicaragua is), then of what value are his opinions about the current government there? This point is similar to one made by Dalton Camp in a recent article:

> This hardy Gallup perennial is not so much a poll as it is a table of nonsequiturs: "Do you approve of the job John Turner is doing leading the Liberal Opposition as much as you approve of the way Brian Mulroney is leading the government or Ed Broadbent is leading the NDP?" . . . How can you approve or disapprove of Broadbent's handling of his job when you don't know what it is?[15]

Camp was probably jesting, but the underlying point is serious.

One response to this line of criticism is to point out that it is one of the prices of a democratic system in which citizens can vote whether knowledgeable about the issue or not. Yet if people are being asked to respond to questions about issues that, but for the pollster's having said, would not be on their minds, then you can wonder whether polls are merely reporting attitudes and preferences. Are they helping to create them? (This question is similar to the question about whether the news media, in their attempts to cover events, sometimes create them.)

To conclude, it is crucial for the consumer to have certain information when a poll is reported and most newspapers omit such information. Humphrey Taylor, president of the Louis Harris Organization, says:

On the whole the media do a lousy job of distinguishing between good, bad, and indifferent polls. They focus on sensational results, not validity.[16]

The citizen who is not equipped to process news reports of surveys and polls is thus at an extreme disadvantage in this society. If "poll-ution" is here to stay, we should prepare ourselves so that we suffer least from the fallout![17]

Questions for Reflection and Discussion

1.   Why would you not need to taste more soup to get a sample from a five-gallon pot than to get a sample from a one-gallon pot?

2.   Why does Johnson say that although sampling may be a science, the construction of good questions for polling is an art? Do you agree with him?

3.   Why is the man-in-the-street sample bound to be unrepresentative?

4.   Can you think of a question that you might not be able to answer accurately on a poll because you did not know what your own beliefs were? Give an example, if possible.

5.   What are the dangers of polls that insist that respondents rate persons or things (for instance on a one-to-ten scale) and will not permit "no opinion" for an answer?

Notes

1. "The Delicate Art of Polling the Public," *The Globe and Mail* (7 September 1985): 10.

2. Harold Mendelsohn and Irving Crespi, *Polls, Television and the New Politics* (Scranton, Penn.: Chandler Publishing Company, 1970), 134–135.

3. A more serious problem is that telephones are usually answered by women (about 70 percent) of the time. Also, researchers have discovered that elderly people are more reluctant to speak over the telephone than to interviewers. On many telephone surveys, between 15 percent and 25 percent of those reached refuse to participate. Four percent terminate any lengthy interview, a much higher proportion than in the case of face-to-face interviews. "I guess it's easier to hang up on someone than to throw them out of your living room." Cf. Kevin McKean, "The Fine Art of Reading Voters' Minds," *Discover* (May 1984), 67.

4. Of course, these situations are not equally likely. It is after all a probability distribution in which each outcome is less probable as one moves away from the mean.

5. *The Globe and Mail* (7 September 1985).

6. R.E. Nisbett and T.D. Wilson, "Telling More Than We Know: Verbal Reports on Mental Process," *Psychological Review*, 84 (1977): 231–259. Cf. Steven Penrod, *Social Psychology* (Englewood Cliffs, N.J.: Prentice-Hall, 1986), 115.

7. Jerry Falwell, "An Open Letter from Jerry Falwell," *Detroit Free Press* (22 March 1983).

8. *Windsor Star* (10 March 1982).

9. *The Globe and Mail* (10 August 1982).

10. William Kastan, "Letter to the Editor," *The Globe and Mail* (29 August 1985). In late 1986, the Canadian government decided not to participate in this initiative "government to government."

11. Elmo Roper, in McKean, "Reading Voters' Minds," 68.

12. Bruce Lenett, "Opinion Pollsters: Testing the Pulse of the Public," *The London Free Press* (6 November 1986): C6.

13. There have been some attempts to test the "bandwagon" hypothesis, specifically using situations where the media is not blacked out. See, for example, John Jackson, ed., "Election Night Reporting and Voter Turnout," *American Journal of Political Science,* 27, no. 4 (1983): 615–635. Some other literature is cited in this article.

14. In November 1986, John Turner was the leader of the Liberal Party in Canada, Brian Mulroney was the prime minister and the leader of the Progressive Conservative Party, Jean Chretien was a former member of Parliament from Quebec who unsuccessfully ran for the position that Turner won, and Ed Broadbent was the leader of the New Democratic Party.

15. Dalton Camp, "At Least One Poll Is Meaningless," *Calgary Herald* (1 September 1985).

16. McKean, "Reading Voters' Minds," 69.

17. The author, being an amateur in these matters, has had to attempt to educate himself over the years. I wish to express my gratitude to Professor Larry LeDuc, Department of Political Science, University of Toronto, for his patient tutelage over the years. I also wish to thank him for reading and commenting on an earlier draft of this paper.

15

Of Crime, Cause, and Correlation*

Stephen Jay Gould

In most mammals, sex is seasonal, whereas in humans it is not. This fact tends to make scientists look for remnants of seasonality in human sexual behavior and in male aggressive behavior. In exploring such issues, however, it is easy even for well-known scientists to confuse correlation with cause. One example of this error is postulating sexual seasonality as a cause for assaults. Cause has been mistakenly inferred from correlation, and alternative explanations of the data are neglected. Fascination with hypotheses about how human behavior traits may be inborn makes it all too easy to ignore these alternative explanations. Thus, the logical error of reasoning from a correlation to a cause is easy to commit.

Since sex can be gentle and a thing of great beauty, it may seem peculiar that so many animals are most touchy and aggressive during their mating seasons. Nonetheless, this apparent paradox makes sense in light of evolutionary theory. An organism's success in the evolutionary race may be measured by the number of offspring raised to carry its genes into future generations. For a male, more copulations with more females mean more offspring, and this biological imperative can engender severe competition among males and zealous defense of females within a male's orbit—hence the link of sex with aggression. Females may also struggle among themselves to win the attention of best fit males or to discourage inappropriate suitors.

In most mammals, sex is seasonal—and periods of nastiness and aggression therefore ebb and flow in correlation with mating activity throughout the year. Yet writings on human evolution usually cite a loss of seasonality in mating as a key feature of our biological history. Human females ovulate at regular intervals

---

*"Of Crime, Cause, and Correlation" by Stephen Jay Gould first appeared in *Discover* Magazine in December, 1983. It is reprinted here by permission of the author.

throughout the year, and both males and females seem interested in and capable of indulging in sexual activity at any time. Indeed, the invention of adaptive reasons for this loss of seasonality forms a common theme in treatises on human evolution—the advantages of monogamy and a strong pair-bond for raising children, for example, and the role of continual sexual receptivity among females in maintaining a male's interest in sticking around. I regard most of these scenarios as pretty silly and purely speculative, but they do attempt to explain a fact of evident importance—why humans are the most persistently sexy of primates.

Yet this very loss of evident seasonality has prompted many scientists to wonder whether some small or subtle remnant of our evolutionary past might still be preserved in modern humans. Does any vestigial seasonality of sexual behavior and its correlates in aggression still remain with us? Does the animal still lurk beneath a human guise?

Since we have no direct evidence for seasonality in human sexual behavior, scientists who seek some sign of it must search the dossier of human activity for conduct that cycles with the seasons and might be linked with sexuality. Various types of aggressive behavior form a promising area for investigation.

This style of research faces, unfortunately, one enormous and daunting problem—it falls so easily into what is probably the most common error of human reasoning, the confusion of correlation with cause. We may illustrate the fallacy with some simple examples. Halley's comet was approaching the earth and was steadily drawing nearer to us for many years. During the same time, my pet hamster had been aging continually and the price of an ice cream cone had risen steadily in Boston. If I computed what scientists call a correlation coefficient between any two of these events (comet distances, hamster ages, and cone prices), I would get a nearly perfect relationship—a quantitative value near the maximum of one. Yet everyone understands intuitively that none of these correlations has any causal meaning—lots of things are moving in the same direction independently.

Even more difficult to interpret are correlations between phenomena that seem to have some causal relationship, but in which the potential causal pathways are both great in number and varied in style. The simple existence of a correlation does not permit a distinction among these myriad pathways. Seasonality, for example, has numerous consequences—variation in temperature and length of daylight are the most direct and prominent. When we find a kind of human behavior that cycles with the seasons, and not by accident, how can we know which of the astronomical number of facets of seasonality it reflects? The causal pathways are often subtle, indirect, and complex. Why, for example, do we play baseball in the summer and football in the fall and winter? Nothing intrinsic to the games dictates such a custom, especially in our modern, all-weather domed stadiums. The reason is linked with seasonality, but by a most indirect and historical route. Baseball has old and populist origins as a game of ordinary folk in rural and urban communities. Our great-grandfathers played it when they could, and when their families would enjoy watching—when it was warm enough, in summer. But football had its origin as a collegiate sport, and colleges (for reasons originally and indirectly linked to the warmth of seasons and the timing of agriculture) are not in session until the fall.

Of Crime, Cause, and Correlation

Thus is the problem in using correlation with seasons as a method for making inferences about the vestigial existence of human sexual cycles: We may expect to find many seasonal fluctuations in potentially indirect correlates of sex—aggressive behavior most prominently—but we cannot infer cause, because the simple correlation cannot, by itself, tell us which of the numerous aspects of seasonality has engendered the behavioral cycle. The discovery of yearly cycles in aggressive behavior does not permit the inference that human biology still records a vestige of primate mating seasons, for two reasons: Firstly, too many unrelated aspects of seasonality may be causing the correlation, and these must be identified and eliminated before we have any right to assert an evolutionary hypothesis; second, underlying sexual cycles are not (by far) the only cause of human aggression. Nonetheless, psychiatrist Richard Michael and ethologist Doris Zumpe recently published a study in the *American Journal of Psychiatry* that made just such a claim and elicited a flurry of press commentary about our vestigial animality.[1] Michael and Zumpe fall right into the fallacy of confusing correlation with cause: They find a simple correlation of aggression to season and ascribe its cause to vestigial sexual cyclicism without any supporting evidence and without even discussing an old and sensible alternative explanation that fits the data far better.

Michael and Zumpe considered the frequency of four crimes—forcible rape, aggravated assault, murder, and robbery—throughout the year in sixteen American localities from Maine to Honolulu. They found that rape and assault showed nearly the same pattern in all but two localities for rape and all but four for assault: The greatest number occurred in summer, within an eight-week period between July 7 and September 8. They conclude, "Because of the close relationship between assault and rape, and because rapes are invariably less numerous than assaults, we postulate that rape comprises a subcategory of assaultive behavior." Robberies, on the other hand, tend to show a reversed pattern, with the greatest number in winter, while murders are scattered throughout the year and display no seasonal peaks. The authors also found no significant differences in frequencies of the various crimes among their sixteen places—especially no tendency toward more violence in hotter climates.

Michael and Zumpe's data provide nothing more than a correlation between frequency of some crimes (but not others) and seasonal fluctuations of climate. They clearly do not have enough information to make causal assertions—for the correlation of crime and season may have a host of potential reasons (or even no reason at all), and the correlation itself does not permit a distinction among numerous possibilities.

Nonetheless, Michael and Zumpe present a single hypothesis about cause, providing no alternative at all and implying that their data are sufficient to make such an assertion. They claim that seasonal fluctuations in hormone levels probably underlie cycles of crime—and suggest that these fluctuations record a vestige of primate mating cycles. They write, "The view that environmental factors may act via neuroendocrine pathways in the human to influence our behavior is consistent with the known role of these factors in socially living, nonhuman primates, which show increased aggressivity at the start of the mating season."

I believe that two debilitating objections can be raised against this far-fetched conclusion: Firstly, some of the authors' own data contradict (or at least fit uncomfortably within their hypothesis); secondly, an explanation that they never consider—the old and "classical" explanation for crime's well-known seasonal cycles—fits all the data and fits them better and more simply than the hormonal hypothesis.

If rape correlates with assault because, it constitutes "a subcategory of assaultive behavior," and aggression cycles with the season as a result of environmentally-entrained variation in hormone levels, then why does murder show no seasonal pattern? Surely murder is aggression. Moreover, though we may regard robbery as premeditated behavior for gain and not, therefore, as another category of aggression expected to cycle with rape and assault, we still cannot understand, on Michael and Zumpe's hypothesis, why robbery shows a reversed seasonal pattern. If their hypothesis has general merit, it should explain the cycles of all the crimes they consider. Michael and Zumpe's batting average, in short, is poor. Their speculation fits only half their data; a third crime (murder) does not show the expected pattern, while a fourth (robbery) displays a different cycle, which they do not attempt to explain at all.

Michael and Zumpe have discovered nothing new. The four patterns that they cite "have been known by criminologists and the beat cop for many years" (to quote Mark Fox, who outlined the same objections in a letter to *Science News,* commenting on a previous favorable report of Michael and Zumpe's article.)[2] The same criminologists and policemen have a standard explanation that fits all four patterns—not just two of them—and seems eminently direct and reasonable to me. It relies upon an immediate, nonbiological reason for correlations between seasons and crime. Quite simply, and to put it somewhat crudely, rapes and assaults peak in summer because winter is a hell of a time to lurk in alleyways—more contact and greater availability in summer provide more opportunity. Robberies show a reversed pattern because weapons are more easily concealed under winter attire. Murders show no pattern because more are unplanned acts of violence committed against friends and family members at moments of extreme stress. I do not assert that this classical explanation must be correct, but it explains everything simply and should not be omitted from discussion. Yet Michael and Zumpe ignored it in favor of exclusive speculations about evolutionary vestiges. The potential pathways from correlation to cause are always numerous.

Michael and Zumpe seem to think that their demonstration of similar peaks in rape and assault for their coldest (Maine) and warmest (Hawaii and Puerto Rico) regions argues for biology and against the idea that "higher temperatures facilitate increased social interaction." But this fact is irrelevant to the debate because both explanations predict it. In particular, the social hypothesis simply requires that summers be warm—and it is hot enough during a Maine summer to populate the alleyways. Similarly, Michael and Zumpe's demonstration that regions with greater seasonal change in temperature show greater annual fluctuations in frequency of rape and assault, if anything, fits the social hypothesis better—it really is too cold during a Maine winter, but is quite possible in Honolulu.

I wrote this essay primarily to illustrate, by egregious example, the cardinal fallacy of confusing correlation with cause. But Michael and Zumpe's article raises two other interesting and general points about scientific explanation.

Why, first of all, do so many scientists show a preference for arcane, complex, indirect, and implausible causal pathways when simple (if less intriguing) explanations are so clearly available? (I have previously argued that the higher batting averages of lefties really can be explained by the unexciting and classical observation that lefties hit right-handed pitching better and that most pitchers, like most of us, are right-handed—and not by newfangled, high-faluting notions about differences between left and right brains, as two overenthusiastic doctors have suggested.) We should start with the immediate and obvious (they usually work) and move to the complex and indirect when our initial efforts fail. Have a healthy respect for simple answers; the world is not always a deep conundrum fit only for consideration by certified scholars.

Secondly, why are we so fascinated by explanations that invoke innate and inherited biology (vestigial mating cycles in this case), when simpler hypotheses based upon the interaction of a flexible personality with the immediate environment explain things better and more fully? We seem drawn, in the absence of good evidence, to biological hypotheses for differences in social and intellectual behavior between men and women or the activities of criminal and law-abiding citizens. I suspect that this preference reflects one of the oldest and most unfortunate biases of Western thought, dating back at least to Plato's search for essences. We want to know what we are "really" like, why we behave as we do. Somehow, we feel that a claim for something inborn and inherited must be more fundamental or essential than an undetermined response to an immediate environment. We prefer to believe that more men are driven to rape in summer by a rise in hormones reflecting an evolutionary past than by a simple increase in availability of targets. But if humans have an essence, it surely lies in the remarkable flexibility that permits such an enormous range of unprogrammed responses to environment. This flexibility defines us and makes us human. We should not only cherish and foster it but also learn to recognize and take interest in its manifestations.

Questions for Reflection and Discussion

1.   Why is it wrong to infer a causal relationship from a correlation? Give an example from Gould's article and an example of your own where this is obviously a mistake.

2.   From what correlation did Michael and Zumpe infer what causal hypothesis?

3.   According to Gould, does the fact that robberies tend (in their sample, at least) to occur more frequently in winter and sexual assaults more in summer tend to confirm or to disconfirm Michael and Zumpe's hypothesis? What does Gould's view here depend on, logically? Do you agree with him?

4.   Is Gould suggesting that explanations of human behavior in terms of what is "inborn" are generally wrong? If so, would you agree or disagree? What sorts of evidence could be brought forward to support or to disconfirm this view?

Notes

1. Richard Michael and Doris Zumpe, "Sexual Violence in the United States and the Role of Season," *American Journal of Psychiatry* (July 1983).

2. Mark Fox, "Letter to the Editor," *Science News* (24 September 1983).

ſ

16

Violence and Domination as Metaphors in Academic Discourse*

Maryann Ayim

Metaphors can have important effects on thinking. In academic life an amazing prevalence of metaphors exist that involve domination, war, and violence. These metaphors are found in science, philosophy, and education. They are often linked with imagery of sexual domination, especially in science, where Nature is often regarded as something female that the male scientist sets out to conquer and dominate. Within philosophy, argument is understood as a confrontation between one person who defends a position and another who attacks. Such metaphors also exist in education; although more cooperative metaphors, such as those of nurturing or participating in a quilting bee, have more positive associations. If we could alter our ways of thinking and switch metaphors, there might be beneficial effects both for scholarship and for human relations.

"In metaphor, a system of belief gets new life in a foreign land; it takes root among the alien corn."[1] In this account, itself metaphorical, Roger Tourangeau provides some indication of how metaphors work. Blown on the winds of change, like dandelion seeds, perhaps, they take tentative root "in a foreign land." Not all of them will survive. In a place too alien, the metaphor will "languish and die," to borrow Israel Scheffler's words.[2]

But of those that do survive, some will establish their roots deeply, and in so doing, will become central to the "process of creating new meaning."[3] They may actually take over the corn field, changing the chemical composition of the soil. This soil will prove either hostile or conducive to the development of other new ideas, rendering the metaphors themselves central to the shape and growth

---

*Used with permission of Maryann Ayim.

of meaning. Hence the metaphors that survive and flourish will become "organizing element[s] in inquiry";[4] as such, they will come to exert powerful influence not only on the perception of what counts as a good solution to a problem but also on the logically prior perception of what constitutes a problem in the first place.[5] In this paper I examine a powerful type of metaphor—one employed in academic discourse generally and especially prevalent in the language of science and philosophy.

The following personal anecdote illustrates the nature of this genre of metaphor. A colleague of mine decided to include a component on a specific language in a computer science course that he teaches. Although he was relatively unfamiliar with the language himself, he deemed his students' exposure to it to be sufficiently worthwhile to merit its inclusion. This decision entailed concentrated work to familiarize himself with the language to the point of being able to teach it. After about two weeks, devoted almost exclusively to this task, he triumphantly declared that he had "beaten the language into submission."

It is important to emphasize that this colleague is by no means a violent, nasty, or even particularly aggressive person. As an academic, however, the image that occurred to him as a natural fit for his achievement in learning the computer language was one of violence. This picture of "beating into submission" captures all too aptly our standard perception of the nature of academic and intellectual success. Thus academic achievement is so closely calibrated with acquiring control over the subject matter that the notion of mastery is perceived as virtually synonymous with that of learning. The definition of the verb "to master" in the *Concise Oxford Dictionary* corroborates this perception. "Master" is defined as "overcome, defeat; reduce to subjection; acquire complete knowledge of (subject) or facility in using (instrument, etc.); rule as a master."[6]

This paper will identify and analyse this type of metaphor as it occurs in academic discourse. In scientific language, the metaphors of dominance, subjugation, manipulation, and control are many. In philosophical discourse, the most powerful metaphors connote not only dominance and subjugation but also violence and outright warfare. Such metaphors also can be found in educational literature. Alternative metaphors do exist for learning, metaphors more closely aligned to nurturance than to subjugation. I argue for the superiority of the nurturant metaphors and suggest that they should replace the violent metaphors so much in vogue in our academies of learning.

Science and the Pursuit of Truth—A Case Study in Manipulation and Control

Nowhere has the notion of success been more closely identified with mastery, control, and maleness than in the discipline of science. To illustrate, I cite two voices from the scientific tradition—Francis Bacon, whose work was among the most powerful in determining the shape and direction of scientific thought, and Richard Feynman, a contemporary scientist who achieved the ultimate hallmark of approbation and honor among his peers in being selected as a Nobel prize winner.

Although the identification of science with mastery pre-dated Bacon, it has probably been expressed most graphically in his writing. In his *On the Dignity and Advancement of Learning,* he admonished the scientist "but to follow and as it were hound nature in her wanderings, and you will be able, when you like, to lead or drive her afterwards to the same place again."[7] The image of scientific knowledge emanating from the control and manipulation of nature arises clearly and directly from this passage. Another more indirect image is that of dualism, with definite boundaries between knower and the knowable, between the scientist and nature. The scientist comes to know nature by controlling it, manipulating it, or in Bacon's words, by leading it, driving it, or hounding it.

Another dualism basic to Bacon's picture of the scientific endeavor is the dualism between male and female. The scientist is, of course, male and nature female. In a subsequent passage in *Of the Dignity and Advancement of Learning,* Bacon fills out his metaphorical account of the nature of the enterprise of science, "Neither ought a man to make scruple of entering and penetrating into those holes and corners, when the inquisition of truth is his sole object."[8] This passage, with its clear allusion to sexual intercourse, metaphorically links scientific inquiry to male penetration of a female body. The earlier admonition to "hound," "lead," and "drive" nature suggests that where nature does not easily render itself to the scrutiny of the scientist, forcible entry or rape may be justified to further knowledge. Nature, then, is characterized as knowable, passive, female, and rapable,[9] and the scientist is active knower, male, and justified in committing rape in the name of science.[10]

Richard Feynman's identification of science with masculinity is equally graphic and equally worrisome from a feminist point of view. In a public lecture in which he described the work that led to his Nobel prize, Feynman likened the process of formulating a scientific theory to falling in love. He said:

> That was the beginning, and the idea seemed so obvious to me and so elegant that I fell deeply in love with it. And, like falling in love with a woman, it is only possible if you do not know much about her, so you cannot see her faults. The faults will become apparent later, but after the love is strong enough to hold you to her. So, I was held to this theory, in spite of all difficulties, by my youthful enthusiasm."[11]

He concluded his address by developing the metaphor further, describing the theory (and the woman) in its old age:

> So what happened to the old theory that I fell in love with as a youth? Well, I would say it's become an old lady, who has very little that's attractive left in her, and the young today will not have their hearts pound when they look at her anymore. But, we can say the best we can for any old woman, that she has been a very good mother and has given birth to some very good children. And, I thank the Swedish Academy of Sciences for complimenting one of them. Thank you.[12]

This characterization of the perceived nature of scientific undertaking is by no means original. It is evident in most of the contemporary feminist critiques of science and the philosophy of science. Lloyd, Keller, and Harding, for example, all provide vivid and abundant evidence for the metaphorical identification of scientific progress with conflict, mastery, manipulation, dominance, male sexuality, and even violent rape.[13]

The metaphors of science have been among the most powerful in terms of shaping our thoughts, legitimating traditional scholarship, and virtually exerting the power of veto over radical innovations in the academic arena. As Harding says, "Neither God nor tradition is privileged with the same credibility as scientific rationality in modern cultures."[14]

Hand in hand with the vision of truth and reality given to us by science is the notion of the method of science as being objective and rational. Because science is not side-tracked by the emotional, its product is not someone's mere subjective account of reality by an objective picture of the world as it really is.

So the picture of science, which most of us hold, is one of an objective quest for the truth, untrammeled by the purely subjective and the emotional, and proceeding in a logical way toward its goal. We also have tended to see science as politically neutral, unfettered and untarnished by affiliation with particular political ideologies. We have somehow envisaged science, in its pursuit of knowledge, as pure and disconnected from the practical applications and consequences of that knowledge. This picture of science is related in obvious ways to our view of the scientist as someone relatively uninterested in other people, with little empathy, who tends toward "objective thinking with a marked inhibition of any tendencies to project themselves into a situation," and with "a rather passive emotional adaptation."[15] Whatever historical justification such a picture of science may have had, it is clear that such a view is no longer tenable. It is evident that scientific research is now selected for financial backing on the basis of its applicability to very specific practical goals and we can no longer afford to ignore the nature of the context within which science is allowed to operate.[16]

The attainment of pure objectivity, even if it should be desirable (which is itself questionable), is simply not possible. Our scientific research will always be colored by our ideals, our metaphysics, and our metaphors. This will be as true of a feminist approach to science as a traditional male-oriented approach. It is important not to do away with values and presuppositions but to make clear what these values and presuppositions are. The most worrisome assumptions are those that go undetected and hence unexamined.

As Harding argues, the alignment of science with maleness, domination, and control should be discountenanced not only because such a view is sexist, but also because it "makes bad science. It leads to false and oversimplified models of nature and inquiry that attribute power relations and hierarchical structure where none do or need exist."[17] Hence feminist criticism will contribute not only to the achievement of higher moral standards in science through its emphasis on sexual egalitarianism, but it will also contribute to raising the standards of the scientific concerns themselves. In the advent of feminist criticism, science should become not only more just but also more fully scientific.

Violence in Academe—Philosophy as a Paradigm

Our much-prized rational "man" has projected a single, consistent image throughout the history of philosophy—the image of violence. The philosophical literature abounds in metaphors of battle, confrontation, sword fights, arm wrestling, knifings, throwing, bull fights, torture, poisoning, and even cold-blooded analyses of the resultant corpses. Out of a multitude of examples, consider the following four: "The weapon behind logical analysis, behind the appeal to reason, is nothing more serious than the sharp edge of inconsistency."[18] "When you disagree with something, the logically appropriate response is to aim your critical arrows at that position itself."[19] The battle metaphor appears even in the context of advice to the logic student about how to respond supportively to an argument: "Having done your best to attack the argument, you should now turn around and do your best to defend it."[20] And the author of a book on the philosophy of social science states that his "aim was to attack a current conception of the relations between philosophy and the social sciences."[21]

Thus philosophers teach students about arguments and provide for them what they believe are models of excellence. They expose the skeleton arguments of the historical giants, most of which they then proceed to tear apart. They are careful not to let students know with which world pictures their own sympathies lie, for it is not the particular metaphysical theories they want them to acquire and to value but rather the philosophical manner of operation. Thus they teach how to lay bare an argument, how to identify the most critical premises and go for the heart of the discussion, which they move into to attack. They want students to learn how to pinpoint and reject the merely extraneous and peripheral, so they will probably provide them with Ockham's Razor as a ready tool.[22]

Philosophers tend to value "sharper" students, whom they may openly praise for their "penetrating" insights. Occasionally they find students of "piercing" intelligence, one or two perhaps with minds like "steel traps." Philosophers regard such students as important: They require "tough-minded" opponents with whom they can "parry" in the classroom, so they can exhibit to the others what the "thrust" of philosophical argumentation is all about. This "battle of wits" is somewhat risky, however, and a "combatant" must take care always to "have the upper hand," to "win thumbs down," to "avoid being hoist by your own petard." If you find yourself pressed for time at the end of a lecture, with your "back to the wall," or as it is occasionally even more colorfully expressed, "between a rock and a hard place," you may have to resort to "strong arm tactics," to "barbed" comments, to "go for the jugular," to "cut an opponent's argument to pieces," or to "bring out the big guns or heavy artillery." If caught in the throes of a real dilemma, you may even have to "take the bull by the horns" or rebut the dilemma by advancing a "counter" dilemma.[23]

Philosophers can justify such behavior—for by engaging in it, they are providing students with further grist for the mill of reason. They are giving them a view of the "cutting edge" of philosophical research. If necessary, this can be made clear in the next class session by performing a "post mortem" of the previous day's battle of ideas. It is interesting that much of this lexicon (for example, "piercing," "thrust," and "penetrating") has overt sexual connotations not unconnected with the image of the violent duel.

Philosophers insist that the strongest argument will be the one that provides a rebuttal to the archrival of its conclusion. In other words, as Janic Moulton points out, philosophical attention becomes focused on attempting to undermine the position of someone who holds the completely opposite point of view, with little time left over to "provide any positive reason for accepting a conclusion . . . or show how a conclusion is related to other ideas."[24]

Philosophers warn students about such fallacious reasoning as "poisoning the wells," *ad hominem* (against or attacking the man), appeal to authority, and *ad baculum* (the use of covert threats as means of persuasion).

Consider as an example the appeal to authority: Dropping an important name or appealing to a person's importance as evidence for the truth of a claim is frequently illicit and always suspect. The claims of authorities, like those of anyone else, philosophers say, must be supported by confirming evidence or compelling reasoning; it is to this evidence that we should turn, not to the status of the authority, when gauging the reasonableness of attaching belief to any particular claim.

At the same time that students are warned of the dangers of sliding into such shabby inference patterns as judging a statement's truth-value solely by virtue of the status of one of its proponents, classroom speech is liberally sprinkled with none too subtle reminders as to where the power of authority really rests.

The metaphors that both describe the interactions of the typical philosophy classroom have not developed from pure coincidence. As Lakoff and Johnson claim, "People in power get to impose their metaphors,"[25] and so we operate with images of confrontation, duelling, and aggressiveness—in brief, the image of the battlefield is projected as the exemplary philosophy classroom. So deeply is this notion embedded, that when I talk in class of developing a critical analysis of an argument's position that is largely supportive of the position in question, my students have great difficulty in understanding me. The notion of a critical analysis is so thoroughly welded into their minds as a purely negative and largely destructive response, that they view the terms "critical" and "supportive" as antithetical.

I believe it is time to stop focusing our attention exclusively on proving arguments that run counter to our own as wrong. We need to turn to the more integrating tasks of asking how these arguments mesh with other different experience sets, different belief systems, different value codes, and even different reasoning styles.[26] The danger of the first focus (proving counterarguments wrong) is that it enables us to isolate tiny chunks of reasoning and never go much beyond; the second focus will lead us to examine a much broader academic context. Whereas the first focus permits, and even encourages, a narrow, segmented approach, the second encourages an approach to philosophy that is more bound up in social consequences. The second approach will integrate philosophy into broader social issues such as sexism, racism, and the nuclear arms race—whereas the first will tend to encourage a focus on building stronger and stronger counterarguments against a rival's position, while we fail to notice its context in a disintegrating universe. The separateness of the first approach is often mistakenly confused with objectivity, although the second's concern with social issues may lead it to be dismissed as an abandonment of reason.

The rejection of the emotional and affective realm in the name of reason may be one facet of the rejection of femaleness in the realm of philosophy. This rejection comes as no surprise in a tradition in which prominent theorists have labeled the female sex as "being as it were a deformity" (Aristotle)[27] and "a sugary sliminess . . . the obscenity . . . of everything which gapes open" (Sartre).[28]

When such misogyny disappears entirely from the academic realm, a radical shift in philosophical parlance may occur. In the philosophy classroom of the future, perhaps words such "seminal," now reserved to bestow the highest praise on an insight or an idea, will be supplemented with words like "ovarian" or "mammarian." There is much work to be done before we reach such a stage, however. Can we expect that education will provide a vehicle capable of contributing to such reform?

Education—A Vehicle for Reform?

Although violent, controlling, aggressive metaphors may be apparent in the realms of science and philosophy, by no means are they confined to these quarters. We live in a world saturated with violent talk. Even the medical metaphor for the body's response to disease is one of the battlefield, with fighter blood cells attacking the invading viruses. Our everyday parlance describes a man who nicks himself shaving as "bleeding like a stuck pig"; a frantically busy person "runs around like a chicken with its head cut off"; an efficient person who accomplishes more than one thing at a time "kills two birds with one stone"; an employee who helps an organization over difficult problems is a "trouble-shooter"; an employer who must let workers go is a "hit-man," "an axe-man," or a "hired gun." Universities who manage to attract a big name to a faculty pull off an academic "coup." When smaller league faculty members consistently fail to "hit the mark," the dictates of reason may compel those in the bigger league to "shoot their ideas down."

Children's fairy tales and nursery rhymes teem with woodsmen who chop off the heads of wolves, old witches who are baked in ovens or otherwise unpleasantly disposed of, hateful stepmothers who reap their due, and tiny babies who plunge out of cradles suspended high in treetops. Our children are initiated as babies into this violent parlance by the traditional stories read to them. Somewhat later the children's cartoons on television carry on. As they grow into early adolescence, the tradition continues with video games and even educational materials selected for use with computers, in which either the object or the reward of the game is to "shoot down" or "eat up" some enemy force. And needless to say, as children grow older, or even in adolescence, an endless supply of violent pornographic materials and a surfeit of violent shows are available on television.

Discourse in the Canadian parliament, now publicly broadcast, is almost a caricature of the confrontational style. Small wonder that education should reflect this tradition and that teachers' instruction manuals for reading should describe the phonetic and structural analysis that precedes the child's learning to spell as helping "to recognize and attack new words" and describe word recognition as encouraging "children . . . to attack new words." Reading specialists tell teachers that "using phonics is only one means for attacking unknown graphic representatives." They advise teachers to place particular emphasis on "determining whether the pupil is attacking unknown words.[29]

Nevertheless, education gives us grounds for optimism. In the last ten years, even the literature on reading itself has shifted away radically from mechanistic models of teaching reading, in which the violent metaphors particularly flourished. These models were in their prime until that time, and both works cited fit this time frame. The latest move in reading has been toward a whole language approach, and with this shift violent metaphors have largely disappeared. Interestingly in the whole language approach, language is viewed as a social art, in which the context of student, teacher, text, and other students are integrated. The behavioristic model that broke reading into small, separable subskills has been abandoned.

Current guidelines as specified by the Ontario Ministry of Education are remarkably free of controlling, violent, sexist language. The broad goals specified for intermediate and senior education are closely linked to dynamic learning, creative thinking, problem-solving skills, and personal responsibility in a social context. What little controlling language there is is centered in the Ministry's guidelines for the primary division, which lists "master[ing] number facts an objective of arithmetic," "master[ing] a vocabulary that enables him or her to name, describe, reason, explain, and use qualitative words as he or she plays, observes, manipulates, creates, and experiments with stimulating material" as an objective of speaking, and "master[ing] a vocabulary of words, phrases, and expressions" as an objective of writing. For the junior division category, the only reference to mastery is in the reading guidelines, where "master[ing] the essential word recognition strategies," is listed as an objective.[30] These are more than balanced, however, by the cooperative, interactive, social objectives specified in the guidelines.

Although these changes provide some legitimate basis for hope that academia ultimately may abandon controlling, manipulative, and violent metaphors for thought, debate, and learning, our optimism may be dampened if we reflect on the current disillusionment at the university level with elementary and secondary school systems. Perhaps this disenchantment reflects a greater attachment by these "higher" institutions to the domination and violence metaphors.

I conclude by examining a manual prepared for use in the university classroom that advocates a cooperative model of learning as opposed to the standard model in which the professor delivers the text or the form of knowledge to the student. In his *Learning Thru Discussion,* William Hill sketches what the objectives of such a classroom would be and offers practical suggestions for the realization of such objectives.[31] In a classroom governed by metaphor of discussion, some of the specific skills to be developed are giving and asking for reactions, giving examples, clarifying, synthesizing, standard setting, sponsoring, encouraging, and group tension relieving. Aggressing, blocking, competing, status seeking, and dominating are deemed by Hill to be absolutely nonfunctional classroom behavior, and only when they are excised does he believe real learning will occur. Ironically, in his introduction to this book, Herbert Thelan seems to have missed Hill's point. In a passage whose language is utterly incongruous with the spirit of Hill's advice, Thelan describes Hill as showing "the variety of ways in which the material can be pinched, punched, squeezed, kicked, and ultimately, mastered."[32]

The model of supportive interaction rather than self-aggrandizing confrontation is one that is developed systematically in the pragmatic philosophy of C.S. Peirce. Peirce sees scientific progress as attainable only through the cooperative efforts of a community of scientists. He says:

> One generation collects premises in order that a distant generation may discover what they mean . . . One [scientist] contributes this, another that. Another company, standing upon the shoulders of the first, strike a little higher.[33]

Interactional cooperation offers a better means of achieving such a goal than does adversarial exchange. It may well be the case that women can provide the models for this interactional exchange. Empirical studies of gender specific language patterns show that in mixed-sex conversations such constructive interactions are consistently present in women's speech and consistently absent in men's.[34] As woman have traditionally been tutored in the battlefield metaphor by men, perhaps women will become the tutors within the context of this new metaphor. A quilting bee provides an explicit example of a particular cooperative community where the excellence of any one quilter's contribution is not undercut or negated by the excellence of another quilter's work. Contrast this with the duelling metaphor, in which achievement of success entails that others come out losers. The quilting metaphor, which commits us to no such problematic stance, is generalizable in a way in which the duelling metaphor is not.

Jane Roland Martin provides an insightful analysis of the inadequacy of traditional models of academic excellence.[35] These models provide a picture of the ideal, which is not fully human. They focus on the rational and cognitive aspects of human development, to the exclusion of the affective and the emotional. They have, furthermore, brought us to the brink of peril in terms of objectification of nature, depletion of natural resources, and a nuclear arms race that threatens us with extinction. A superior model would be a nurturant cooperative one, one which puts humanity in its proper place—as part of the natural world and very much dependent on it. Caring, compassion, and nurturance should be as integral to our truly educated person as objectivity, scientific rigor, and rationality itself. I urge that our classrooms could be improved only by adopting this wider notion of education that Martin depicts. Reason itself will be better served if we abandon the metaphor of the battlefield for the more humane and more human metaphor of the cooperative community.

Questions for Reflection and Discussion

1. Why does Ayim believe that it is harmful to think of science as a male pursuit in which something metaphorically female (Nature, a subject matter, or a theory) is mastered and dominated by a male scientist? Would such a metaphor of science tend to be harmful to women hoping to participate in science? Why or why not?

2. Why, according to Ayim, can science not be purely objective?

3. Is there such a thing as a "dead metaphor"? (Note: This itself is a metaphor!) Would a dead metaphor be one in which misleading associations did not arise from the metaphorical use of a word?

4. If we did not use the confrontational metaphors for argument, what alternatives might there be? What might be the results if we thought of two persons arguing with each other as partners in a dance, or as parents with offspring to nurture?

Notes

1. Roger Tourangeau, "Metaphor and Cognitive Structure," *Metaphor: Problems and Perspectives,* ed. David S Miall (Sussex: The Harvester Press, 1982), 34.

2. Israel Scheffler, *Beyond the Letter: A Philosophical Inquiry into Ambiguity, Vagueness, and Metaphor in Language* (Boston: Routledge and Kegan Paul, 1979), 129.

3. Mary Gerhart and Allan Melvin Russell, *Metaphoric Process: The Creation of Scientific and Religious Understanding,* foreword by Paul Ricoeur (Forth Worth: Texas Christian University Press, 1984), 98.

4. James Fernandez, "The Performance of Ritual Metaphors," *The Social Use of Metaphor: Essays on the Anthropology of Rhetoric,* eds. J. David Sapir and J. Christopher Crocker (Pennsylvania: The University of Pennsylvania Press, 1977), 101.

5. Donald Schön, "Generative Metaphor: A Perspective on Problem-Setting in a Social Policy," *Metaphor and Thought,* ed. Andrew Ortony (Cambridge, Eng.: Cambridge University Press, 1979), 255.

6. *The Concise Oxford Dictionary,* ed. J.B. Sykes, 6th ed. rev. (Oxford: Clarendon Press, 1976), 672.

7. Francis Bacon, *The Works of Francis Bacon,* eds. James Spedding, Robert Leslie Ellis, and Douglas Denon Heath, vol. 4 (London: Longman and Company, 1860), 296. This passage is cited in Sandra Harding, *The Science Question in Feminism* (Ithaca:Cornell University Press, 1986), 237.

8. *Ibid.*

9. Harding, *The Science Question in Feminism.*

10. This violent imagery is developed in more detail in the section of the paper that focuses specifically on philosophy, but it is important to notice its presence in the language of science as well.

11. Richard Feynman, "The Development of the Space-Time of Quantum Electro-dynamics," *Science,* 153, no. 3737 (12 August 1966), 699–708.

12. *Ibid.,* 700.

13. Genevieve Lloyd, *The Man of Reason; "Male" and "Female' in Western Philosophy* (Minneapolis: University of Minnesota Press, 1984), especially pp. 10–17. Harding, *The Science Question in Feminism,* especially pp. 168–169, 237.

14. There is ample historical evidence that scientists have identified the purpose of science with controlling, manipulating, and dominating nature, according to Harding. it is now clear that a select group (largely middle class white males) has benefited most from this manipulation. See Harding, *The Science Question in Feminism,* especially p. 16.

15. Mary Ann Roe, *The Psychology of Occupations* (New York: Wiley, 1956), 218.

16. Harding, *The Science Question in Feminism,* 16.

17. *Ibid.,* 121.

18. Michael Scriven, *Reasoning* (New York: McGraw-Hill, 1976), 34.

19. Ralph H. Johnson and J. Anthony Blair, *Logical Self-Defense* (Toronto: McGraw-Hill Ryerson, 1977), 42. Notice that the very title of this book connotes violence.

20. David Hitchcock, *Critical Thinking: A Guide to Evaluating Information* (Toronto: Methuen, 1983), 215.

21. Peter Winch, *The Idea of a Social Science and Its Relation to Philosophy* (Boston: Routledge and Kegan Paul, 1958), 2. For a fuller exposition of the "argument is war" metaphor, see George Lakoff and Mark Johnson, *Metaphors We Live By* (Chicago: The University of Chicago Press, 1980).

22. The reference here is to a principle identified with William of Ockam, a medieval philosopher who advocated "shaving off" unnecessary metaphysical entities because you should not multiply entities beyond necessity.

23. Lionel Ruby, *Logic: An Introduction* (Chicago: J.B. Lippincott, 1950), 295–297.

24. Janice Moulton, "A Paradigm of Philosophy: The Adversary Method," *Discovering Reality: Feminist Perspectives on Epistemology, Metaphysics, Methodology, and Philosophy of Science,* eds. Sandra Harding and Merrill B. Hintikka (Dordrecht, Holl.: Reidel, 1983), 161.

25. Lakoff and Johnson, *Metaphors We Live By,* 87, 157. For another interesting account of the adversary method as paradigm, see Janice Moulton, "Duelism in Philosophy," *Teaching Philosophy,* 3, no. 4 (Fall 1980), 419–433. This adversary paradigm is further developed by Susan R. Peterson, "Are You Teaching Philosophy, or Playing the Dozens?" *Teaching Philosophy,* 3, no. 4 (Fall 1980), 435–442.

26. This point is also developed by Moulton in "A Paradigm of Philosophy: The Adversary Method," especially pp. 161–162.

27. Aristotle, *Generation of Animals,* eds. T.E. Page and others, trans. by A.L. Peck (London: William Heinemann, 1953), book 4, ch. 6, p. 461, Becker ref. 775a15–18.
  Ironically, in the same passage, Aristotle admits that "in human beings, more males are born deformed than females" (*Ibid.,* 459, Becker Ref. 775a4–7). This he attributes to the inherent superiority of the male embryo that, being "much hotter in its nature than the female . . . move[s] about more . . . and [hence] . . . get[s] broken more" (*Ibid.,* Becker Ref. 775a5–12).

28. Jean Paul Sartre, *Being and Nothingness; An Essay on Phenomenological Ontology,* trans. by Hazel E. Barnes (London: Methuen, 1957), 609, 613. This passage is cited in Angela R. Miles and Geraldine Finn eds., *Feminism in Canada: From Pressure to Politics* (Montreal: Black Rose Books, 1982), 160.

29. Marion E. Cross and Jan Hulland, *Teacher's Guidebook for Starting Points in Reading (C), With Notes on Starting Points in Language (C),* Book 2 (Canada: Ginn and Company Educational Publishers, 1975), 12. Walter T. Petty, Dorothy C. Petty, and Marjorie F. Becking, *Experiences in Language; Tools and Techniques for Language Arts Methods* (Boston: Allyn and Bacon, 1976), 328.

30. Ontario Ministry of Education, *Ontario Schools, Intermediate and Senior Divisions (Grades 7–12/OACs); Program and Diploma Requirements* (Ontario: Ontario Ministry of Education, 1984), 3. Ontario Ministry of Education, *The Formative Years; Circular P1J1,*

Provincial Curriculum Policy for the Primary and Junior Divisions of the Public and Separate Schools of Ontario (Ontario: Ontario Ministry of Education, 1975), 6, 8, 10, and 13.

31. William Fawcett Hill, *Learning Thru Discussion,* with introduction by Herbert A. Thelen (Newbury Park, Calif.: Sage, 1962), especially pp. 33, 38.

32. Herbert A. Thelen, "Introduction," *Learning Thru Discussion* (Newbury Park, Calif.: Sage, 1962), 9.

33. 70. Peirce, 7.87.

34. See, for example, Pamela Fishman, "Interactional Shitwork," *Heresies: A Feminist Publication on Arts and Politics,* 2 (May 1977): 99–101. See also D.H. Zimmerman and Candace West, "Sex Roles, Interruptions and Silences in Conversation," *Language and Sex: Difference and Dominance,* eds. Barrie Thorne and Nancy Henley (Series in Socio-linguistics, Series ed. Roger W. Shuy) (Rowley, Mass.: Newbury House Publishers, 1975), 105–129.

35. Jane Roland Martin, "The Ideal of the Educated Person," *Educational Theory,* 31, no. 2 (Spring 1981): 97–109.

Bibliography

Addelson, K. "The Man of Professional Wisdom." *Discovering Reality: Feminist Perspectives on Epistemology, Metaphysics, Methodology, and Philosophy of Science.* Edited by S. Harding and M. Hintikka. Dordrecht, Holl.: D. Reidel, 1983.

Altheide, D. *Creating Reality: How TV News Distorts Events.* Newbury Park, Calif.: Sage, 1976.

Altheide, D., and R. Snow. *Media Logic.* Newbury Park, Calif.: Sage, 1979.

Angus, I. *Technological Enlightenment: Limits of Instrumental Reason.* Washington, D.C.: University Press of America, 1984.

Arendt, H. *The Life of the Mind.* San Diego, Calif.: Harcourt Brace Jovanovich, 1978.

Aristotle. *Generation of Animals.* Edited by T. Page and others. Translated by A. Peck. London: William Heinemann, 1983.

Arlen, M. *30 Seconds.* New York: Farrar, Straus and Giroux, 1980.

Aronson, J. *The Press and the Cold War.* Indianapolis, Ind.: Bobbs-Merrill, 1970.

Austin, J. *How to Do Things with Words.* Oxford: Oxford University Press, 1971.

Bacon, F. *The Works of Francis Bacon.* Edited by J. Spedding, R. Ellis, and D. Heath, vol. 4. London: Longman and Company, 1860.

Bambrough, R. "Conflict and the Scope of Reason." *Ratio* 20, no. 2 (1978).

Barber, B. *Strong Democracy.* Berkeley and Los Angeles, Calif.: University of California Press, 1984. (No relation to author of "Resistance by Science.")

Barber, B. "Resistance by Scientists to Scientific Discovery." *Science* 34 (1961). (No relation to author of *Strong Democracy.*)

Barry, V. *Good Reason for Writing.* Belmont, Calif.: Wadsworth, 1983.

Beardsley, M. *Practical Logic.* Englewood Cliffs, N.J.: Prentice-Hall, 1950.

Bentham, J. *Bentham's Handbook of Political Fallacies*. Rev. ed. with preface by A. Larrabee. Baltimore: Johns Hopkins Press, 1952. Originally published as *The Book of Fallacies: From Unpublished Papers* by J. Bentham, by a friend, 1824.

Bernard, J., trans. *Kant's Critique of Judgment*. New York: Hafner, 1951.

Bok, S. *Lying: Moral Choice in Public and Private Life*. New York: Pantheon Books, 1978.

Boulding, K. *The Image*. Ann Arbor, Mich.: University of Michigan Press, 1956.

Brandt, W. *The Rhetoric of Argumentation*. Indianapolis, Ind.: Bobbs-Merrill, 1970.

Broverman, I. and others. "Sex Role Stereotypes: A Current Appraisal." *Journal of Social Issues* 28, no. 2 (1972).

Camp, D. "At Least One Poll Is Meaningless." *Calgary Herald* (1 September 1985).

Canadian Broadcasting Corporation. "The Politics of Information." Transcript of CBC "Ideas" series program. Toronto: May 1–22, 1983.

———. "Propaganda." by Jan Fedorowicz. Transcript of CBC "Ideas" series program Toronto: March 29–April 19, 1983.

———. "The Pundits." Transcript of CBC "Ideas" series program Toronto: May 9–May 23, 1984.

Cantril, H. *The Invasion from Mars: A Study in the Psychology of Panic*. Princeton, N.J.: Princeton University Press, 1940.

Capaldi, N. *The Art of Deception*. Dubuque, Iowa: Brown, 1971.

Carlson, C., Hersen, M., and R. Eisler. "Token Economy Programs in the Treatment of Hospitalized Adult Psychiatric Patients." *Mental Health Digest* 4 (December 1972).

Casebier, A., and J. Casebier. *Social Responsibility and the Mass Media*. Washington, D.C.: University Press of America, 1978.

Cavalieri, L. "New Strains of Life—or Death." *New York Times Magazine* (22 August 1976).

Cederblom, J., and D. Paulsen. *Critical Reasoning*. Belmont, Calif.: Wadsworth, 1982.

Chargaff, E. "Letter to the Editor." Reprint in *Science* 192 (1976).

Chase, S. *The Tyranny of Words*. London: Methuen, 1938.

Chomsky, N., and E. Herman. *The Political Economy of Human Rights*. Vol 1, *The Washington Connection and Third World Fascism*. Vol. 2. *After the Cataclysm*. Montreal: Black Rose Books, 1979.

Cohen, B. "Principles and Situations: the Liberal Dilemma and Moral Education." *Proceedings of the Aristotelian Society* 76 (1975–1976).

The Concise Oxford Dictionary. Edited by J. Sykes. 6th ed. rev. Oxford: Clarendon Press, 1976.

Copi, I. *Introduction to Logic*. 5th ed. New York: Macmillan, 1978.

Crable, R. *Argumentation as Communication: Reasoning with Receivers*. Columbus, Ohio: Charles E. Merrill, 1976.

Crawshay-Williams, R. *Methods and Criteria of Reasoning: An Inquiry into the Structure of Controversy*. London: Routledge and Kegan Paul, 1957.

Cross, M., and J. Hulland. *Teacher's Guidebook for Starting Points in Reading (C), With Notes on Starting Points in Language (C)*, book 2. Toronto: Ginn and Company Educational Publishers, 1975.

Dahl, R. *The Guardianship of Nuclear Weapons*. Syracuse, N.Y.: Syracuse University Press, 1985.

Dewey, J. *Logic: The Theory of Inquiry*. New York: Holt Rinehart, and Winston, 1938.

Edelman, M. *Political Language: Words That Succeed and Policies That Fail*. Orlando, Fla.: Academic Press, 1977.

Ehninger, D. *Influence, Belief, and Argument: An Introduction to Responsible Persuasion*. Glenview, Ill.: Scott, Foresman, 1974.

Ehninger, D., and W. Brockriede. *Decision by Debate*. 11th ed. New York: Dodd, Mead, 1973.

Ehrenreich, B., and D. English. *For Her Own Good*. New York: Anchor, 1978.

Eisenberg, A., and J. Ilardo. *Argument: A Guide to Formal and Informal Debate*. 2nd ed. Englewood Cliffs, N.J.: Prentice-Hall, 1980.

Ellul, J. *Propaganda: The Formation of Men's Attitudes*. Translated by K. Kellen and J. Lerner. New York: Knopf, 1965.

Ennis, R. "Rationality and Educational Practise." *Philosophy and Education*. Edited by J. Soltis. Chicago: National Society for the Study of Education, 1981.

Epstein, E. *News from Nowhere*. New York: Random House, 1973.

Falwell, J. "An Open Letter from Jerry Falwell." *Detroit Free Press* (22 march 1983).

Feinberg, J. "The Idea of a Free Man." *Educational Judgments*. Edited by James Doyle. Boston: Routledge and Kegan Paul, 1973.

Fernandez, J. "The Performance of Ritual Metaphors." *The Social Use of Metaphor: Essays on the Anthropology of Rhetoric*. Edited by J. Sapir and J. Crocker. Philadelphia: The University of Pennsylvania Press, 1977.

Feyerabend, P. *Against Method*. London: New Left Books, 1975.

———. *Science in a Free Society*. London: New Left Books, 1978.

Feynman, R. "The Development of the Space-Time View of Quantum Electro-dynamics." *Science* 153, no. 3737 (12 August 1966).

Finocchiaro, M. *Galileo and the Art of Reasoning*. Dordrecht, Holl.: D. Reidel, 1980.

————. "Fallacies and the Evaluation of Reasoning." *American Philosophical Quarterly* 18, no. 1 (January 1981).

Fischer, D. *Historians' Fallacies: Toward a Logic of Historical Thought*. Boston: Routledge and Kegan Paul, 1971.

Flew, A. *Thinking About Thinking*. 2nd ed. Glasgow: William Collins Sons, 1978.

Fodor, J. *The Modularity of Mind: Faculty Psychology*. Cambridge, Mass.: Massachusetts Institute of Technology Press, 1983.

Fogelin, R. *Understanding Arguments: An Introduction to Informal Logic*. 2nd ed. San Diego, Calif.: Harcourt Brace Jovanovitch, 1982.

Ford, D. *The Cult of the Atom*. New York: Simon and Schuster, 1982.

Gardner, H. *Frames of Mind: The Theory of Multiple Intelligences*. New York: Basic Books, 1983.

Gardner, M. *Science: Good, Bad, and Bogus*. Buffalo, N.Y.: Prometheus Books, 1982.

Gerhart, M., and A. Russell. *Metaphoric Process: The Creation of Scientific and Religious Understanding*. Fort Worth: Texas Christian University Press, 1984.

Giere, R. *Understanding Scientific Reasoning*. New York: Holt, Rinehart, and Winston, 1979.

Gilbert, M. *How to Win an Argument*. New York: McGraw-Hill, 1979.

————. *The Buddy System: Moving from Conflict to Cooperation*. Unpublished manuscript circulated by the author, Department of Philosophy, York University, Toronto, Ontario.

Gitlin, T. *Inside Prime Time*. New York: Pantheon, 1983.

Goffman, E. *Frame Analysis: An Essay on the Organization of Experience*. Cambridge, Mass.: Harvard University Press, 1974.

Goodfield, J. *Playing God*. New York: Random House, 1977.

Gould, S. *The Mismeasure of Man*. New York: Norton, 1981.

Govier, T. "Ad Hominem: Revising the Textbooks." *Teaching Philosophy* 6 (1983).

————. *A Practical Study of Argument*. Belmont, Calif.: Wadsworth, 1985.

————. "What's Wrong with Slippery Slope Arguments?" *Canadian Journal of Philosophy* 12 (1982).

————. "Who Says There Are No Fallacies?" *Informal Logic Newsletter* 5, no. 1 (1982).

Grice, G. "Logic and Conversation." Reprinted in R. Fogelin. *Understanding Arguments: An Introduction to Informal Logic.* 2nd ed. San Diego, Calif.: Harcourt Brace Jovanovitch, 1982.

Grobstein, C. "Recombinant DNA Research: Beyond the NIH Guidelines." *Science* 194 (1976).

Guthrie, W. *The Sophists.* Cambridge, Eng.: Cambridge University Press, 1971.

Habermas, J. *Knowledge and Human Interests.* Boston: Beacon Press, 1968.

Halpern, D. *Thought and Knowledge: An Introduction to Critical Thinking.* Hillsdale, N.J.: Erlbaum, 1984.

Hamblin, C. *Fallacies.* London: Methuen, 1970.

Hardwig, J. "The Achievement of Moral Rationality." *Philosophy and Rhetoric* 6, no. 3 (Summer 1973).

Harding, S. *The Science Question in Feminism.* Ithaca, N.Y.: Cornell University Press, 1986.

Hare, W. *In Defence of Open-Mindedness.* Kingston and Montreal: McGill-Queens University Press, 1985.

Harris, D. "On Differential Stigmatization for Predelinquents." *Social Problems* 15 (Spring 1968).

Harrison, A. and R. Bramson. *The Art of Thinking.* New York: Berkeley Books, 1982.

Harvard Nuclear Study Group. *Living with Nuclear Weapons.* New York: Bantam Books, 1983.

Hayek, F. *The Counter-Revolution of Science: Studies in the Abuse of Reason.* New York: Free Press, 1955.

Hempel, C. *Philosophy of Natural Science.* Englewood Cliffs, N.J.: Prentice-Hall, 1966.

Hill, W. *Learning Thru Discussion.* Introduction by H. Thelen. Newbury Park, Calif.: Sage, 1962.

Hinman, L. "The Case for *Ad Hominem* Arguments." *Australasian Journal of Philosophy* (1982).

Hitchcock, D. *Critical Thinking: A Guide to Evaluating Information.* Toronto: Methuen, 1983.

Hoffer, E. *The True Believer.* New York: Harper and Row, 1951.

Hofstadter, D. *Goedel, Escher, Bach: An Eternal Golden Braid.* New York: Basic Books, 1979.

Hopkins, H. *The Numbers Game.* London: Secker and Warburg, 1973.

Illich, I. *Medical Nemesis.* London: Calder and Boyars, 1975.

Innis, H. *The Bias of Communication.* Toronto: University of Toronto Press, 1951.

International Society for Animal Rights. *Newsletter* (June 1985).

Irvine, J., and others. *Demystifying Social Statistics.* London: Pluto Press, 1979.

Jackson, J., ed. "Election Night Reporting and Voter Turnout." *American Journal of Political Science* 27, no. 4 (1983).

Johnson, R., and J. Blair. *Logical Self-Defense.* 1st ed. Toronto: McGraw-Hill Ryerson, 1977. (2nd ed., 1983.)

Johnson, R. and J. Blair (Eds.). *Informal Logic.* Point Reyes, Ca.: Edgepress, 1980.

Johnstone, H. *Philosophy and Argument.* University Park, Penn.: Pennsylvania State University Press, 1959.

Jowell, R., and G. Hoinville. "Public Opinion Polls Tested." *New Society* (7 August 1969).

Kahane, H. *Logic and Contemporary Rhetoric.* 3rd ed. Belmont, Calif.: Wadsworth, 1980.

Kamin, L. *The Science and Politics of I.Q.* Hillsdale, N.J.: Erlbaum, 1974.

Kaplan, F. *Wizards of Armageddon.* New York: Simon and Schuster, 1984.

Kilgalen, R. "Hydrotherapy—Is It All Washed Up?" *Journal of Psychiatric Nursing* 10 (November-December 1972).

Klapp, O. *Opening and Closing: Strategies of Information Adaptation in Society.* Cambridge, Eng.: Cambridge University Press, 1978.

Kuhn, T. *The Structure of Scientific Revolution.* 2nd ed. enlarged. Chicago: University of Chicago Press, 1970.

Kurtz, P. "Debunking Neutrality and Skepticism." *The Skeptical Inquirer* 8, no. 3 (1984).

Lakoff, G., and M. Johnson. *Metaphors We Live By.* Chicago: University of Chicago Press, 1980.

Lasswell, H., and A. Kaplan. *Power and Society: A Framework for Political Inquiry.* New Haven, Conn.: Yale University Press, 1950.

Leach, E. "Animal Categories and Verbal Abuse." *Reader in Comparative Religion.* Edited by W. Lessa and E. Vogt. New York: Harper and Row, 1979.

Leach, G. *The Biocrats.* Harmondsworth, Eng.: Penguin, 1972. (Especially the chapter on priorities.)

Lehrer, K. "Social Information." *Monist* 50, no. 4 (October 1977).

Lenett, B. "Opinion Pollsters: Testing the Pulse of the Public." *The London Free Press* (6 November 1986).

Lippman, W. *Public Opinion.* 3rd ed. New York: Macmillan, 1960.

Little, F. *Critical Thinking and Decision Making.* Toronto: Butterworths, 1980.

Lloyd, G. *The Man of Reason; "Male" and "Female" in Western Philosophy.* Minneapolis: University of Minnesota Press, 1984.

McCloskey, H. "Liberalism." *Philosophy* 49 (1974).

McCuen, G. *Basic Skills for Critical Thinking* (with *Teacher's Manual*). St. Paul, Minn.: Greenhaven Press, 1979.

McElroy, E., and A. Narciso. "Clinical Specialist in the Community Mental Health Program." *Journal of Psychiatric Nursing* 9 (January-February 1971).

McKean, K. "The Fine Art of Reading Voters' Minds." *Discover* (May 1984).

Mackie, J. "Fallacies." *Encyclopedia of Philosophy.* Edited by J. Edwards. New York: Macmillan, 1967.

MacLean, E. *Between the Lines.* Montreal: Black Rose Books, 1981.

McLuhan, M. *The Gutenberg Galaxy.* Toronto: University of Toronto Press, 1962.

McPeck, J. *Critical Thinking and Education.* Oxford: Martin Robertson, 1981.

McPhail, T. *Electronic Colonialism.* London: Sage Publishers, 1981.

Manner, J. *Four Arguments for the Elimination of Television.* New York: Quill, 1978.

Meiland, J. *Thinking: How to Get the Best Out of College.* New York: Mentor, 1981.

Mendelsohn, H., and I. Crespi. *Polls, Television, and the New Politics.* Scranton, Penn.: Chandler, 1970.

Merelman, R. *Making Something of Ourselves: On Culture and Politics in the United States.* Berkeley and Los Angeles, Calif.: University of California Press, 1984.

Meynell, H. "Science, the Truth, and Thomas Kuhn." *Mind* 84 (1975).

Michael, R., and D. Zumpe. "Sexual Violence in the United States and the Role of Season." *American Journal of Psychiatry* (July 1983).

Miles, A., and G. Finn, eds. *Feminism in Canada: From Pressure to Politics.* Montreal: Black Rose Books, 1982.

Mill, J. "On Fallacies." *A System of Logic Ratiocinative and Inductive.* Book 5. Edited by J. Robinson. Toronto: University of Toronto Press, 1974.

Mishan, E. *Twenty-One Popular Economic Fallacies.* New York: Praeger, 1973.

Montefiore, A., ed. *Neutrality and Impartiality: The University and Political Commitment.* Cambridge, Eng.: Cambridge University Press, 1975.

Moulton, J. "A Paradigm of Philosophy: The Adversary Method." *Discovering Reality: Feminist Perspectives on Epistemology, Metaphysics, Methodology, and Philosophy of Science.* Edited by S. Harding and M. Hintikka. Dordrecht, Holl.: D. Reidel, 1983.

———. "Duelism in Philosophy." *Teaching Philosophy* 3, no. 4 (Fall 1980).

Munson, R. *The Way of Words*. Boston: Houghton Mifflin, 1976.

Naess, A. *Communication and Argument: Elements of Applied Semantics*. London: George Allen and Unwin, 1966.

———. "Toward a Theory of Interpretation and Preciseness." *Theoria* 15 (1949).

Nisbett, R., and T. Wilson. "Telling More Than We Know: Verbal Reports on Mental Process." *Psychological Review* 84 (1977).

Oran, D. "Judges and Psychiatrists Lock Up Too Many People." *Psychology Today*. (August 1973).

Oxford English Dictionary. Oxford: Oxford University Press, 1933.

Owen, D. *None of the Above*. Boston: Houghton Mifflin, 1985.

Passmore, J. *Man's Responsibility for Nature*. New York: Charles Scribner's Sons, 1974.

———. *Philosophical Reasoning*. London: Duckworth and Company, 1961.

Paul, R. "Teaching Critical Thinking in the 'Strong' Sense." *Informal Logic Newsletter* 4, no. 2 (1982).

Penrod, S. *Social Psychology*. Englewood Cliffs, N.J.: Prentice-Hall, 1986.

Perelman, C. *The Idea of Justice and the Problem of Argument*. Boston: Routledge and Kegan Paul, 1963.

———. *The New Rhetoric and the Humanities. Essays on Rhetoric and Its Applications*. Dordrecht, Holl.: D. Reidel, 1979.

———. *The Realm of Rhetoric*. Translated by William Kluback. Notre Dame: Notre Dame University Press, 1982.

Perry, T. *Moral Reasoning and Truth: An Essay in Philosophy and Jurisprudence*. Oxford: Clarendon Press, 1976.

Peterson, S. "Are You Teaching Philosophy or Playing the Dozens?" *Teaching Philosophy* 3, no. 4 (Fall 1980).

Petty, W., Petty, D., and M. Becking. *Experiences in Language; Tools and Techniques for Language Arts and Methods*. Boston: Allyn and Bacon, 1976.

Polanyi, M. *Personal Knowledge*. Chicago: University of Chicago Press, 1960.

———. *Science, Faith, and Society*. Chicago: University of Chicago Press, 1964.

———. *The Tacit Dimension*. New York: Doubleday, 1966.

Polanyi, M., and H. Prosch. *Meaning*. Chicago: University of Chicago Press, 1977.

Popper, K. *The Logic of Scientific Discovery*. London: Hutchinson, 1959. (First published in German in 1935.)

————. *The Open Society and Its Enemies*. 5th ed. Princeton: Princeton University Press, 1971.

————. *The Poverty of Historicism*. Boston: Beacon Press, 1957.

Postman, N. *Amusing Ourselves to Death*. New York: Viking, 1985.

————. *The Disappearance of Childhood*. New York: Delacorte, 1982.

————. *Teaching as a Conserving Activity*. New York: Delacorte Press, 1979.

————. *Teaching as a Subversive Activity*. New York: Delacorte, 1969.

————. "TV's Disastrous Impact on Children" (Interview). *U.S. News and World Report* (19 January 1981).

Poundstone, W. *Big Secrets: The Uncensored Truth About All Sorts of Stuff You Are Never Supposed to Know*. New York: Quill, 1983.

Quasthoff, U. "The Uses of Stereotype in Everyday Argument." *Journal of Pragmatics* 2 (1978).

Report of the Working Party on the Experimental Manipulation of the Genetic Composition of Micro-Organisms. Presented to Parliament by the Secretary of State for Education and Science. Cmnd. no. 5880, 3 (1975).

Rescher, N. *Dialectics*. Albany, N.Y.: State University of New York Press, 1977.

Rivers, C. "Genetic Engineers—Now That They Have Gone Too Far, Can They Stop?" *Ms.* (June 1976).

Robinson, J. "Television's Impact on Everyday Life: Some Cross-National Evidence." *Television and Social Behavior*. Edited by E. Rubinstein and others. Washington, D.C.: U.S. Department of Health, Education, and Welfare, 1972.

Roe, A. *The Making of a Scientist*. New York: Dodd, Mean, 1952.

————. *The Psychology of Occupations*. New York: Wiley, 1956.

Rosten, L. *The Joys of Yiddish*. New York: Washington Square Press, 1968.

Rubin, B. *Questioning Media Ethics*. New York: Praeger, 1978.

Ruby, L. *Logic: An Introduction*. Philadelphia: J. B. Lippincott, 1950.

Russell, J. *Mephistopheles. The Devil in the Modern World*. Ithaca, N.Y.: Cornell University Press, 1986.

Rutherford, P. *The Making of the Canadian Media*. Toronto: McGraw-Hill Ryerson, 1978.

Said, E. *Covering Islam*. New York: Pantheon, 1980.

Sartre, J. *Being and Nothingness; An Essay on Phenomenological Ontology*. Translated by H. Barnes. London: Methuen, 1957.

Scheffler, I. *Beyond the Letter: A Philosophical Inquiry into Ambiguity, Vagueness, and Metaphor in Language*. Boston: Routledge and Kegan Paul, 1979.

————. *The Language of Education.* Springfield, Ill.: Thomas, 1960.

————. *Science and Subjectivity.* Indianapolis, Ind.: Bobbs-Merrill, 1967.

Schickel, R. *Intimate Strangers. The Culture of Celebrity.* New York: Doubleday, 1985.

Schön, D. "Generative Metaphor: A Perspective on Problem-Setting in Social Policy." *Metaphor and Thought.* Edited by A. Ortony. Cambridge, Eng.: Cambridge University Press, 1979.

Schudson, M. *Advertising: The Uneasy Persuasion. Its Dubious Impact on American Society.* New York: Basic Books, 1984.

Scriven, M. *Evaluation Thesaurus.* 3rd ed. Inverness, Calif.: Edgepress, 1981.

————. *Reasoning.* New York: McGraw-Hill, 1976.

Searle, J. *Speech Acts: An Essay in the Philosophy of Language.* Cambridge, Eng.: Cambridge University Press, 1969.

Siegel, H. "Critical Thinking as an Educational Ideal." *The Educational Forum* (November 1980).

————. *Educating Reason: An Essay on Rationality, Critical Thinking, and Education.* Boston: Routledge and Kegan Paul, in press.

————. *Relativism Refuted: A Critique of Contemporary Epistemological Relativism.* In press.

Simring, F. "Letter to the Editor." Reprint in *Science* 192 (1976).

Sinsheimer, R. "Inquiring into Inquiry: Two Opposing Views." Hastings Center Report (August 1976).

————. "Potential Risks," *National Academy of Sciences, Research with Recombinant DNA,* (1977).

————. "Troubled Dawn for Genetic Engineering." *New Scientist* 168 (1975).

Smith, A. *The Geopolitics of Information.* London: Faber and Faber, 1980.

Smith, C., and D. Hunsaker. *The Bases of Argument: Ideas in Conflict.* Indianapolis, Ind.: Bobbs-Merrill, 1972.

Smythe, D. *Dependency Road: Communications, Capitalism, Consciousness, and Canada.* Norwood, N.J.: Ablex, 1981.

Staunard, D. "Ideological Conflict on a Psychiatric Ward." *Psychiatry* 36 (May 1973).

Stebbing, S. *Thinking to Some Purpose.* Harmondsworth, Eng.: Penguin, 1945.

Steel, R. *Walter Lippman and the American Century.* Boston: Little, Brown, 1980.

Stephenson, M., and J. Weal. *Nuclear Dictionary.* New York: Longman, 1985.

Struggle for Justice. Prepared for the American Friends Service Committee. Philadelphia: Hill and Wang, 1971.

Sunley, R. "New Dimensions in Reaching-Out Casework." *Social Work* 13 (April 1968).

Taylor, R. *Film Propaganda. Soviet Russia and Nazi Germany.* New York: Barnes and Noble, 1979. (No relation to the author of *Good and Evil.*)

Taylor, R. *Good and Evil: A New Direction. A Forceful Attack on the Rationalistic Tradition in Ethics.* 2nd ed. Buffalo, N.Y.: Prometheus Books, 1984. (No relation to the author of *Film Propaganda.*)

Theall, D. *Understanding McLuhan: The Medium Is a Rearview Mirror.* Montreal and London: McGill-Queen's University Press, 1971.

Thouless, R. *How to Think Straight: The Techniques of Applying Logic Instead of Emotion.* New York: Simon and Schuster, 1939. Originally published as *Straight and Crooked Thinking,* 1930.

Toby, J. "An Evaluation of Early Identification and Intensive Treatment Programs for Predelinquents." *Social Problems* 13 (Fall 1965).

Toulmin, S. *An Examination of the Place of Reason in Ethics.* Cambridge, Eng.: Cambridge University Press, 1953.

―――. *Foresight and Understanding: An Enquiry into the Aims of Science.* 2nd ed. New York: Harper and Row, 1975.

―――. *The Return to Cosmology: Postmodern Science and the Theology of Nature.* Berkeley and Los Angeles, Calif.: University of California Press, 1982.

―――. *The Uses of Argument.* 2nd ed. Cambridge, Eng.: Cambridge University Press, 1969.

Tourangeau, R. "Metaphor and Cognitive Structure." *Metaphor: Problems and Perspectives.* Edited by David Miall. Sussex, Eng.: The Harvester Press, 1982.

Tuchman, G., and others, eds. *Hearth and Home: Images of Women in the Mass Media.* Oxford: Oxford University Press, 1978.

Vetterling-Braggin, M., and Elliston, F., and J. English, eds. *Feminism and Philosophy.* Totowa, N.J.: Littlefield Adams, 1977.

Walton, D. *The Arguer's Position: A Pragmatic Study of* Ad Hominem *Attack, Criticism, Refutation, and Fallacy.* Westport, Conn.: Greenwood Press, 1985.

―――. "The Fallacy of Many Questions." *Logique et Analyse* 24 (1984).

Walton, D., and J. Woods. *Argument: The Logic of the Fallacies.* Toronto: McGraw-Hill Ryerson, 1982.

Wellman, C. *Challenge and Response: Justification in Ethics.* Carbondale, Ill.: Southern Illinois University Press, 1971.

West, W. ed. *Orwell: The Lost Writings.* New York: Arbor House, 1985.

White, R. "Propaganda: Morally Questionable and Morally Unquestionable Techniques." *Annals of the American Academy of Political and Social Science* 398 (1971).

Wicklein, J. *Electronic Nightmare*. New York: Viking, 1981.

Will, F. "The Uses of Argument." *Philosophical Review* 69 (1960).

Williams, T. *The Impact of Television: A Natural Experiment in Three Communities*. San Diego, Calif.: Harcourt Brace Jovanovitch, 1986.

Wilson, B. *Rationality*. Oxford: Oxford University Press, 1973.

Winch, P. *The Idea of a Social Science and Its Relation to Philosophy*. London: Routledge and Kegan Paul, 1958.

Windes, R., and A. Hastings. *Argumentation and Advocacy*. 4th ed. New York: Random House, 1969.

Young, M. *Knowledge and Control*. London: Collier Macmillan, 1971.

Ziegelmueller, G., and C. Dause. *Argumentation: Inquiry and Advocacy*. Englewood Cliffs, N.J.: Prentice-Hall, 1975.